OUT OF THE WILDERNESS

April ~ May 1954

In the Youth Employment Office Mr Marley ground out his cigarette in an ashtray, no doubt fantasising the receptacle to be a vital organ of my body, and glared at me. He was tall, sinister and balding, with heavy horn-rimmed glasses and reminded me of Reginald Christie, the notorious Rillington Place murderer who had featured in the newspapers during the early Fifties.

'I guess you're getting as sick of seeing me as I am of seeing you!' he snapped. 'Have you ever considered working in a shop?'

'I'll have a try,' I piped up manfully as he handed me a chitty.

His parting words rang in my ears. 'And for goodness sake put a decent shirt and tie on. And if you don't get the job come straight back here.'

He was quite right of course. I didn't intend to return home jobless this time. Fear can be a terrible spur and I suppose I had tried his patience somewhat. It wasn't that I was work-shy. As a child I simply lived for each day as it came along without giving much thought to the future. I vaguely assumed that when I left school I would inevitably work at the Kodak factory in Harrow with much the same certainty that I would have to start shaving one day. As it happened Kodak didn't want me and neither did the Stationery Office (vacancy filled), neither did a local machine shop (no knowledge of machinery). From then on in panic I suggested training to be a chef, landscape gardening – even a child film actor. No wonder Mr Marley was losing his patience with me.

If I failed this one I was really dreading facing the bald and bespectacled ogre. He would probably tear my throat out. For one mad moment I considered asking him if I could be employed in his office as an office boy but somehow I didn't think this suggestion would go down very well.

On my way home I studied the chitty. The firm was called *G.A. Dunn & Co. Ltd. Hatters and Outfitters*, and the address was 259 Station Road. I just couldn't recall the place, which irked me as I lived at 50 Station Road. On the way home I checked all the shops and found it. I must have passed it hundreds of times with its two square oak-framed windows and narrow central lobby. Indeed, I recalled from my infant days being utterly fascinated by the display of headwear on show. Many were the times when I would drag my mother up to the window and ask, 'how old will I have to be before I can wear one of those hats?'

Cautiously I peeped in the shop doorway. The interior looked dark and gloomy in contrast with the bright sunshine outside. Suddenly a figure appeared. A dark-suited authoritative figure who seemed to glare at me with haughty indignation as if I were some foul rodent trespassing on hallowed ground. I took flight and fled, hoping that I would not be recognised when I returned for my interview.

I hurried indoors and donned my Sunday Best clothes. Fawn check double-breasted sports jacket, brown trousers, brown brogue shoes, cream shirt and the final touch of which I was particularly proud. A dark brown tie with vivid yellow piping round the edges. My, we were snappy dressers in the Fifties!

Thus attired, I set off to meet my destiny. This was it! This was the 'biggie'! I just had to succeed this time. The entrance of the shop seemed as forbidding as ever and I timorously ventured into the shadowy interior, holding out my employment chitty like some holy offering. A suave and sleek young man with pale blonde hair plastered back across his narrow skull approached me and asked if he could help.

'I've come about the job vacancy,' I whispered in the tones of one confiding to his doctor the symptoms of some embarrassing complaint.

The young man quirked a thin smile. 'One moment,' he replied. 'I'll get the manager.'

A tall, immaculately-suited figure emerged from the oaken gloom and I repeated my request. 'Oh, no,' he rumbled at last, casting a lofty glance of appraisal over my person. 'You're much too young. We require someone in their Twenties.'

I felt crushed and defeated as he loomed over me, waving aside my plea for employment. I thanked him for his time and dejectedly left the shop, dreading another session with Mr Marley.

I had only walked a few yards up the road when someone tapped me on the shoulder. It was the young assistant from the shop.

'He's changed his mind,' he grinned. 'He does that a lot. Anyway I think you've got the job.'

I was to learn that this was a characteristic of Ronald Harvey, the manager. He nearly always changed his mind. Yet another little characteristic of his was the ability to pass the blame for his own errors onto others.

I returned to the shop where Mr Harvey was on the phone to the Area Supervisor. Phrases such as 'refined manner' and 'tidy appearance' were

DEDICATION

Many thanks to John and Anne for publishing this book,
Pamela and Jan for their encouragement,
and Lauren Asare for her splendid cover design.

uttered and I mentally preened myself. In retrospect, I can afford to be cynical. My 'refined manner' was more of a nervous funk, reducing my voice to a mouse-like squeak. And as for my 'tidy appearance', well I suppose it was tidy but what with my sartorial taste and the Manager's standard of judgement it was more a case of compensating errors.

Mr Harvey was, as I said, immaculate. About six feet tall, heavily-built without being fat and of that swarthy complexion which many Europeans acquire having lived for many years in the tropics. In fact he had lived in Sudbury for many years and had been no further south than Portsmouth.

He was in his late forties and round-faced, made even rounder by his short cut black hair and centre parting. Add to this a pair of mud-coloured eyes and he looked like a reproachful chimpanzee – albeit a very reproachful chimpanzee.

I was told that would be expected to perform many menial tasks in the shop before I was let loose on a customer. Tasks such as sweeping the pavement area of the shop front, making the tea, cleaning the fascia with a dustpan and brush, making the tea, hoovering out the shop – and making the tea. In due course I would be called to help out at other branches during holiday periods. Also I was to wear a suit and in due course a hat. But that would depend on whether or not I survived my trial period of employment. I was told to be at the shop promptly on Monday morning at 8.50. Yes, I had got the job!

I left the shop in a state in stratospheric rapture. After all those weeks in limbo I had finally made it. I was far too elated to go straight home so I opted for the back roads. I didn't trust myself encountering someone I knew as I might gibber with incoherent glee and end up being certified. Ecstasy, LSD and Crack had not been invented but I was displaying the symptoms of their combined effects. I was going to make the ten! I was going to wear a hat! It was with great difficulty that I resisted the urge to perform cartwheels and somersaults down Welldon Crescent.

Eventually I arrived home and having calmed down I sat in my father's armchair and waited for my mother to come home. 'Why are you dressed up like that?' she gasped, staring at my Sunday finery.

'I've got a job,' I proudly informed her.

Her face paled and her jaw dropped open. 'Where?' she managed to croak.

'In a shop.'

'Oh, my God!' she whispered. 'Not a greengrocer?'

I was justifiably hurt by her reaction. And what if I had? I would have been able to get her cheap veggies. 'No,' I retorted. 'In a clothes shop. Dunn & Co. And I will be earning fifty shillings a week.'

Mum looked aghast. 'Fifty ...? Are you sure they didn't say fifteen?'

'No, they didn't.' I was beginning to feel less than gratified by the reception of my joyful tidings. 'Fifty shillings – two pounds ten shillings.'

My father was over the moon when he heard. Dunn's were one of the best outfitters outside the West End. Yes, dear old Dad was really proud and the next day my parents took me to a more modest outfitters to buy me my very first suit.

As I tried on the dark grey suit my mother just couldn't resist confiding my expectations to the sales assistant. 'He's going to work at Dunn & Co.'

The assistant, leaning languidly against the counter with his tape measure draped around his neck like a symbol of office, smiled a world-weary smile. 'Is he indeed,' he murmured. 'I suppose he could do worse.'

It certainly surprised my grandparents who, like my aunts and uncles, had written me off as best a no-hoper and worse an embryonic criminal. 'Dunn's is a very posh shop,' announced Grandma. 'He'll have to look smart. I've got some things of his Grandad's that will be just right.'

And she produced a horrible mud-coloured raincoat which came down to my ankles and a black bowler hat which all but obscured my face if it hadn't been for my ears holding it up.

Tactfully the offerings were accepted but Dad did murmur something about it being a long wait until Bonfire Night. In any event, I never saw the hat and coat again.

And so at last the stage was set for the next phase of my life, ready to commence at 8.50 Monday morning. Fair enough, I thought as I got ready for bed, I had got a job to be going on with while I could be on the lookout for something else.

THE FIRST DAY

31 May 1954

There were three of them. Three figures in trilby hats, and they were watching me as I approached. It felt like the last reel of *High Moon*. I had set out that Monday morning for my first day at my first job, attired in my double-breasted dark grey birds-eye suit and the most sober tie I could find and quite understandably nervous. And the scrutiny of the hatted trio did nothing to ease my feelings.

The tallest, a fair-haired chap with rimless glasses and in his mid-twenties turned out to be James Fenton the senior assistant. His sardonic smile and aloof manner were somewhat daunting and he had a tendency to look down his nose at those he considered his inferiors. Which really goes to show just how wrong first impressions can be. His stiff, aloof manner was due to a crop of angry boils on the back of his neck which curtailed such head movements as friendly nods.

Derek Carstairs proved to be much more sociable from the outset. He had large glasses and a small face. But the third member of the trio was something of a contrast. He was rather on the short side, pale, and wearing the widest brimmed hat I had ever seen outside a Western film. Also the brim was turned up all round and seemed to dominate him. It was more a case of the hat wearing him. He was clutching a large brown paper parcel nearly as big as himself. 'You the new sprog?' he asked.

'Yes, Sir,' I dutifully informed him. I thought it best to play safe and call them all 'Sir' until I was sure of their rank and station. It transpired that Derek Carstairs and 'Little-Man-Big-Hat', whose name was David Hopton, were ordinary rank and file junior assistants about my own age.

'Dunno how long you'll have to wait,' David Hopton told me. 'Old Ronnie's probably missed his bus. It won't be his fault, of course. Never is.'

I was mystified. This trio had not been in evidence when I applied for the job and there was no sign of the assistant I had spoken to then. And who was 'Old Ronnie' anyway?

'Old Harv,' sneered the large-hatted one. 'Harvey – the manager.'

I really felt like a fish out of water. I must have seemed very naïve to these worldly young men. I soon learnt that the missing assistant had been helping out at Harrow for a week and had since returned to his base shop at Kilburn. Furthermore, David Hopton was based at Wembley and had only called in to deliver a garment required for a customer, which explained the brown paper parcel.

Then the immaculate figure of Mr Harvey hove into view, wearing an expensive-looking grey hat and an expression of hurt resentment on his swarthy face. This was his normal expression when his features were in repose. 'Good mornings' were grunted back and forth then Mr Harvey proceeded to open the shop. Proceeded to, as it was quite a ritual. The door looked like something out of Westminster Abbey; solid oak with three stained glass panels. First of all a thumping great padlock had to be removed, along with its slotted-in plate. Then an ordinary mortise lock followed by a Yale lock. After 'The Ceremony of the Keys' we all trooped into the darkened interior in the wake of the manager.

Then came a scream and a crash. In the darkness Mr Harvey had fallen over a chair. For such a burly man he had a very high-pitched scream. 'Who left that chair there?' he complained, glaring accusingly at Derek Carstairs who was obviously his whipping boy. 'I could have broken my neck.'

'Pitty you didn't,' I heard David Hopton snigger behind me.

Lights were switched on and my new companions set about their various tasks. All except Dave Hopton who deposited his parcel and sauntered off, no doubt to find the most time-consuming and leisurely route back to Wembley. I stood in the middle of the shop like a condemned man waiting by his three-sided topless office desk which, for no reason I could think of, reminded me of a chicken coop – albeit a very elegant oak panelled stained glass chicken coop. 'Carstairs will show you what to do,' he said. And that was that.

Derek Carstairs was probably the best person to have on hand with new recruits. He possessed a kindly and sympathetic nature, and that first day I didn't actually do anything. I watched him brush the dust from the ledges of the shop front, I watched him sweep the front step and I watched him hoover the floor and dust the shelves.

While this industry was in progress Mr Harvey and Mr Fenton were busy with different coloured sales tickets and different coloured bottles of ink. It all looked horribly complicated and I despaired of ever mastering the mental skill involved which surely must be necessary for such work.

The next item on the agenda was a visit to the bank to collect the night safe wallet and Saturday's receipts, and then the most important task of all

– getting the manager's lunch. In those days banks were hallowed ground. You spoke in hushed whispers and deferred politely to the immaculate male staff and elegant female cashiers. The interior of the bank was all oak panelling and brass fittings and I began to suspect that it was another branch of Dunn & Co. Derek signed the collection book and stuffed the night safe wallet in his brown carrier bag. 'Next stop *Sainsbury's*,' he grinned.

I was to learn that buying the manager's lunch could prove to be the most mortifying, humiliating and embarrassing task of any. It was all right if the person who served you was familiar with Mr Harvey's foibles. They just grinned understandingly and complied. Alternatively, you could be regarded with such contempt that you wished only to dwindle to nothing and become part of the mosaic pattern on the tiled floor.

Two ounces of ham; that was what he wanted. Nothing more and nothing less. The fact that the ham was sliced into four ounce portions, each portion neatly stacked on its own little square of greaseproof paper, meant nothing to him. Two ounces. So one portion had to be sliced neatly in half and almost lost inside a paper bag. And he didn't want any fat on it either.

Sometimes he would decide on a piece of veal and ham pie. This was even worse. *Sainsbury's* delicious veal and ham pie was a long rectangle which was sliced off in required portions and it also contained the bonus of two hardboiled eggs. But Mr Harvey's demands left no doubt as to his requirements. 'A piece about 1/9d,' he would say, 'and I don't want an end piece with all that pastry. Tell them to slice a bit out of the middle with some egg in it.'

After *Sainsbury's* Derek led me back, past the shop and over the road to a modest little establishment called *Danny's Café*. It was squashed between *Bunting's Garage* and a short row of terrace cottages. I liked *Danny's Café* on first sight. It was obviously a cottage knocked into a café with two large windows flanking the door. Inside were a number of small tables covered with blue and white checked oil cloth with the counter at the far end. The atmosphere was friendly, smelling of cigarette smoke and brown sauce. There were several workmen in their flat caps and overalls drinking mugs of tea that looked strong enough to creosote a fence.

The counter had two glass cases displaying various bread rolls and sandwiches with assorted fillings. Behind the counter stood Danny himself, a little man, reminiscent of an unshelled tortoise and as Cockney as Bow Bells. He was in his rolled-up shirtsleeves, black waistcoat and a floral-patterned apron. Incongruously, an elegant curly-brimmed black hat topped the apparition, held up by his large ears which also supported a pair of horn-rimmed spectacles as misty and spotted as his display cases. 'Yus?' he asked.

'Two buttered rolls please,' said Derek, placing sixpence on the counter. These were duly placed in a paper bag and handed over. At least it didn't seem as complicated as *Sainsbury's* and was to be part of my daily routine. Danny was a very amiable little man and his wife, *Mrs Danny*, a large and homely grey-haired lady. They had a waitress, Lil, a thin lady swathed in a blue overall coat who compensated for her emaciated face with a frantic explosion of blonde hair.

Back at the shop all the bookwork had been completed and it was now time for the morning tea break. While Derek attended to this I took the opportunity to study my workplace. The shop was quite long but narrowed to almost half its width towards the back. This was due to the interior staircase of the upstairs flat. The cupboard beneath the stairs was where the cardboard boxes and Hessian sacks of waste paper were stored. The front area of the shop was dominated by looming oak fixtures flanking each side, the shelves containing stacks of hats in leather buckets. Below the shelves a counter and below the counter vast drawers for the caps and 'overflow' hat stock. The smaller area towards the end of the shop was the clothing department. After all, Dunn & Co were first and foremost Hatters.

But one item puzzled me. Halfway down the shop by the cupboard, on a level with the manager's office, was an oaken plinth about three feet high and fitted into the top was a gleaming copper cylinder with a long spout jutting out at an angle. It was obviously a boiler of some sort for it would bubble away merrily and then, for several seconds, a jet of steam would billow forth. Then would come a clicking noise from a hidden thermostat and that steam jet would abate and the whole cycle would begin again.

At first I thought it was some device installed for asthmatic staff members but then I realised it was for steaming hats. Derek had mentioned it on the way to the bank. It fascinated me but there were more important things to be dealt with such as the manager's tea.

This was duly served to him in his office in a bone china cup and saucer while the staff had to rough it with any available unbroken teacup in the hidden recesses of the shop. This leisure period took place behind a large oak wing mirror on casters which effectively screened the horrible spectacle of the staff imbibing their beverage from the delicate eyes of the public. I half expected to find an oak teapot and kettle and wondered if the shop had been built out of a forest of oak trees that had originally grown there. It certainly is no exaggeration to say that *Danny's Café* would have looked like the Savoy Tea Rooms compared to our little hovel. It was close by the fitting-room and consisted of a rickety table covered with a sheet of brown paper. This paper was changed once a week or whenever the tea stains became unbearable. Chairs were a luxury denied the staff. Mr Harvey had a high stool in his 'office-coop' and there were a couple of 'doctor's-waiting-room-style' wooden chairs in the shop for weary customers but we had no such facilities in the tea section. The only seating accommodation was a short flight of three wooden steps leading to the washrooms and toilet, both these areas each being about the size of a telephone box.

Tea over and we were back to work. Mr Harvey was on the telephone to another shop. I later discovered that there was a sort of jungle telegraph which traced the movements of any illustrious visitor from Head Office such as our Staff Supervisor.

Mr Fenton was busy with a customer and Derek was filling me in on the requirements for the day. 'If the window cleaner comes in,' he said, 'tell him that the manager said the front step hadn't been washed down properly this morning. And we're getting a stock delivery today, too.'

Another customer came in and Derek went forward to attend to him. Left to my own devices I thought I had best put on some show of earning my living so I grabbed a duster and made a few token passes at the all-surrounding woodwork. But I was intrigued by the hat steamer. I wanted to make its acquaintance. It drew me to it like a copper magnet. I surreptitiously peered around the back of the wooden plinth. There was a black plastic knob at the base of the cylinder; obviously some sort of control. Well I had to learn what it was all about so I turned it full over.

Instantly a gout of boiling chalky water squirted out of the spout and across the shop with alarming intensity. Fortunately my actions were not noticed and I hastily removed all evidence from the red stone floor with my duster. I would keep my hands off things in future. I didn't want my first day to be my last day.

Just then someone else entered the shop. Even I realised that it wasn't a customer. He walked in purposefully and stood by the office but Mr Harvey was still on the phone. Remembering Derek's words regarding the window cleaner, I approached the newcomer. 'Mr Harvey's on the phone at the moment,' I timidly explained, 'but he says that you didn't wash the doorstep down properly this morning.'

The newcomer's eyes widened behind his gold-rimmed spectacles and his brown moustache quivered with surprised indignation. 'Bloody cheek!' he began.

I'd done it again, I thought, dismayed. This wasn't the window-cleaner. Then I noticed the bundle of clothing under his arm, loosely wrapped with brown paper. 'Sorry,' I quickly added. 'You must be the delivery man.'

Both Mr Fenton and Derek had finished with their sales and were enjoying my discomfort immensely. The former with his customary sneer but Derek with more sympathetic amusement. 'It's Mr Weiss the tailor,' he explained. 'He does our alterations.'

Happily enough Mr Weiss had a sense of humour and could see the joke. Thankfully too, Mr Harvey, who was still on the phone, missed that particular little episode.

A few minutes later the stock delivery arrived. A large brown and cream van – the Dunn & Co colours – pulled up outside and a tubby man in a brown double-breasted suit with brass buttons and a brown uniform cape with a shiny peak, emerged from the cab and strutted into the shop. I didn't like the look of him one little bit. He had piggy little eyes, a thin moustache and the foulest tongue I had ever heard. I immediately decided not to include him on my Christmas card list.

Strangely enough, although he was only the delivery man Mr Harvey deferred to him as if he was one of the directors. Probably he was frightened of him. He snapped his fingers at me. 'John – make Mr Regan a cup of tea and help unload the delivery.'

Mr Regan echoed these instructions in his own peculiar way with the stress placed on speed, all peppered with fruity and unrepeatable adjectives. I felt very angry. Enough was enough! And what was all this business about the manager calling me 'John'? That wasn't my name. I slopped some hot water into the teapot, swirled it around and poured it out into an unused mug. A hefty splash of milk and a couple of scoops of sugar – and that was all he was going to get out of me. The worm was turning!

Mr Regan blundered into the tea area and grabbed the mug. True, it probably was not the best cup of tea that I had ever made. It looked like lemonade without the fizz. But I took a very dim view of Mr Regan's criticism after the first swig. He grimaced and made a distasteful remark concerning gnats.

I was shocked. I had never heard an adult speak like that. Outside my family the only adults I had ever had any dealings with were school teachers and those at Sunday School. 'I'm sure I wouldn't know,' I coldly retorted. 'I'm not in the habit of drinking that – even if you are.'

I stalked out to help unload the van, leaving Mr Regan staring after me with a funny sort of grin on his face. Oddly enough, I think he found my reaction amusing and approved of it.

Mr Harvey had a very good sense of timing. The van had gone and we were left with cardboard cartons, all bulging with clothing, to unpack. He glanced at his watch. 'Lunch time,' he grunted, grabbed his paper bags of bread rolls and ham and vanished into the fitting-room where he always had his lunch. There was a chair there and a little flap table and he could make himself quite comfortable.

Mr Fenton stood aside waiting for customers – unpacking stock was beneath his dignity – so Derek and I got busy with the delivery. I was glad of something to do and while I counted the quantities of the various items Dave checked them off on the invoice.

During the course of this activity a customer came in to look at a suit. I didn't notice, being fascinated by the wonderful assortment of hats we were unpacking. Then Mr Fenton tapped me on the shoulder. 'Tell Mr Harvey that a customer wants to try on a pair of trousers.'

That's no big deal, I thought, making my way to the fitting-room. Of course the customer wants to try on a pair of trousers. Do we have to tell the manager every time a customer wants to try on a pair of trousers? Then the penny dropped. He wanted to try them on in the fitting-room – and Mr Harvey was having his lunch in the fitting-room. No fool, that Mr Fenton. What was that saying about killing the messenger who bears bad news? I was soon to find out.

'Please, Sir,' I murmured nervously, tapping on the door. 'A customer wants to try on a pair of trousers.'

The door opened six inches and an angry bull glared out at me, showering me with a spluttering of breadcrumbs. Mr Harvey growled, uttered a short but blood-curdling expletive and, with a great show of reluctance, gathered up his plate and newspaper. By this time the customer had joined us and was also anointed with a shower of breadcrumbs from a very resentful manager, 'I don't fancy finishing my lunch in there afterwards!' Mr Harvey grumbled loudly. 'You never know what sort of germs these people carry!'

It was Murphy's Law that whenever Mr Harvey went to the fitting-room for his lunch a customer would want to try on a pair of trousers. Mercifully I was saved by Derek glancing at his wristwatch. 'Want to take your lunch hour, Keith?'

Did I just! I was out of that shop like a rat up a drainpipe. Funny things, lunch hours. They are sixty minutes like any other hour but always seem shorter. I was to find that the hours that sag and seem longer are the mid-afternoon hours. As I lived near the shop I was home in about seven minutes. Happily my mother never asked if I had got the sack. I think she still hadn't taken it in that I was no longer one of the unemployed masses.

I soon disposed of my Marmite sandwiches, Eccles cake and Penguin wafer washed down with two cups of tea and was hot-footing it back to the shop. The delivery had been sorted out and while Mr Fenton and Derek Carstairs finished their lunch break, I was given the boring but necessary job of tearing up all the soft cardboard cap boxes into fist-sized fragments and cramming them into the Hessian salvage sacks.

Lunches over, Derek told me that our next job was to take a parcel down to Harrow and Wealdstone Station.

I frowned. 'What's wrong with the Post Office?'

'It's too big to go by post,' he explained. 'It's got to go by rail, and it will need both of us to carry it there.'

He was right too. I never realised clothing could weigh so much. Apart from the address it was vitally important that the parcel bore the legend in blue crayon 'London Ledger Account 7717. Camden Goods'. I had no idea what this meant. It could have been a magic spell to protect the parcel during its journey from wicked fairies. Eventually we struggled down to the station with it and deposited it in the goods section.

On the way back to the shop Derek told me about the firm I now worked for. Dunn & Co was founded in 1886 by George Arthur Dunn, a Quaker and philanthropist. The beginnings were humble; a little shop in Shoreditch. But due to the excellent quality of the goods the business rapidly expanded until there were one hundred and eighty branches throughout the United Kingdom. The Head Office, which also combined the warehouse was in Camden Town, and it was from this one point that the entire firm was controlled – and controlled most efficiently.

Mr Dunn retired from the business in the 1920s, leaving the firm in the tried and trusted hands of a Board of Directors who adhered to his principle of how the firm should be run. He died in 1939 – coincidently the same year I was born. I toyed with the idea that I might be a reincarnation of the Great Man. Well you never know ...

'We've got his picture hanging in the shop,' concluded Derek. 'All the shops have got them. Haven't you seen it?'

I recalled a sepia portrait whose eyes seemed to follow me around the shop like General Kitchener's poster.

The afternoon passed without incident. A few customers sauntered in. Some purchased, some didn't. The afternoon tea break came and went. I had no direct dealings with the customers and simply made myself useful by putting away any stock which they had been looking at. Mr Harvey sometimes deigned to serve a customer if that person looked prosperous enough or was accompanied by an attractive lady. For the most part he roosted in his 'office-coop' muttering down the telephone to unseen colleagues in Wembley, Watford or Edgware.

As six o'clock approached the booking up of the daily sales and the banking up of cash was dealt with. I decided to have a good look at the Founder's picture. I found the photographic portrait of George Arthur

Dunn in the minuscule clothing department. It was a large oval sepia print in a square frame and just like all those Victorian photographs. The slightly penetrating dark eyes glowering and the massive black moustache, almost challenged by a beetling pair of eyebrows. And the hot-looking three-piece suit in some woollen weave must have been sheer murder to wear in the summer, as was the restricting stiff collar with its tightly knotted tie. But on looking closer at the face I could see that it was not as old as it first appeared. There was a shrewdness and sensitivity there and I could well believe that this was a man who had created a successful and thriving clothing empire.

However, there was another picture which caught my eye. It was an excellent study in light, bright colours of a very well-dressed and smug-looking man reclining in an armchair and smoking a cigarette. Before him on the floor was an Oriental-style lamp and standing by the lamp was the inevitable genie, complete with massive turban, baggy pantaloons and curly-toed slippers. It was bowing obsequiously before the smug man and holding out a trilby hat as if it was a peace offering. I hate to think what the Race Relations Board would have made of the scene. Below the picture was the legend, 'No sooner said than Dunn'. I suppose it indicated that somewhere in the firm there was someone with a sense of humour, obvious though it may be.

LEARNING THE ROPES

May ~ June 1954

During that first week we received a visit from Mr Drew our Area Supervisor. He was a tall man, fresh-complexioned with the aquiline features usually associated with naval officers in war films. He proceeded to explain my humble functions as junior assistant in a most avuncular manner, half-sitting on the counter, probably to put me at my ease. And then he actually took off his hat, eliciting a shocked gasp from Mr Harvey. After all, executive members of Dunn & Co never – but never – removed their hats. As no ladies were on the staff the question of etiquette did not arise.

Mr Drew went on to explain that during the early days of my employment I would be called upon to deal with menial tasks but in the fullness of time when I had qualified for the rank of senior assistant I may well become a manger.

His manner throughout was almost apologetic. Probably he had some idea of the menial tasks I was to undertake working for Mr Harvey.

Chat over, he donned his hat and turned to the manager. 'Right, Mr Harvey. Let's have a look at the windows. Get your hat.'

I knew Dunn & Co were Hatters but they acted as if a hat was a life support system like an astronaut's space helmet. They would never dream of stepping outside bareheaded – not even to look at the window display.

'That suit display looks very good, Mr Harvey,' I heard Mr Drew comment. 'A very nice arrangement.'

'Yes, I thought it would,' came the reply. 'When I put it in I thought it would look very good.'

'Not so sure about that coat though,' remarked Mr Drew. 'It doesn't quite balance the window grouping very well.'

'No, it doesn't,' Mr Harvey's voice rumbled and grumbled. 'I told Fenton that when he put it in that it didn't quite balance the grouping.'

That was the manager all over. I was soon to learn that if something was good, he had done it. If it wasn't, somebody else had. Another of his little characteristics when he was grumbling came out as a clicking of the tongue combined with a sucking in of the breath. I don't know how he quite managed this but it came out as a 'sluck'. 'You blokes – sluck – it was your fault – sluck …'

With Mr Drew's departure Derek decided to acquaint me with the stock. 'Nobody expects you to take it all in first go,' he reassured me. 'You'll pick it up as you go along.'

Inevitably we started with the hats. These were ranged along the shelves in leather buckets stacked inside each other; smallest on top and biggest at the bottom. Derek jotted down a list of the mainstream sizes. They ranged from 6½ up to 7¼ going up in eighths. 'Eighths of what?' I queried. 'Surely not inches? There would only be three-quarters-of-an-inch between the smallest and the biggest.'

Derek raised his eyebrows and took a deep breath. 'Well it's not quite as straightforward as that. True, the sizes are based on the Imperial measurement but it is the sum of the length of the hat from back to front plus the width, then divided by two.'

Even I, a fresh young sprog, had to be amused at this. How very typically English to complicate the matter with this little bit of mystique. Evidently there was also the metric system which simply involved the circumference of the head in centimetres.

'Don't worry about it,' Derek chuckled. 'It's one of those things you'll soon pick up. The extreme size headwear, large and small, we keep in one of the drawers under the hats as we don't really get much call for them. I might as well tell you now that glove sizes are in inches, the sizes arrived at by the measurement round the hand just above the thumb joint.'

But I was intrigued by the hats. I had investigated one stack and was amazed to find that the crowns were not dented in with a crease at the top but only had two dents down each side. 'They're fur felts,' Derek informed me, 'and have to be shaped by the hat steamer. The dents at the side are so they stack in easier. The cheaper wool felts have to be blocked into shape at the factory under great pressure. There are something like twenty processes to making a fur felt hat when the fur is blown onto a metal cone in strands and worked into what is termed a hood.'

'Something like a candy floss machine,' I murmured, in the hope of sounding as if I had made an intelligent comment.

Derek looked at me somewhat askance. 'They're made from rabbit's fur but the really expensive ones are made from beaver. Only the West End and City shops stock those.'

'You mean this isn't the only Dunn & Co shop?' I asked.

This time Derek burst out laughing. 'We've got one hundred and eighty of them all over England, Scotland and Wales!' He pointed to a row of hat buckets on a topmost shelf. 'Those are what we call velours. The best ones are Austrian velours but there are some English velours but they are harder to the touch. Here, feel the difference.'

I did so and he was quite right. And the colours were magnificent. As well as the black, grey and brown there were bottle green and a golden brown, all in that soft velvety texture. The dearest one retailed at the stratospheric price of 75/- or £3.75 in today's decimal currency.

Derek's next words made me start. 'After lunch I'll show you how to sling a stiff.'

Heavens above! Were we in the undertaking business too? I wasn't sure about this job now.

'A stiff is the trade term for a bowler hat,' Derek patiently told me, pointing to a row of green bags on an upper shelf. They appeared to be tucked in around the sides with a piece of square cardboard inserted, bearing the style number, size and price written on the surface. They looked like a row of shelled peas. 'Top hats are termed silks,' Derek added, 'and Homburgs or Anthony Edens are known as frames.' This last was a very heavy-looking black hat with a straight crease and a silk-bound brim. He went on to explain the various shapes of the soft fur felt hats.

Most of them were called the 'Polo' style but I never found out why. The turn-down brim style was known as a snap brim and these could be steamed into the porkpie style, or completely round with no front dents, the pear-shape which was with the two front dents – also known as the trilby style after the female character in the Svengali story, or simply the straight crease, with or without frontal dents. Some of these straight crease hats were worn with the brim curled up in the off-the-face style.

There were a couple of others which took my eye. One was a blended wool/fur felt with a stitched gabardine covering in fawn or grey called the 'Wethergard' and a lightweight and very dramatically-sloped crown called the 'Cresta' after the famous Cresta Slope ski run.

Derek dragged me away from these fascinating styles to show me the cheaper wool felts. They were, on appearance, very attractive-looking hats but when you touched them they were as hard as wood. 'They don't take the rain very well,' Derek told me. 'Once they get wet they go as limp as flannel.'

Nevertheless they looked good. Many of them had fancy bands in leatherette. One such was called the 'Montana' style with little stars cut into the band. Derek had one of these hats so they couldn't have been all that bad. But one very interesting thing I found was that I was able to distinguish between the quality of the hats when I was steaming them. The fur felts smelt of apricot, the blended felts of strawberries, and the wool felts of Marmite!

Looking back from over half a century I cannot help but notice one glaring anomaly. In recent years the television has screened a number of dramas set in the wartime era. Usually they get the settings right but in *Foyle's War* all trilby hats have wide flat brims, almost like scouts' hats instead of the usual curl or dish as it was known on the brim. Obviously they must be the cheaper quality wool felts that have been ironed to get any kind of kinks and wrinkles out. But to one who remembers what trilby hats did look like the effect jars. Possibly the programme planners involved in the series were too young to realise this. But to resume ...

My baptism of fire as far as the hats were concerned wasn't over. Derek led me to the 'Dreaded Conformature'. This infernal machine was used to make bowler hats fit as, unlike soft felt hats, they contained a large amount of shellac. The conformature resembled the skeleton of a top hat and was comprised of many Bakelite keys which formed the crown and the brim. These were held in position by a metal spring encircling the edge of the brim. This fiendish contraption was placed on the customer's head so that the keys were pushed out to the individual shape of his head. On the top the keys terminated in an oval of upward-pointing metal spikes which expanded to reproduce the head shape in miniature. A piece of white card was placed in a metal frame above these spikes and pressed down, leaving a small-scale shape of the head. The shape was then cut out and placed in a wooden block made up of an oval of wooden pegs. The pegs were shuffled around the edges of the card and held in place by tightening up several brass wing nuts thus bringing the paper template shape back to life-size. This was then placed inside the bowler hat and heated over an electric fire which softened the shellac and formed it to the customer's individual head shape. So we were actually creating hats made-to-measure.

In passing, Derek informed me that the inventor was said to have gone mad. I wasn't really surprised. It was an evil looking device and the first time I attempted to use it I almost trepanned the customer.

We passed on to other accessories used in headwear. The curved brim brushes which could only be used by right-handed people, the brass circular hat measure and the stretching blocks. These latter items, resembling medieval knuckle-dusters, consisted of two half circles of heavy wood joined together by a brass handle, screw-threaded at both ends so that they could be expanded within the hat.

By this time I was in a state of utter confusion. How could I take this all in? I just hoped that I was somehow accumulating all this information by osmosis. And as for all the bookwork with the stock sheets, invoice books and so forth as well as the different coloured inks of red, black and green. And they had to be real ink, not ballpoint pens. I despaired of ever getting the hang of it all and would probably retire as the oldest junior assistant ever.

We then passed on to the clothing which proved to be a great deal more straightforward. Coats simply came in chest sizes from thirty-four inches up to forty-six. The same went for jackets but they also did long and short fittings as well as regular fittings. With the suits the size range was the same but with even more permutations. Whereas say, a regular, long or short fitting had a thirty-eight inch chest there was a drop of four inches to the waist size. But they also did stout and short stout where the chest and the waist were the same and portly and short portly with only a two inch drop to the waist size. Later they were to toy with an extremely limited range of long portly fittings and also slim fittings where the drop to waist size was six inches.

But the quality of that merchandise was obvious even to a fifteen year-old such as I. All those splendid gabardine raincoats lined up on the racks as smart as guardsmen. The elegant lounge suits, queuing up neatly on their rails, all awaiting a good home, and their weekend counterparts in soft woollens of lovat, brown and green. You could see the quality in the way they hung. A firm called *Crombie* did the Rolls Royce of Winter overcoats but they also did a limited range of sports suits. The colours and patterns were highly distinctive. But alas – the sports or weekend suit is now a thing of the past.

I felt something was missing. 'Do we stock trousers?' I asked Derek.

He opened a cupboard near the front of the shop and pulled out three shelves on which lay a meagre range of trousers. Grey, fawn and lovat. Compared with the rest of the clothing stock the trousers seemed hard done by. Also the way they were withdrawn from the wooden cabinet had something macabre about it. It put me in mind of a cadaver being removed from a mortuary cabinet.

But on the bottom shelf were waistcoats. 'We don't carry many waist-coats this time of the year,' Derek explained. They're more of an Autumn and Winter range. Very popular as Christmas presents. You wait until you see the Winter stock. Silk brocade, red, yellow tattersall check. Every pattern and colour you could imagine.

I could well believe it and my love affair with waistcoats began there and then. The Spring and Summer range were only plain woollen or satin finish in grey, fawn and maroon but I could see how elegant they looked with a dark suit.

It can be imagined that my mind was in a whirl with this surfeit of information. How could I possibly cope? How could I possibly take it all in? But it does happen. I was so fascinated with the variety and quality of the garments that I quickly absorbed all this information over a short period without being aware of it. Even so, I was still kept to the menial tasks and not let loose on a customer until I had a fair idea of the salesmanship required.

But I felt that I had managed to get one foot on the lowest step of the ladder. Mr Harvey now called me Keith instead of 'John' which was the stock name by which all junior members of staff were known. But I still managed to get into trouble of some sort with Mr Harvey. For instance, he had his tea in a bone china cup and saucer while we all made do with thick china or enamel mugs. Now a bone china cup and saucer in a shop with a stone floor is not really practical. It was a case of an accident waiting to happen. And it did.

I was washing up the tea things in the little barred window condemned cell which passed for the washroom when I let slip the manager's cup. I'll admit that I was probably miles away on some daydream. But that is not an excuse, it is a reason. I watched in astonishment as the cup actually bounced off the stone floor. Then it bounced again with the same result. But on the third bounce it wasn't so lucky and shattered with a loud crash. Then Mr Harvey's roar erupted from the shop of which 'you' and 'clumsy' were the only words I feel able to record with any decorum.

On another occasion Mr Harvey casually tossed a postcard onto the table and told me to get rid of it. I took him at his word and made a thorough job of tearing it into sixteen pieces before his disbelieving eyes and tossing the fragments into the wastepaper basket. He said get rid of it, not post it was my only possible plea of defence to Mr Fenton and Derek who were almost ill with laughter.

But there was one occasion when the boot was on the other foot. Not only did I have to get the manager's lunch for him but quite frankly do some of his domestic shopping as well. On this particular occasion it was a Saturday and I had to get a pound of sprats for Winkie the family cat. I had a fair knowledge of the pecking order in the Harvey domicile and it was, starting from the top, Mr Harvey's mother-in-law who lived with him, his wife, Winkie the cat and finally Mr Harvey himself.

Trade had been a bit on the slack side that week as the weather was too fine for wandering around hot shops, also the holiday season was just about beginning, and Saturday wasn't much of an improvement either. Sir was not a very happy bunny. Booking up at six o'clock he chuntered on about the trade – or lack of it – as if it were our fault. Just to be really awkward he made no effort to close the books at a decent time and we didn't get out of the shop until 6.30.

Even then we weren't off the hook. The day's takings had to be deposited in the night safe at the bank and we had to accompany him. So there we were. Mr Fenton, Dave and yours truly, all trooping behind Sir while he strode along still grumbling and complaining about us. 'It was your fault, Carstairs – sluck – losing that suit sale on Tuesday. I don't know – sluck – you blokes.'

By then we had reached the bank. Still carping on at us, Mr Harvey opened the night safe, but instead of depositing the leather night safe wallet with the day's takings in it – he put in Winkie's pound of sprats. And it was a very hot weekend!

TRIBULATION AND PROBATION

Summer 1954

We never did learn the outcome of Mr Harvey returning home spratless, to face the wrath of his wife, mother-in-law and Winkie the cat. No doubt he shifted the blame. 'It was their fault; those blokes – sluck – they should have been watching.' Yes, I can just hear it.

Despite these little setbacks and crises I settled in well enough to the weekly routine. Monday was taken up with bookwork and the stock delivery, and Tuesday, being generally a quiet, in-between sort of day, would be when we dressed one of the windows. This could prove something of an ordeal as Mr Harvey was called upon to do some work. All merchandise had to be removed from the window and returned to stock after first making sure that it hadn't faded. The display stands were put out of the way and then the window had to be cleaned. This meant a zinc bucket of water and a leather, a yellow duster for drying purposes and finally a wad of tissue paper for polishing. This was made even more difficult as the shop faced east and the sun would dry the glass out before the smears could be removed. Mr Harvey would go outside and peer at the glass while I stood inside, limp and sweating, waiting for him to point an accusing finger at a near-invisible smear that I had missed.

Then it was a question of sweeping and polishing the linoleum floor. The sweeping was necessary on account of the baker's next door which held a great attraction for wasps. Whether or not it was a sinister reflection on their cakes raised an unanswered question but dozens of wasps would find their way into our windows and grandly expire on the displays.

From then on my duties were easier and I had nothing more difficult to do than make up the various price tickets required for the fresh display. But if there was one thing that spoiled the display it was the price tickets. These consisted of a metal slide into which the individual digits which made up the price were placed. These were thin pieces of white plastic and as some of them had become yellowed with age they gave the impression of a set of bad teeth.

I kept well out of the manager's way as window dressing always put him in an ill-humour. He grumbled and grunted his way through the task but we usually managed to get it all done by about three in the afternoon.

Wednesday was a breathing space. It was half-day which meant that we closed at one o'clock. But it was a full morning as, apart from my regular chores, there were the stock sheets to be filled in and posted to Head Office. While Mr Harvey and Mr Fenton dealt with the hats and clothing, Derek and I saw to the caps. It was a simple enough business of one calling out the reference numbers and sizes and the other jotting them down on the stock sheets.

Wednesday morning was when our red stone floor received its weekly polish. This was done by a Mrs Briggs who was what was known then as a charwoman. Mrs Briggs was the stage image of a charwoman. Squat, aproned, wearing a red beret – although I had doubts about her ever being in the Parachute Regiment – and her one-tooth grin with her usual cheery greeting of, 'hullo, ducks.'

For her labours she received the princely sum of 7/6d which was duly recorded on the Petty Cash Sheet 'Floor Cleaner 7/6d'. Evidently Mr Harvey had previously received admonition from Head Office for putting 'Woman 7/6d'.

'We don't pay for your women, even if they are only 7/6d,' came the Olympian rumbles from our lords and masters.

But Thursdays were often quite different. 'We'll both be going to Kentish Town to collect some extra stock for the weekend,' Derek told me.

I felt the blood drain from my face. 'All that way?' I quavered. 'Isn't that down near the South Coast?'

Derek stared at me blankly. 'Kentish Town is in North London and our Head Office and warehouse are there.'

I hadn't been told about this part of the job and I had visions of us with a horse and cart, stacked to capacity with hats and clothing, negotiating our way across the North Circular Road at Stonebridge Park but, of course, it all turned out to be a much more straightforward and less worrisome procedure.

Derek and I were sent on our way with several letters to various departments, requesting stock. 'This is a doddle,' Derek assured me as we strolled down to Harrow and Wealdstone station. 'At least we'll be out of Ronnie's way for the morning.'

We had to change at Willesden Junction as the trains only ran through to Camden Road during peak hours. This entailed climbing a flight of stairs, darting down a sooty, twisting wormhole and then another flight of stairs which led up to what was rather grandly called Willesden High Level.

But oh, the view! Scrapyards of discarded cars on one side like the graveyard of metallic elephants and a panoramic view of Heinz factory with the Taylors Lane cooling towers looming up, complete with cumulus clouds of polluted vapour towering above them. It was a sight to stir the blood and rot the lungs.

The High Level Line ran from the salubrious environs of Richmond and through Acton which was definitely not. From Willesden it looped around the outer edges of Kilburn and Hampstead, to join up with our original line at Camden Road.

This station looked as if it had been carved from living rock; its greyness only relieved by the maroon nameplates and the unexpectedly ornate canopy edging above the platform, all in maroon paint. British rail must have bought a job lot of the stuff.

We passed through the cathedral-like, rocky-walled ticket office into the street and around a few corners to the citadel of our masters. The Head Office was an off-white building which took up a triangular block between forked roads, save for an establishment at the apex which manufactured artificial Christmas trees. Facing us in the wall was a large metal folding door. Derek pressed a button on the wall and the doors ponderously folded aside, allowing us entrance.

Yet another illusion shot down in flames. I had imagined entering Head Office through glass doors of purest crystal, beyond which we would find ourselves in a spacious foyer with ankle-deep dove grey fitted carpets. There we would await our collection and take our ease in modern Scandinavian furniture whilst being served coffee by elegant ice maiden secretaries.

What confronted us resembled Fingal's Cave. A dark loading bay for the delivery lorries and a raised stone walkway along one side. Derek led the way along this uneven and precipitous track to a wooden door with two glass panels. No photo-electric doors here! Derek rattled the door and in response one of a row of bespectacled clerks in their shirt-sleeves in an office beyond the inner reception area, reached under his desk and pulled a piece of knotted strong. This string ran through a hole in the office wall, through the reception area to the doorknob which duly clicked open, allowing us to enter.

'Watch out when we leave,' Derek warned me. 'They try to catch us in those folding doors on the way out.'

I thought we had stepped into a junior production of an Al Capone film. Several fellows about my own age, all suited and wearing hats tilted rakishly back from their foreheads, lounged against the wooden counter and glanced at us with critical appraisal. Being the only un-hatted one I felt quite inferior. These youths were obviously what we now term as 'street-wise', though probably cocksure and arrogant would be nearer the truth. It emerged that they were junior assistants from various branches in the London area on a similar mission to ours.

'Where's your papers?' demanded an irascible voice.

No svelte blonde secretaries here. Instead, a harassed and angry little white-haired man in a dusty, blue chalk stripe suite. This was Mr Bristow the Warehouse Manager. Derek dutifully handed him our letters. Mr Bristow glared at him. 'We've got enough to do here without you lot coming in for stock. Pests! You can all clear off for half an hour. There's a café over the road.'

We obediently trooped off to this villainous-looking establishment and bought coffee, although I was inclined to believe it was British Rail soot. The air was thick with cigarette smoke as my peers vied with each other loudly over such issues as how they really ran their shops instead of their 'imbecile managers'. Inflated egos floated through the air like barrage balloons.

Eventually we all wandered back to the warehouse where Mr Bristow awaited us, surrounded by large packages of black waterproof paper tied up with coarse white string.

'Took your time, didn't you?' he greeted us accusingly. 'Sign for your parcels and clear out. We've got work to do.'

Somehow we all got sorted out and went our separate ways. Derek and I had four large and bulky parcels between us and that string really cut into the hands and raised blisters. It was a great relief to drop them on the platform while we waited for our train back.

But the worst wasn't over. On arriving back at Harrow and Wealdstone we were faced with the arduous journey back to the shop. It was no use trying to get a bus; the parcels were too big. So we had to walk the mile-plus, slightly uphill. As we staggered into the shop, weak-kneed and perspiring, Mr Harvey's plaintive voice challenged us with, 'Where have you been? I want my lunch.' Then, to me, 'get me a piece of veal and ham pie with an egg in it.'

Friday was a day of suppressed excitement for that was the day we got paid. That depended, of course, if there was enough cash in the till. It was common practice in those days to draw your wages that way as very few of the lower ranks had bank accounts, and credit cards had not been thought of.

Usually, about four in the afternoon, Mr Harvey would call us up in turn to sign for our wages on a pad which was half-hidden by a piece of blotting paper so that you couldn't see what the others were getting. For some reason in those early days commission was signed for and paid on a Monday.

Having some real grown-up money of the folding kind was almost intoxicating and I well remember my first purchase. It was from *Sopers*, a nearby departmental store, and it was a splendid cravat in gold and wine red hexagons at the princely sum of 10/6d. In those days Dunn & Co only sold outer clothing. Derek plainly thought I was mad lashing out on a cravat but, surprisingly, Mr Fenton sided with me. He was a very clothes-conscious young man; probably the only thing we had in common.

Saturday lunchtime soon became the 'happy hour' when I would treat myself to something special. Occasionally it was a new tie, as we didn't stock ties in those days. Other days it might be a book or a record. Whatever it was entailed a hurried journey home by bus, have my dinner and get back to the shop – and I always managed it within the hour.

As the days trundled by and the Summer got hotter, I learnt that Mr Harvey was due to take his fortnight's holiday and would hand over stock on the coming Friday. Hand over to whom? In those days the senior assistant never took on relief work at his own shop. It was customary for someone from another branch to take on that mantle, and on this occasion it was an assistant from the West End.

Simon Delgado proved to be quite the opposite of Mr Harvey. A dapper man of middle years and a very natty dresser. On first impression one recalled the line in reference to Oscar Wilde, 'not as other men', but this was quite the wrong assumption. He was simply a dandy who discreetly enjoyed female company despite not being exactly what you would call handsome. What hair he still possessed was fair, but most of it growing in a trim line beneath his long nose and his features gave the impression of a surprised weasel. But his clothes! An immaculate silver-grey bowler hat which matched his elegantly waisted single-breasted suit and a silk waist-coat that must have been torn from a rainbow. But he had the sort of personality to carry it off.

Those two weeks were certainly a refreshing change from 'Sir's' grumbles and he taught me more about the job than Mr Harvey ever did. He taught me how to string up a parcel securely for post and the procedure involved if it was to be sent registered post. This was when the value of the contents was above a certain amount and the preparations involved were like some Druidic ritual.

After the parcel was strung up '1/– Fee Paid' was written on it in blue crayon. Then red sealing wax and matches were produced and the molten wax was dropped on every knot and join of the parcel's string.

Simon's attitude to the clerical side of the job was dismissive. He was partially colour blind and the various coloured inks entailed with completing the weekly sales sheets confused him. Inevitably he would say, 'I've had enough of this. Let Head Office sort it out,' and cram the whole lot into an envelope and post it.

He lived in Wembley in his own flat with his housekeeper, an elderly lady who had been his nanny when a child. He travelled to work on one of those motorised bicycles with some sort of engine fixed to the rear wheel we used to call a putt-putt. And couldn't he shift on it! He would come hurtling down Watford Road, seemingly at the speed of light in his grey suit, flamboyant waistcoat and bowler hat tilted forward over his brow. Crash helmets were yet to become compulsory.

One evening at about 5 o'clock Simon glanced at his watch and nodded at Derek and me. 'You two can go,' he announced.

Go? I gaped at him in astonishment. Go for good, did he mean?

'An early night,' he generously elaborated.

James Fenton looked up from his bookwork and smirked.

'He's never heard of an early night. Harvey doesn't believe in them.'

Simon primly placed his fingertips together. 'Silly man,' he murmured. 'Silly, silly man.'

Simon was a first class salesman. I soon learnt that he could get away with saying the most outrageous things to customers that no one else could get away with. He could flannel and flatter with the best of them, but if he felt someone was messing him about and wasting his time he had his own technique which made me cringe.

On one such occasion he had a cap customer. Being a West End salesman he started with the top quality but the customer found some fault with all of them. It was obvious that he wanted a top quality cap but at the lowest price. Simon stuck with it until the man finally said that he wanted one of the 6/6d caps. 'Oh, you want a **cheap** cap?' declared Simon. He carelessly flung open the drawer of cheap caps and sauntered away, nose in the air and his hands held out in an expressive gesture of dismissal.

On the other hand, he could be Prince Charming himself. He was endeavouring to sell a customer a suit but was having an uphill struggle due to the customer's wife who criticised every suit her husband tried on. Simon paused in his sales pitch, fixed the lady with a bright blue eye and exclaimed, 'Madam, what a beautiful dress! My wife has been looking for one like that but yours is obviously exclusive!'

The lady simpered and underwent a complete change of character. The fact that Simon was a bachelor was academic. Within five minutes he had made a sale and the suit was being wrapped up.

But he could also be a bit of a rebel – a big bit in fact. On one occasion he did a fortnight's relief at the Brighton shop. This shop's Area Supervisor was a Mr Rouse better known as 'Hookey' Rouse on account of his thin, aquiline nose. He had been an Area Supervisor for some time and knew all the wrinkles, and that nose of his was like a radar system for sniffing out any irregularity. So much so that one Saturday he took himself down to Brighton to see how Simon was making out at the shop. It must have been a very strong instinct to compel him to do this as Area Supervisors rarely if ever visited their shops on a Saturday.

On arriving at Brighton he found the shop locked, barred and bolted with the lights out. The Hookey Radar System went to work again and led him through the town to the sea front where he found Simon and the three assistants sitting on the promenade, wearing white caps out of stock and eating ice-creams!

They were marched back to the shop despite Simon's plaintive arguments that nobody went shopping on such a beautiful day. The shop was reopened and the caps returned to stock. Strange as it may seem there were no dismissals. In those days murder would have to have been committed before anyone was sacked from Dunn & Co.

This incident made me wonder why a man of Simon's years of experience had never become a manager. I was later told he had been offered a manager's position at a branch in Bristol but had refused it because it would have meant selling his flat which would have resulted in his housekeeper being homeless. My respect for Simon Delgado rose and has never lessened.

I can still see him now on a fine day when there was nothing much to do. He would stroll outside, lean against the railings at the kerbside with his arms stretched out each side of him along the top rail. Completely relaxed with his ankles casually crossed and his head tilted back in the bright sunshine, he looked as if he had been crucified.

But all good things come to an end and the fortnight passed all too quickly. Mr Harvey returned and Simon went back to the glamour and clamour of the West End. Derek Carstairs also departed, having been transferred to our Harlesden branch. I was sorry to see him go as he had greatly helped me through those early days. He left the firm a few weeks later and I never saw him again.

However, we were to receive a replacement. When I first saw him I thought he must be a younger brother of Mr Harvey. He was about the same build, black hair, but his complexion was sallow. Also there was a puckishness in his face which hinted at a nature alien to anything in the Manager's genes. This was Norman Hurst who was our new First Sales.

Mr Fenton had replaced him while he was off sick. The fact that he had off for the best part of a year with tuberculosis which, in the Fifties, could often prove fatal, was of no consequence to the firm. It is to their credit that they kept him on the payroll for the whole time he was off work.

Mr Hurst, in his early thirties, had a schoolboy's sense of humour; that wonderful sense of the ridiculous which cheered the atmosphere tremendously. He was wildly erratic in some things which made each day an adventure of the unexpected which I found most welcome. I never had much to do with James Fenton and he kept himself pretty much to himself as far as I was concerned. All I really knew about him was that he was diabetic and had to give himself daily injections of insulin.

I wasn't the only one who found him aloof. Mr Drew didn't get on with him too well and once lost his temper and told him to 'wipe that smug smile off his face!' After that it was only a matter of time before he handed in his notice.

The Saturday he left Mr Harvey let him off early. He hadn't been gone five minutes when I noticed that he had left his hypodermic and other medical paraphernalia behind. Scooping it all up, I chased after him and caught him up at the bus stop. Imagine my amazement when he thanked me and said that it didn't matter as he had the necessary medication at home. Then he shook hands with me and wished me well – and then his bus came along. I was astonished. He had hardly acknowledged my existence in the weeks I had been at the shop. It just goes to show how you can never tell with some folk.

As we were down to three staff – the Manager, Norman Hurst and myself – I had been allowed access to the unsuspecting headwear customers. Not the clothing customers – I might cause too much damage. Happily I found that I had an inborn knack of shaping the hats. As far as dealing with public went I no doubt grovelled and toadied in those early days but I soon learnt to adopt civility rather than servility.

Every so often we would have a visit from the Shop Inspector to make sure that we were abiding by the rules and regulations as laid down by the Shop Acts notice displayed prominently in the fitting-room-cum-staff room. This listed the hours we should work and the specified amount of break time we were entitled to. Although they seemed hot on safety measures they never picked up the fact that there was no rear entrance to the shop. The only way in or out was through the front door.

I mentioned this to Norman Hurst one day.

'Just supposing a car crashed into the front of the shop and caught fire. We would be trapped.'

But Norman had a ready answer. 'The best thing to do would be to each grab an overcoat, soak it under the tap, wrap it round you and crash your way out through the display windows, using the clothing stands to break the glass.'

Judging by his grunt of disapproval I don't think that this survival plan was shared by Mr Harvey. I suppose he was thinking of the hole made by the stock deficit of damaged goods in his Annual Trade Bonus. Happily the problem never arose.

One Saturday a customer asked for a bowler hat. I found one, apparently left out of display, and it fitted perfectly. This was one of the new range which did not need conforming to the customer's head shape. The crunch came when Mr Harvey demanded, 'where's my new bowler hat?'

I could have said that it was just crossing the road to the Granada cinema but felt that he would miss the humour of this. I was right too. He chuntered and puffed for ages and the fact that Mr Hurst found it amusing didn't help either.

Then just as we were about to close the shop Mr Harvey said he wanted a word with me. Hadn't he had enough already? After all, he could order another hat, couldn't he?

But I was to be surprised. 'You've passed through your probationary period,' he told me, 'so you are now eligible for purchases at staff discount. A third off coats and suits and 30/– off your first hat.'

He then produced one of the Polo style trilbies in dark grey-blue. It was the lower medium quality range in fur and wool mixture, priced at 28/6d.

I put it on and peered into the mirror. It looked odd. Too high in the crown and too wide at the top. I would have preferred something more racy. I looked like a hat on legs.

Nevertheless, I knew that I had passed into full staff membership and could appreciate just how Queen Elizabeth II had felt the previous year. This was my Coronation – even if I didn't think much of the crown.

THE WINDS OF CHANGE

Autumn 1954 ~ Autumn 1956

I never really learnt to love that first hat. In fact I came to detest it. It could cause acute embarrassment on a windy day and it was difficult to maintain nonchalance when pursuing it down the street. Apart from holding it in place I had to walk in a steady crouch with my head down. This probably accounts for my tendency to cringe when walking.

The other and even worse ordeal was when I made my daily visit to *Danny's Café* for Mr Harvey's buttered rolls. I had to pass a coffee bar and this particular place was a rendezvous for the local Teddy Boys. Previously I had been ignored but now I stood out like a sore thumb. Big hefty chaps they were, with their Tony Curtis forelocks, long jackets and drainpipe trousers. Their leader was a red-headed fellow in a garish black-and-white houndstooth-check jacket which almost reached his knees. And once they had noticed me I was doomed to ridicule.

'Rotten 'at!' they would shout, and I would favour them with a sickly grin and nod, which probably gave the impression that I was the local halfwit. But I soon solved the problem by keeping a folded hat bag in my pocket, and as soon as I was out of the shop that hat was in the bag until I was on my way back.

I really don't know why I was worried. The firm had these small show-cards displaying monochrome photographs of young men wearing various styles of hats. They didn't look any better than I did. But there was something odd about those pictures. Nearly all of them had chimney pots in the background. I later discovered that they were not professional models but Head Office staff who had been herded up to the flat roof of the office and photographed. It gave me cause to wonder what the general public made of them and it beggars description; all those well-dressed young men, strolling around the chimney pots.

Despite my hat troubles I seemed to be coping with the job sufficiently enough, apart from one incident of incurring managerial wrath. Mr Harvey had a habit of not bothering to extinguish his cigarettes and would just drop the butts in the ashtray. This incident occurred one day when I was sweeping the floor with one of the old electric cylinder cleaners with the long flexible tube. To save time emptying the ashtrays I flicked the nozzle over them. A minute later Sir bellowed, 'something's on fire! I can smell burning!'

I turned and saw a fierce jet of black smoke billowing out of the rear of the sweeper. Obviously the cigarette butt had set fire to the dustbag. What to do? The answer came in a flash. I had heard that if you were cornered just brazen it out; it can sometimes work. So acting on this I looked Mr Harvey straight in the eye and announced, 'If you think it has something to do with the cleaner, Sir, you are gravely mistaken.' This, with black smoke roiling and coiling around me. Unfortunately the ploy didn't work.

I had trouble with that machine on another occasion. The tube was blocked and I was vainly poking a length of wire down it to clear the obstruction. 'I'll show you how to clear it,' Mr Hurst offered. He took the tube from me, disconnected it and screwed it onto the exhaust. Then he pointed the nozzle out of the shop doorway and switched it on. It cleared all right. A horrible great ball of dust shot out across the pavement and hit a lady in the rear. Mr Hurst thrust the tube into my hands and vanished, while the lady peered around indignantly for her molester. Luckily I went unseen, skulking and quaking in the shadows of the doorway.

Without doubt the most physically arduous task I had to do was buffing the floor. Thankfully this was not often, but usually when a Head Office bigwig might be paying us a visit. The red stone floor was polished once a week by Mrs Briggs but every so often I would have to give it an extra shine with the floor buff. This instrument of torture was a thick wooden pole about six feet long, hinged to a great slab of iron with a thick felt pad over it. I had to pump this horror back and forth until the floor shone like glass. I must have sweated pounds and could well imagine how the galley slaves of Ancient Rome must have suffered.

As the weeks drifted into the Autumn I was granted three days leave; one day for each full month that I had worked. Usually I went to Suffolk with my parents to visit relatives but any such holiday was out of the question. But three days was three days and I was glad to take them.

One afternoon I decided to have a look at our Piccadilly shop. It was our 'flagship' branch and I was curious to see it. The store was vast compared to Harrow. Massive windows packed with clothing, and inside I glimpsed 'Ye Olde Oak Tudor' fittings, complete with a baronial staircase. Even the wall clock was wooden! It looked like Westminster Abbey with price tickets. And then the shock. A figure suddenly materialised in front of me. A tall man in a black curly-brimmed hat and a long black overcoat, his hands thrust deep into the pockets as he seemed to glare at me!

I took fright and beat a hasty retreat. It must have been one of the directors – and here was I, sauntering around Piccadilly without a hat! I was halfway down the subway steps of Piccadilly Circus when I realised that even if he was a director he wouldn't have known me from Adam. But I decided to leave Dunn's shops alone for the rest of the three days.

On my return to work I found that we had a new member of staff. Ivor Powell had worked for Dunn & Co previously and had just finished his term of National Service in the Army. He had applied for a job in Head Office as Assistant Buyer but had agreed in the meantime to work at Harrow through the Christmas period.

Yes he was a Welshman. Well, he had to be with a name like that! Furthermore, he claimed to be a cousin of the actor Richard Burton. We got on famously. He was bluff, rough and tough; a stocky young man with a hideous taste in suits. I recall one in particular. It was black-and-white houndstooth with a red panel check. His technique with customers was hilarious. Instead of tapping discreetly on the fitting-room door and inquiring how the garment fitted, he would mount the three steps leading up to the washroom, lean over the top of the fitting-room and ask, 'how are you getting on, boyo?' With his bluff humour and Mr Hurst's erratic wit, Mr Harvey's overbearing personality inevitably dwindled.

On returning from the bank one Autumn morning Mr Harvey said, 'You've got to go to help out at Wembley today. Mr Penrose hasn't got any staff.'

They say a change is as good as a rest so on the way to the station I called in my home to say that I wouldn't be in for lunch but would get something at Wembley. I knew where the shop was so that didn't present a problem. It was squarer than Harrow but had a spacious upstairs department with windows at each end. But it was located on the railway bridge of the station and whenever an express train thundered through – they were steam trains in those days – the light fittings would rattle alarmingly and even a few of the parquet tiles would be shaken loose from the floor. More than a few times a sale was lost when a customer fled the shop, fearing an impending earthquake.

Mr Penrose was a charming man. Not fat but squarely-built with the appearance and bearing more befitting a member of the higher echelons of statesmanship. He greeted me as an old friend. 'Hello, John. There's just a few things need attending to. We could do with some change from the bank and there's two parcels to be posted. When you've done that we'll have a nice cup of tea.'

He even brought his own lunch with him; a neat little packet of sand-wiches which he ate in his office-coop with a white napkin spread across the desk top. 'What do you do at Harrow for lunch?' he asked me when he had finished.

'I only live a short distance from the shop,' I told him, 'so I go home for lunch. I'll pop over to *Lyons* and get some sandwiches.'

He dismissed the idea with a wave of his hand. 'Oh, no. You're helping me out today. You go home and have your lunch. And take your full hour, too – never mind the travelling time. And tell me how much your fares are and I'll reimburse you out of the petty cash.'

Now this was totally different from Mr Harvey. On my return from lunch Mr Penrose suggested another cup of tea, and as trade was quiet he suggested several that afternoon. At 4.30 he glanced at his watch. 'Don't forget your dental appointment at 5 o'clock,' he murmured.

What dental appointment? He had lost me completely. Then the penny dropped. This was his way of giving me an early night.

He thanked me graciously for helping out and I realised the sense of the philosophy that starting with a difficult boss would therefore make me appreciate the others.

By this time Christmas was fast approaching and our plain brown hat bags were replaced by plain brown hat bags with a sprig of holly printed on them. Our display showcards which read 'Dunn & Co. – To Be Sure' were replaced by ones which read 'Dunn & Co. – To Be Sure – Happy Christmas'. Also, discreet pieces of cardboard holly were fastened to all the display stands.

Dunn & Co were very generous to their employees. Not only had we received earlier in the year a Summer bonus, we also got a Winter bonus – and a Christmas Box. And if the Christmas holiday fell midweek it was not unusual for them to grant us an extra day, just to make the holiday worthwhile.

With the arrival of 1955 Ivor Powell ascended to his senior post at Head Office and we had a succession of junior staff begged, borrowed or stolen from other shops to make up the number. Once you get into a routine it is surprising just how quickly the time passes and Mr Harvey's summer holidays came round again. But it was not Simon Delgado who did the fortnight's relief this time; it was Rupert Higgs, the Senior Assistant of Watford branch. I had met him briefly before when he was relieving the Kilburn branch. I had been sent there with a parcel and was met by this plump young man with a tranquil, almost oriental expression and slightly slanted eyes. So, on my return to Harrow I announced, 'They've got a Chinaman working at Kilburn.'

Even Mr Harvey laughed at this. In fact, anything to do with Rupert Higgs created mirth. His fortnight at Harrow was a laugh from beginning to end. One quiet afternoon I was tidying up out the back – or the staff area concealed by the large wing mirror – and Norman Hurst and Rupert were chatting in the shop. Rupert had a stock of extremely funny stories and he told them in his own particularly understated way. It is a sad fact that you can never remember more than a couple of jokes at such a marathon of merriment, but what I do remember is my stomach really aching with laughter.

After my fortnight's summer holiday – I was now eligible for full holiday entitlement – Mr Drew paid us a visit one afternoon. I was always a bit leery about his visits as they frequently involved shunting off junior staff to some remote corner of the Dunn & Co empire and I always wondered if and when it was going to be my turn, and where would they send me anyway?

On this occasion he had come to check the stock which was a long and boring business of counting, recounting and then noting all the totals on a new set of stock sheets as the opening figures. I was entrusted to count the caps which I managed to get wrong by some quite spectacular amounts. Also we had to count the hangers. The wooden clothing hangers were charged to the shop at 2/6d each and the green wire trouser hangers at 1/–. And those totals had to be right. If any of the wooden hangers were damaged they were written off and taken away by the Area Supervisor who had to personally dispose of them. I was told this was done when they had a bonfire in their gardens.

On this particular visit I was informed that I would be required to work at our Wembley branch to cover for their junior who was on holiday. At least they had the decency to give me a week's grace so it wasn't a matter of dashing off at a moment's notice.

This gave me time to get things sorted out. It would be quite unreasonable for me to expect to go home for lunch. That was only a one-off, and as Mr Penrose had just retired the new manager could well be a carbon copy of Mr Harvey. To this end I acquired a lunch box of which I was very proud. It went with my new hat and my new double-breasted gabardine raincoat (belted in airforce blue, I looked like an American serviceman) even if it was rather on the big side and looked as if I had stolen it from a giant. All in all, I felt quite the man about town. Actually the lunch box resembled a miniature suitcase but it would suffice to hold my newspaper, liver sausage sandwiches, Eccles cake and Penguin wafer.

What a pleasant surprise Wembley turned out to be! Mr Benson the new manager was probably the finest manager I have ever worked for. He was middle-aged, quite tall with grey 'wings' to a good head of hair. In his dark three-piece suit and horn-rimmed glasses he looked and had the manner of the much-missed family doctor. I don't think he ever asked or accepted anything without saying 'please' or 'thank you'. When the magic time for a tea break came around he would murmur, 'shall we have a cup of tea, laddie?' He was known as 'Bertie' Benson for some obscure reason but his Christian name was William. Not that I had the temerity to call him 'Bertie', even though I thought of him thus. It was always 'Sir' or 'Mr Benson'. Likewise with senior staff it was always 'Mr'.

His one and only assistant was Roy Manson, a tall, athletic fellow in his mid-twenties. He had the appearance – to me at any rate – of one of those dangerous characters who played Poker on Mississippi riverboats with his darkly saturnine features and long sideburns. He also did a bit of boxing which fitted in well with his image.

But he was a friendly enough person and the three of us jogged along famously. The tea breaks were very laid-back sessions. Bertie would have his downstairs in his little office-coop while Roy and I retired to one of the two spacious fitting-rooms upstairs where I would let him read the sports pages of my newspaper. Customers were considerate. They never interrupted us and on reflection it is a wonder how we stayed in business. But to even the balance Saturday trade was really hectic.

Being built on a railway bridge the shop had a rear entrance into the booking hall which was a mixed blessing as some members of the public would simply use it as a short cut to the High Street. But at least a few of them had the grace to buy something en route – even if it was only a 7/6d cap.

If there was anything to carp about it was the lack of toilet facilities. We had a little hand basin in a minuscule staff room designed for a dwarf but for the toilet purposes we were obliged to use the amenities on the main line platform of the station. The same went for tea leaves. This was long before the discovery of the space-age tea-bag and all the grouts were tipped into a bucket, taken down to the main line platform and poured down a cavernous drain.

All went well until the penultimate day of my sojourn. That Friday Bertie said to me, 'laddie, my brother has brought a suit and the trousers needed altering. The tailor has just bought them back. Would you mind delivering them to his home later this afternoon? You can go straight home afterwards.' That was typical of Bertie. He never told you to do anything; he asked you to.

There didn't seem to be any problem involved. The address was in Northolt and Bertie gave me very careful instructions how to get there. A bus to Sudbury Town, through the subway to Bridgewater Road. The only snag was that he didn't tell me the bus stop wasn't the one immediately outside the subway and I had travelled to Hanger Lane before I realised that I was going the wrong way.

As is always the case I had to wait ages for the right bus to get to Northolt and finally completed the delivery at 6.30 in the evening. Then I had to wait for a bus back to Harrow, eventually arriving home at 7.15. Poor old Bertie was most apologetic about it next morning – my last day at Wembley – and let me off at 4.30 in the afternoon to make up for it.

On my return to Harrow the following Monday I was most gratified and surprised to learn from Mr Harvey that Bertie had given a good account of me. Gratified that I had scored a couple of Brownie points and surprised that the manager had bothered to pass the compliment on. Whether or not this had anything to do with my work status or just a coincidence but I was let loose on clothing customers as well as the headwear.

One Wednesday morning in November I woke up feeling decidedly rough. This was unusual, especially when Wednesday being half-day afforded the prospects of a free afternoon left to my own sinister devices usually put me in good spirits. I was alone in the flat as both my parents had gone to work. I struggled up and ventured out into the passage. I felt very shivery and then I had this impression of falling on a pile of freezing cold spanners. The mind can play funny tricks in the morning. I became aware that I was lying face down on the cold and very hard passage floor. I had blacked out. Feeling very wobbly I dragged myself up and tottered off to the bathroom to assess the damage. Probably growing pains, I told myself. The bathroom mirror revealed a nasty gash on my forehead which I cleaned up sufficiently not to frighten the horses. Then I washed, shaved, dressed and had a cup of tea. I couldn't face any food and decided that I could always buy myself something to eat at the baker's next door to the shop.

It was a typical murky, foggy and dank November morning, which quite suited my mood. Halfway to work I had to remove my hat as the cut on my forehead had developed into a bump the size of an egg. Roll on 1 o'clock, I thought.

They didn't seem overly concerned about me at the shop and being Wednesday it was a pretty easy morning. But I did have to take a pair of trousers to our alteration tailor, Joe Weiss at Kenton, as they were wanted for Friday.

When Joe's wife opened the door to me she must have thought it was the Grim Reaper. 'You shouldn't be at work in your state!' she shrieked. 'You should be at home in a nice warm bed already! What's that fool of a manager thinking of?'

Well, it's good to have friends, I reflected as I groped my way back through the fog to the bus stop. I was feeling worse by now and had started to cough. The fog, I thought. Anyway, it's nearly 1 o'clock.

I think the cut on my head must have opened up again as Norman Hurst said I looked like Banquo's ghost when I returned to the shop. Thankfully they let me off early and I went straight to bed.

The next day I felt worse so we had the doctor in. He made no bones about it. Bronchitis. Well that was that. I was stuck in bed for two weeks which was a bit of a bore as I was supposed to be appearing as a Wise Man in the Church Nativity play. Well that was one Oscar or Emmy I would have to write off.

But there was a brighter side which said a lot for dear old Dunn & Co. On the two Fridays I was off sick Norman Hurst called in with my wages. And that is something you don't hear much of these days.

As soon as I was signed off I returned to work, feeling a little shaky but all the better for being in the real world. I prefer the definition 'pale and interesting' to 'washed out'. Another member of staff had been taken on, a few years older than me – either a senior-junior assistant or a junior-senior assistant. Jack Davenport was a very self-assured and dapper little chap which didn't greatly endear him to Mr Harvey. I found him easy to get on with and I will always be grateful to him for introducing me to the wonderfully crazy world of that radio programme *The Goon Show*. He could do all the different voices and I picked them up quite well too. Jack was with us for several months until he was finally transferred to our Golders Green branch. But he was only there a short while before he left the company when he and his wife emigrated to Australia.

By this time, I had become reconciled to the obligatory hat. Dunn & Co had introduced a number of new styles which had become very popular. Also their idea of giving the varying styles a name gave them something which could catch the publics' imagination. There was the 'Mambo' which had a completely flat crown with no dents and the ribbon bow at the back. This was very popular with the American servicemen from their base at Ruislip. The 'Berkeley' was a bit of a brute to shape up as the brim was very curly and the front was supposed to be flat. When the brim has a 'dish' in it the curl is very hard to flatten out.

But the one I took to was the 'Corniston', a snap-brim trilby with a dramatically tapered crown. I felt quite at ease with this style and had long since dispensed with the bag used for concealment. Anyway, all the Teddy Boys had disappeared from Harrow and I had good reason to believe that many of them were 'guests' at one of Her Majesty's 'hotels'.

There was great excitement in the Spring of 1956. The Manager was going to have a new desk to replace his office-coop. It was a tall, oaken construction, five-sided with an actual door and an actual lock. It was placed in front of the doorway facing down the shop with a terribly flawed mirror in the top half facing out of the doorway which would surely deter the most hard-boiled customer. The upper structure facing into the shop was true Dunn & Co style with little square leaded panes, embellished here and there with a fragment of stained glass. It looked like an ecclesiastical lighthouse.

Of course, 'Sir' was really full of himself and soon took up residence. Oddly enough it was such a towering edifice it made him look quite small. But for Mr Harvey it was a point of command; the bridge of his ship.

But pride goeth before a fall. He must have jammed the lock somehow because he couldn't get the door open. He looked like a very angry monkey in a cage and I knew if I gave way to the fit of giggles that was bubbling up inside me I would never hear the last of it.

There was only one thing for it. Norman Hurst fetched a ladder so that the Manager could climb up from his desktop via his office stool, out of the top of his wonderful new office and descend safely by the ladder. This went as planned up to a point and I am sure Mr Harvey must have been dysfunctional. He certainly seemed accident-prone. Of course, his bulk didn't help matters and he had just swung himself astride the office top and scrambled for the ladder when he missed his footing and, screaming like a gutted capon, he fell on Norman who was unashamedly cackling with laughter!

Mr Harvey wasn't hurt; he was making too much noise to have suffered any serious injury. And while he was sitting there, hooting, swearing and blaming me of all people, 'you blokes – sluck!' Norman had scrambled up the ladder, into the office and sorted the lock out in a matter of seconds. After that the door of the new office always remained open.

It was about that time I developed three addictions. Horlicks tablets and Ovaltine capsules – although I couldn't abide either concoction as a drink – and Dennis Wheatley books. All three hang-ups took me over completely. The book was one of Wheatley's occult novels *The Devil Rides Out* and I simply couldn't put it down. I didn't want it to finish but I had to keep reading it during every waking moment. It travelled with me to work in my pocket, along with the Horlicks and Ovaltine goodies and I contrived a clever ruse – or so I thought – how I would be able to read the book at work without being discovered.

The wing mirror had been angled across the end of the shop, creating a little triangular space where I could ensconce myself after attending to my regular duties. This worked well for the first couple of times. I would read unseen and scoff my tablets, completely lost in the sinister world of satanic misdeeds. Unfortunately, it was the Ovaltine capsules which brought about my undoing. Horlicks tablets were oblong whilst the Ovaltine were round. I had just reached a particularly exciting passage in the book when I lost my grip on the tins. Twenty Ovaltine tablets rolled out from the mirror and down the shop at high speed. A second later Mr Harvey's voice boomed out, 'what's that bloody boy doing now?'

That was the end of my literary breaks.

Usually I managed to endure Mr Harvey and his difficult ways but after working with 'Bertie' Benson it wasn't so easy to bite the bullet. One day in particular he had given me a really bad time and I was on the point of throwing the job in. The tortures I had gone through to get that job faded into obscurity. I wanted out and that was that.

But Fate moves in remarkably strange ways. There was a film I wanted to see at one of our local cinemas. It was the last of the Ealing comedies and it was called *The Ladykillers*. On reaching the cinema that evening I tried to put Mr Harvey out of my mind and settled down to enjoy the film. And didn't I enjoy it! I hadn't laughed so much in years. It was even funnier than Rupert Higgs and his endless stream of jokes. I left the cinema utterly at peace with the world and Mr Harvey. It certainly is true that laughter is the best medicine.

But the wind of change was breezing through our happy little emporium. Norman Hurst had been made up to manager and would take over our Finsbury Park branch. I was sorry to see him go as his madcap humour was a much-needed counterbalance to Mr Harvey's grumbles.

His replacement was a young Irishman, Michael Flynn. He was slim, dark and serious at first. Well he remained slim and dark but the serious part wore off once he had settled in. He had a mischievous sense of humour and had been responsible for adding a caption to the portrait of our Founder in Ealing, his previous branch, which read, 'There's an evil, black-eyed monster who's forever gazing down on the underpaid assistants from his desk in Camden Town'.

But there were still straws blowing in the wind of change and those straws soon became haystacks. This time it was our Manager who was on the move to take over our branch at Richmond. Mr Ronald-veal-and-ham-pie-with-egg-in-it-Harvey. But the big question – who would be his successor?

LULLS AND STORMS

Autumn 1956 ~ Autumn 1957

It was with great trepidation that Michael Flynn and I waited to learn who Mr Harvey's successor would be. I never found out why he had been transferred but it would have been due to someone either dying or retiring. It needn't necessarily have been the Richmond manager; that would have been too simple. There would most likely have been a whole chain of managers shunted from shop to shop.

We were soon put out of our misery. The new manager of Harrow was to be Bertie Benson. 'What's he like?' Michael asked me, looking furtive and suspicious. But then he always did look like that.

'He's okay,' I assured him. It gave me a warm glow of superiority to be consulted. It was the first time in my working life – short though it had been – that a senior member of staff had asked my opinion on anything.

The day of arrival and departure was a Thursday and Mr Drew officiated at the ceremony; in other words the tiresome business of stock checking and opening the new sales sheets which, when completed, both managers signed with great solemnity. It was like witnessing a peace treaty.

We didn't exactly wave our handkerchiefs in farewell to Mr Harvey, neither did we weep into them. I was still pinching myself to make sure that I wasn't dreaming. Then as soon as Mr Drew had departed, Bertie, true to form, said, 'well, laddie, shall we have a nice cup of tea?' And that set the tone for the future of Harrow.

But however good or bad your manager was, the firm had rigid ground rules regarding how the staff presented themselves for work. Apart from the sacred hat a formal suit was a 'must' and the shirt had to be white. Furthermore, collar-attached shirts were a taboo; they had to have separate collars. These were blue murder to struggle with. Many of our managers – Mr Harvey included – had a box of freshly starched collars, every Monday, delivered to the shop by a firm which specialised in this particular sartorial accessory. The tie had to be slid through the folded collar, judging the lengths correctly for when it was tied. Then the whole thing had to be anchored to a stud in the neck of the shirt collar. This agonising act of self-strangulation required eyes in the back of your head. Once this was secured and you had recovered your breath, the two ends of the stiffly starched piece of fabric had to be secured to a metal stud painfully located on the Adam's apple. Then finally the tie was sorted out. That front stud was a curse. You could always tell a white-collar worker on his day off if he was wearing an open-neck shirt because there would be an angry red mark on his throat and sometimes a greenish patch like mildew from the metal stud.

Dunn's didn't have a particularly strict rule on ties but obviously preferred a discreet item of neckwear. As I tended to err on the flashy (I always preferred distinctive) side Mr Drew was never at a loss to make some caustic comment. I didn't care two hoots. I had acquired a wonderful selection of waistcoats. Cherry red, brown and fawn draughtboard check, the good old yellow Tattersall check. Even a dark brown one with red and yellow spots.

But I was brought down to earth one day. I had set off to the bank (no *Sainsbury's* or *Danny's Café* as Bertie brought his lunch with him) and I felt like Jack-the-Lad. My snappy silver-grey hat, black double-breasted suit and a pair of brown and yellow leather driving gloves. It sounds odd these days to be wearing gloves without a topcoat but I must have seen it in some old film about gentlemen burglars. My silver tie was enhanced by a tie clip with a large round red stone and I felt the bee's knees as I strutted into the bank – only to be rudely deflated by the Chief Cashier who fixed me with a sardonic eye and solemnly announced, 'the law states that you should display two reflector lights.' I don't think that tie clip ever saw the light of day again.

But I must confess that not all my sartorial delights were purchased from Dunn's. I was unfaithful to them on three occasions at three different shops. There was the off-white trenchcoat which looked good with my trilby hat and made me look like a mysterious detective. Well that's what I thought although I probably did look mysterious but not in the way I wished. Then there was the jacket. This was light fawn with long lapels, saddle-stitched with tabs instead of the usual notches at the reverse. It also had a pair of gussets from the back of the shoulder to the waist and reminded me of what the well-dressed cowboy wore for Sunday best.

But the waistcoat was a disaster. I bought it from one of a chain of shops that infested north London. They all had this lurid bright blue fascia and their windows were jam-packed with Teddy Boy suits and looked more crowded than a pub offering free Guinness on St Patrick's Day. The waistcoat was black with a red velvet pattern meandering all over it in a jigsaw design. To my disgust the pattern wore off after three weeks and the garment developed a most repugnant odour of rancid cheese.

I quite liked being sent to other branches to collect or deliver some item of clothing required for a customer. This could knock quite a hole in any morning or afternoon, affording a leisurely train journey – all expenses paid – and a chance to meet some of my contemporaries in other branches.

One afternoon I was sent to collect a parcel from our Ealing Broadway branch. This was new territory for me but Bertie gave me explicit instructions – the correct ones this time – how to get there. A bus to South Harrow Station, a train to Ealing Common and it was about half a mile walk to the Broadway.

I was greatly impressed by the amount of trees at Ealing Common; it looked quite rural. Certainly not the sort of place I would expect to find a Dunn & Co shop. Well, I didn't and it wasn't. As I progressed towards the Broadway 'rural' waned and 'urban' waxed and pretty soon I was wondering down a typical high street of a typical London suburb.

I nearly missed the shop. In fact, I walked past it at first. It had the narrowest frontage I had ever seen. It seemed even smaller than Harrow! I ventured inside and became blind for several seconds. This was often the case with our shops when it was sunny outside. The interiors were so dark and cloistered that it took some time for your eyes to adjust. By that time it was too late for the customer to take evasive action. The salesman had pounced out of the shadows with his tape measure at the ready like a garrotting wire.

What confronted me in the Ealing shop looked like a very long and narrow passage. Running up each side into the far distance were headwear fixtures which made the place seem even narrower. But the most daunting spectacle of all was the silhouette approaching me. He must have been the fattest man ever. How he managed to negotiate the passage that was Dunn's of Ealing was beyond me. I'm sure he glided between those hat fixtures with the sides of his hips on the counter edges like a tram on rails. As he coasted towards me I was surprised to see that he was quite a young man with a fine head of wavy fair hair and a small pointed nose which seemed lost in such an abundance of face. His eyes were very round and held a look of astonishment. I later found this was his normal expression when his features were in repose. Nicholas Willoughby was yet another of Dunn's wide variety of characters and one of the most genial-natured men I have ever met.

'Aha!' he greeted me with a plummy voice. 'The emissary from Harrow.' He handed me a carrier bag. 'Guard this with your life and may the gods grant you safe passage on your journey.'

Well there was no answer to that. I probably touched my forelock, muttered, 'ooh, aye, Maister,' and waddled off. We certainly had some weird and wonderful personalities on our payroll.

These excursions gave me the opportunity to case out the West End shops; Oxford Street, Piccadilly and the Strand. At one time the Strand was the showpiece of Dunn & Co. It was on a corner which is always a good site. But the interior was something else. The fixtures were 'Dunn-oak' but far superior to their suburban counterparts. Concealed lighting gently illuminated a ceiling of pale blue, simulating the sky, with even a hint of fleecy Summer clouds.

Stocks of hats were nowhere to be seen; that would be much too vulgar for the Strand. Instead there were glass showcases ranged around the shop with one hat in each, all of differing colour and style. The customer would indicate certain hats on display and the assistant would depart to the stockroom in the depths of the emporium to find those particular hats in the required size. But not before he had seated the customer at a little table with a mirror and opened a drawer full of cigarettes so the customer could enjoy a quiet smoke while he was waiting.

But this last practice has disappeared. It is said that the Strand assistants all had hacking coughs and ciggies were disappearing by the fistful. So you didn't need to put two and two together …

Nevertheless, I was keen to see the inside of this fabulous shop, and I wasn't disappointed. The interior was magnificent. Oak and glass gleamed and shone with polish. The brass rails of the clothing fixtures were like burnished gold. I collected the package from the assistant and was just exchanging a few words of conversation with him when a bald little man with a white moustache, glasses and a very pink face, appeared. 'Be on your way, boy!' he snapped. 'You're not paid to stand around gossiping!' He was even worse than Mr Harvey.

My other regular excursion was a visit to Head Office for extra stock. This occurred nearly every week. When we closed for half-day on Wednesday Bertie would hand me some letters and say, 'Would you mind going up to Camden Town tomorrow, laddie? There's a few extra items we need for Saturday.'

This was a good arrangement as I could go straight from home while the trains were more plentiful. Also it meant I could catch a Broadstreet train which only ran during peak hours, thus avoiding the tedious business of changing over to the High Level at Willesden Junction.

On the other hand, it meant that I would be travelling on the same train as some of the big bugs from Head Office. I thought it best to keep a low profile and always boarded the last carriage, knowing that any Dunn's staff would be at the front as that end was nearest to the exit at Camden Road.

As the train crossed the bridge just outside Camden Road the Head Office staff could be seen down below in the street. Hatted and suited little figures, all converging on the lofty, off-white building that was Head Office. They looked like people out of an LS Lowry painting.

On one visit I had rather more parcels than usual to carry. It wasn't so much the weight but the bulkiness which made them awkward. It was a case of dot and carry me to the station, and struggling up to the platform was a nightmare. But the relief of collapsing into the comfortable train with my burden dumped on the adjacent seat! This time I didn't mind the roundabout route to Willesden High Level. Probably my hands would have regained their circulation by then.

These trains were really comfortable. Never mind the cloud of dust that billowed up when you sat down; they were spacious and light. Each carriage was divided into two by a swing door. One half had the open plan seating arrangement similar to tube trains but the other half was all little ingle nook seats clustered cosily together like something out of the Aitcheson-Topeka railroad of the Wild West. The only drawback with these trains was the manually operated doors. These were sliding doors which were opened by a lever and if the lock had not been properly engaged the door would slide open of its own accord when the train either accelerated or decelerated. This could be quite unnerving if you happened to be leaning against it.

It wasn't so funny when I got to Willesden Junction and had to negotiate the 'wormhole' down to the ground level line with my load of parcels. And to make matters worse there was a Harrow train about to depart. It was one of the red Bakerloo trains with sliding doors – and they might slide shut at any moment. I frantically kicked, hurled and buffeted my parcels into the carriage – then the doors started to close! Hells bells! The train would go off with my parcels and would be stranded at Willesden! I leapt into the carriage just as the doors slid to and made it by the skin of my teeth – but not the brim of my hat. That item stayed between the doors, squashed flat, snatched from my Brylcreamed skull by the electrical wonders of modern technology. I wrenched it out, much to the amusement of the other passengers, and tried to mould it back into shape. But the guts had been knocked out of it and it really was a sorry-looking sight.

At Harrow I was faced with the arduous trek to the shop with my cargo of hats, coats and jackets. With blistered hands I somehow managed the first few hundred yards and had paused for a breather when help came from an unexpected quarter. A greengrocer in the block where I lived saw my predicament and kindly offered me the use of his potato sack trolley. This was wonderful! I was soon bowling effortlessly along with those hateful parcels. They were of no consequence and I felt that I could move mountains.

When I trundled into the shop Bertie's glasses nearly fell off with shock but he didn't say anything; he just looked a bit askance. I didn't care; I had been saved a very painful and tiring ordeal. I took the empty trolley back when I went to lunch and must have looked a proper drip in my smart suit and hat, wheeling an empty trolley. The wheels rattled noisily without any load to muffle them and although I was grateful for its use I found the journey back somewhat embarrassing.

But by and large 1957 was a good year. I was eighteen years old and working in a shop near home with a manager of the most patient and fatherly disposition. And then a new character entered the arena of my working life. This was 'Long' John Neville; JN as he was usually known. He was held in some degree of terror, especially by the junior staff. This was on account of his official position of Senior Staff Supervisor. He certainly looked the part in his immaculate suit and bowler hat. He was tall, moustached, with coldly piercing eyes of assassin blue. Unfortunately, his nose had a reddish tinge which reminded me of the character in the advertisements for a well-known brand of gin. Thankfully his visits were limited to two a year; one in the Summer and one just before Christmas. The Christmas one was better as he would try to project an air of festive bonhomie. The attempt was pathetic to see. JN just couldn't relate to people but at least the poor old devil tried to make the effort to be genial. He just didn't know how to. Nobody trusted him and anyway, he was one of the bosses. But it was a case of an utter snob with a nice man trapped inside, trying to get out.

The jungle telephone would warn us that he was in the area and we would all start play-acting; brushing hats, suits and so forth. He would have a muttered conversation with the manager and one by one we would be summoned forth for a little pep-talk. Thankfully they never lasted long and we couldn't understand what he said anyway. This was on account of his manner of speech. It was rich and plummy but with a particular buzzing sound. Probably because of his stiff upper lip. It is difficult to convey in the printed or written word the sound that came forth. It was as if he had a mouthful of bees. He would stand before us, leaning on his umbrella with both hands and buzz.

But there was less to JN than I first thought. During one visit Bertie asked him about season's stock.

'Not my department, Mr Benson,' he buzzed. 'I don't know about these things.'

Bertie asked him about the Christmas display.

'I don't know about these things,' the reply buzzed back. 'You will have to speak to someone at Head Office about that.'

It soon became obvious that poor old JN didn't know anything about anything. He was just a figurehead. Also he was treated with utter scorn and derision at Head Office, right down from the directors to the warehousemen.

On one occasion he called me Mr Bradley and asked me how my children were. On another, arriving at our Preston branch, he suddenly withdrew his notebook, scrutinised it and exclaimed, 'Heavens! I'm in the wrong shop!'

Then there was the time when he asked me to pop over the road and put some money in the parking meter for him. I knew he drove a Humber Super Snipe and duly put it in the meter adjacent to the aforesaid car. The silly old duffer had omitted to tell me that he had borrowed his daughter's mini that day and he got a parking ticket.

That Autumn we took on extra junior staff. Bob Sinclair, a very nationalistic young Scotsman who wasn't with us too long, partly because he wasn't allowed to wear his kilt at work, but used to change into it on Wednesday half-days. Yet another Caledonian followed him. Angus Scott (yes, he was actually called Scott) was tall, sleepy-eyed and sleepy-brained with auburn hair – about the most colourful thing about him. He did stay a few weeks longer but left to become – and this is the utter truth – a lighthouse keeper!

Donald Barr didn't come from Scotland; he came from Pinner Green and was fanatically into Skiffle groups. I got on quite well with Don as he had a good sense of fun and a dry wit. He looked a bit of a villain with his long sideburns but thankfully he only looked it.

Dear old Bertie wasn't too happy about me trundling into the shop with the greengrocer's trolley but he was too much of a gentleman to make an issue of it. Instead, when a collection was needed from Head Office, he sent Don and Angus along with me in the event, he said, that they would know where it was if I was unable to go.

Imagine my horror when we rendezvoused at the station on Thursday morning. By bizarre chance all three of us were wearing identical clothing, right down to the last detail. Grey trilby hats, grey double-breasted suits, white shirts and plain maroon ties. We must have looked a sinister trio. Androids and Clones were unheard of in those days but we may well have been responsible for those words becoming familiar in later years.

During the Autumn Dunn's made the most memorable step in their history to date – and probably their biggest blunder. They decided to advertise. It was unfortunate that the item they chose to promote was a new wonder hat which they had just given birth to. It was called the 'Drylon'.

They really went mad with the advertising campaign. On buses and in tube stations were posters displaying a rather mean-looking porkpie-styled hat in jungle green gabardine which was so dark that it could have been anything. At first glance it looked like a tortoise that had withdrawn into its shell. 'The Drylon is coming!' proclaimed the posters. 'The Indestructible Hat! Waterproof, Crushable And Flexible Enough to Be Rolled Up And Stored In Your Pocket!' Or something along those lines.

First of all we had a mass delivery of the new super-hat in a variety of colours, retailing at 30/– which was quite cheap, even in those days. Then came the display unit. This consisted of a green wooden box shaped like the podium for Olympic medallists. Inside was an electric motor with no instructions. Also included were two plastic hands and a yellow plastic duck. One of the hands was like a tightly clenched fist and the other as if grasping something.

We studied it in wonder. The omens were bad. Something was going to go wrong but we didn't know what. Then the jungle telephone rang. It was Norman Hurst who was then managing Wembley. He had it all worked out and was enlightening all the branches in the area as to how the apparatus functioned.

A Drylon was placed on the uppermost central box and the top of its crown filled with water for the plastic duck to float in, thus demonstrating the hat's waterproof qualities. The grasping plastic hand was fitted into the front of the box but a bit lower down with a rolled-up Drylon in its clutch to give visual proof of its resilience. And finally the plastic fist was attached to a metal rod projecting from the box just above the third hat which was placed on the floor of the window. The metal rod was connected to the electric motor and when switched on the fist would rhythmically pound the hat which defiantly returned to its natural contours as soon as the pressure was removed.

We followed these instructions, including the wiring up, and switched it on. There was a bright blue flash followed by an explosion and we were nearly on the phone for a new manager. Norman had literally got his wires crossed and had almost been instrumental in wiping out every Dunn's manager in Middlesex.

I shouldn't have been surprised. Dunn's had a remarkably cavalier disregard for safety measures in all matters electrical that was almost gung-ho. Only the previous Christmas they had decided to brighten up their cardboard holly with paper lanterns, each with a powerful light bulb inside. We improvised with bell wire and there was some pretty serious scorching in those paper lamps by the time we dismantled the display on Twelfth Night. My goodness, it was an exciting life!

Finally, Michael Flynn got it all sorted out and we left the shop that evening with one Drylon secured in a plastic hand, another being slowly pummelled by the plastic fist and the little yellow duck swimming happily in his personal pond atop the third Drylon.

The super-hat sold like hot cakes the next day but we were in for a shock the second morning. The hat in the first seemed to have fossilised and refused to unroll, the duck was high and dry, the water having soaked through the hat's crown, but the third Drylon was most damming of all. The plastic fist had hammered it as flat as a pancake.

This proved to be the case in all our branches throughout the country and we received a tersely-worded directive from Head Office. All Drylon displays were to be removed from the windows and all stocks of Drylon hats were to be removed from the sales points, packed up and invoiced for return to the Warehouse. All customers returning Drylons as complaints were to be reimbursed without quibble. Some unfortunate head must have rolled in the Camden corridors of power but Dunn's drew their horns in as far as advertising was concerned.

Having survived injury and embarrassment we rolled along quite happily. I was enjoying the job and even getting to know some of the regular customers. I worked for a decent manager and got on well with Michael and Don. All in all I was feeling very content and comfortable.

I should have known better for that is when the lightning strikes. One October afternoon Mr Drew paid his customary fortnight's visit and called me over for a few words. He said that Bertie was pleased with my progress and now was the time to 'graze in fresh fields' or words to that effect. In short, I was to be transferred to another shop as an 'admin factotum'.

I wasn't sure what it meant and didn't care for the sound of it. It could be Latin but it sounded a bit North American Indian. In any case I didn't want my cosy little world upset but I had no choice. And where would my new place of work be? Wembley or Watford? Possibly Edgware? No; Kentish Town. Slap-bang in the shadow of Head Office!

TO PASTURES NEW

October 1957 ~ June 1958

It was a cold, damp miserable Monday morning in October 1957. A pathetic-looking character, clutching his lunchbox, huddled in the doorway of the Kentish Town branch of Dunn & Co. I felt quite pathetic, too, despite my new staff discount overcoat and hat. Kentish Town looked a bit dangerous, pretty much like Dodge City with trolleybuses instead of stagecoaches.

I had caught the 8.05 Broadstreet train from Harrow & Wealdstone and arrived at Camden Road by 8.40. A ten-minute walk past our Head Office and along Kentish Town Road had led me to my new place of work, a single-window shop with a lobby and entrance door on the right-hand side.

I had been worried that I would be late on my first day but it was the manager who was late. His name was Bob Figgis and there would be just the two of us. I wondered what he would be like. Would he be a bad-tempered character like Ronald Harvey? Was he young and ambitious? Merciful heavens! Was he possibly strange in more unspeakable ways? And I was to be his 'admin factotum'. My father had told me that this simply was a grand way of meaning 'chief cook and bottle-washer'.

'You my new help?'

I started at the curt voice. I hadn't seen him approach but Mr Figgis had emerged from the tube station opposite and seemed to materialise out of thin air. He was probably in his early forties, stocky and not very tall. His complexion was unusually sallow, full around the jowls with an aquiline nose. His hair was wavy and very black – almost blue-black. This, along with the bluish shadow he always had on his cheeks, somehow made me think of Italian opera singers.

Happily, my private misgivings concerning his personal character proved groundless. He was a rough diamond but easy to get on with. He was married, with a young daughter, and lived in Kings Cross. As with most of Dunn's staff he liked his tea and, most of all, his ciggies.

The customers were more rough and ready than I was used to at Harrow but they weren't so fussy and, all in all, I settled in quite well. The shop was roomy and the fitting-room-cum-staff-room was a good size and located at the end of the shop. It certainly was a vast improvement on Harrow's staff amenities, with a nice little bamboo table, the top covered with a piece of red lino.

We also had a cellar, the door located just by Mr Figgis's office-coop. A flight of treacherous wooden stairs led down to this sinister gothic under-world, lit only by a forty-watt bulb and whatever light managed to filter through the opaque tiles in the pavement above. Stacks of cardboard boxes abounded, most of them disintegrating in the damp to pulpy masses which afforded living accommodation for a truly amazing variety of creepy-crawlies.

The mornings always passed quickly. This was on account of our bank not having a branch in Kentish Town, which meant a journey to Camden Town each day. Mr Figgis had to break his homeward journey every evening to bank the takings and this meant either catching a bus or a tube train.

Travel to and from work was better than I had expected. I usually caught the 8.05 but if I missed it there was another seven minutes later. And in between these there would be a Euston train and a Bakerloo. During peak hours there was never a train out of sight along the line.

The evenings were okay if I got out on time. I usually caught a train about 6.20 which mean that I would be home about 7pm. If I missed that I had to endure a more leisurely chug around the High Level to Willesden Junction where I changed to a Watford train, arriving home about 7.20.

Early closing day at Kentish Town was Thursday and this was a different kettle of fish. No through trains ran to Harrow during off-peak hours so it meant a High Level excursion. I usually got home about 2pm. Even then, I am surprised, looking back at what I could do with that afternoon, such as it was. A bite of lunch then a train up to the West End, a mooch around the shops then home in the evening with the rush-hour crowds. It never occurred to me not to go home and eat out somewhere instead. We could be strange creatures of habit in those days.

All trains were off-peak times on Saturdays. Shop workers didn't count – never have done. This meant I had to start out earlier to allow for the journey via the High Level. But it could be tricky in the evening. If – and it was a big 'if' – I left work promptly at 6pm and I could get to Camden Road by 6.15, I might just catch a shuttle train which ran directly to Willesden Junction where a Watford train would be waiting. But real life isn't like that. Invariably I would scramble up the steps to the platform, which was like scaling the side of an Aztec pyramid, just in time to see the tail light of my train fading away in the distance. A long wait was inevitable and being in the latter months of the year meant that it was dark by that time. Fortunately, the cavernous waiting-room was furnished with a real coal fire which is more than you get these days, even if the railways boast state-of-the-art stations.

But even so, it was a long wait. After fifteen minutes a train would be heard approaching. Now this was a goods train. They did this during weekends on the passenger lines. An endless stream of metal sausages and metal trucks would rattle and rumble through, bound for goodness knows where, and I would be left, gazing at the red signal light, willing it to turn green.

Finally, my train would trundle in – a High Level one of course. On Saturdays there were usually only three people travelling on that particular train; the driver, the guard and a clown in a trilby hat – me. By the time I had made the changeover at Willesden Junction and groped my way home through the fog it was nearly 7.30.

We always had a lot of fog in the Fifties but there always seemed to be more at Kentish Town. And it always seemed to be foggy when I had to deliver a customer's parcel. I would venture from the bright lights of the High Street to be swallowed up in the foggy, smoggy clouds that infested the side roads. Viaduct bridges with their menacing gaslit tunnels seemed to be everywhere and the cobblestones underfoot gleamed with moisture. I felt like the hapless victim out of the first reel of a horror film and was thankful that Jack the Ripper only killed prostitutes and not junior shop assistants.

Fog and prostitutes recall an incident which occurred on the run-up to Christmas. Mr Figgis and I had just locked up the shop and were preparing to go our separate ways when a female figure in a headscarf approached me, looming out of the gloom, 'Hello, dear,' she greeted me.

My reply was something along the lines of, 'go away; it's not pay night' – or words to that effect.

The apparition responded indignantly. It was my sister, Cynthia, who had left home several years ago while I was still at school, got married and was living in Hackney. Well how was I to know? At least sibling contact had been established even if it was in a somewhat unorthodox manner.

One task which I never relished always cropped up the week before Christmas. Dunn's always seemed to be in a dither whether or not they should open or close for half-day on the week prior to Christmas. I would have to visit all the men's outfitters in the area to find out what they were doing. Mr Drew had called in on his usual visit and sent me to a gents' outfitters across the road to find out what their business hours would be.

I put the question to a sales assistant who gave me an old-fashioned look and told me to wait while he spoke to his manager. The latter erupted from his office, almost purple with fury. 'Clear out!' he roared. 'I'm sick to death of you pests! Clear out and stay out!'

Terrified, I fled in a Dunn's-ward direction. Pale but indignant, I told Mr Drew of my reception – or lack of it – expecting some sort of sympathetic reaction. I didn't get it.

'I expect it was because I called there earlier and asked them,' he smirked. 'I just thought I would send you along to confirm it.'

'Funny you should say that,' Mr Figgis commented. 'I phoned them up this morning and asked them the same thing.'

During the Christmas period we engaged a junior assistant as 'another pair of hands' but he wasn't with us more than a fortnight before he was sent to our Golders Green branch. I had done a few days there and he was welcome to it. Mr Karswell, the manager was even worse than Ronald Harvey. Miserable and nit-picking would sum him up. Fortunately, his senior help was Ron Manson whom I had worked with at Wembley which made my time there a bit more bearable.

We picked up another junior, Dave Woddie – Mr Figgis used to call him 'Fly-Blow' – who lasted a few weeks. He was amiable enough but not very bright; a black-haired version of Elvis Presley – even to the blue-suede shoes. Poor boy was transferred to our Camden branch where he worked – wait for it – under the brother of Ronnie Harvey, name of Hubert, though he much preferred to be called Bill. I wonder why?

Mr Figgis was a first class salesman and we got through the Christmas and Winter trade without any extra help. About that time we received a delivery of discontinued stock at knock-down prices. Not content with displaying them in the window he would take a batch home and sell them in his local pub in the evening. He also did the rounds of his local police station and fire station and always sold the lot. How much his sales technique differed from the conventional I couldn't say but it was not unusual for him to appear the next morning sporting a black eye. As I said, he was a very rough diamond.

But his biggest success was with the Russians. In Highgate there was an establishment known as the Russian Trade Legation and Mr Figgis had cultivated their visits to the shop in a most lucrative fashion. Like many foreigners they fell in love with our Harris Tweed and gabardine coats. The manager saw the possibilities in this interest and was soon taking bulk orders for made-to-measure Harris Tweed overcoats and as many double-breasted top quality raincoats as possible.

Even I, still comparatively naïve in worldly matters, could curl a cynical lip at this. Our snow-booted clients were simply buying in bulk to take back to Russia and sell at an exorbitant profit. Scratch a Communist and you will find a filthy, profiteering Capitalist pig underneath.

One day I was sent to the Russian Trade Legation with a prepaid delivery of overcoats. I found the place without difficulty, and a vast, looking edifice it was too, with a front door that would have looked better on a giant's castle. I rang the bell and the door was opened by the giant himself. This was a barrel of a man in an ill-fitting double-breasted suit and a face like a rockslide. 'Da?' he enquired in a throaty and threatening voice.

I politely whimpered my identity and mission, inwardly marvelling at how and why these Russians were so enormous. It must be something to do with the snow, I reasoned. Probably they grew tall to be away from the cold ground; nature's way of compensating.

He studied me balefully with a pair of icy blue eyes for some seconds, then signed the receipt book, took the parcel and disappeared, slamming the door in my face. Mean devil! Not even a half-crown tip!

Although I initially resented any change in my place of work I had settled down at Kentish Town. True, it was totally different to Harrow and doubtless harboured a darker element of crime in those days, but you could safely venture out without fear of being mugged. We had a better class of criminal in those days. In fact, I quite liked the place.

But there was one thing bothering me. It had risen on the horizon of my life several months earlier as a pale and misty cloud. But as the days, weeks and months rolled by it became a thundercloud. National Service. Two years of being hauled off for military training in one or other of the Armed services.

For several months I had anxiously studied the notice board outside Wealdstone Police Station, scanning the black and red print for the dates of birth eligible for the 'call-up' as it was known. Each time I breathed a sigh of relief. They wanted people who were born years before me. Most likely when it was the turn of my year group the whole idea would have been scrapped or they simply might even forget about me.

Then one day, early in January 1958, I saw the year 1939 in bold red print. Doom had overtaken me! I was due to register for National Service that very month!

Just to twist the knife in the wound those of us who were eligible were invited to attend a meeting at a local school one evening where a bright and breezy Army officer gave us a most cosy little chat on what fun we would have once we were in uniform. I was not converted, and the presence of some former school chums whom I hadn't seen for years didn't give me much comfort. I got the impression that they were all for it. But they always had been a mad bunch at school and they didn't seem to have changed.

The day I registered was a Saturday morning and I joined the queue of apprehensive teenagers at the government office given over to the task for the day. There was a choice of which branch of the services we would prefer to be mutilated in but my forlorn request of Salvation Army didn't even raise a titter. On my father's advice I opted for the Royal Air Force.

That over, I set off for Kentish Town feeling strangely relieved. We are creatures of habit and take refuge in such, and I even managed to half-convince myself that I really might be somehow overlooked or forgotten.

The following days slithered into Summer and the annual holiday period was fast approaching. Complying with the system, I had made my usual fortnight's reservation for July but I didn't care to think where I might be then – and it certainly wouldn't be a holiday. Mr Figgis had booked for June and the relief manager was a Mr Banner, a strange-looking and peppery little man known as 'The Martian'. This was due to his slightly slanted piercing eyes, long pointed nose and long pointed ears; otherwise he looked quite normal. We got on well enough for the first week but that old gut feeling about the impending medical had returned.

This finally happened on Tuesday June 10th. Oddly enough, coming home from work in the train that evening I had a feeling that something was about to break, and I was right. There was the sinister brown envelope on the hallstand, informing me that my presence was required the following Tuesday at 8.30am for an x-ray at Tavistock Square, Euston, to be followed by the full medical at Bromyard House, Acton, later the same day.

My poor mother didn't know what to think. She didn't care overmuch for me being called up and possibly used as cannon fodder, but on the other hand she was worried that if I failed the medical I might have some terrible disease like leprosy – or even to be found insane. The week's wait passed in a sombre grey blur and the seemingly endless amount of forms to be filled out bewildered me.

The weather on that fateful day didn't cheer me up much either. It was raining cats and dogs. As for the medical; it was a fiasco. I had, by habit dressed for work, and hat, overcoat and briefcase are cumbersome things to carry around in a state of undress as well as all the other sartorial accoutrements which my job demanded. The x-ray was bad enough but the full medical was worse. I never made it past the example question in the examination for the Royal Air Force. I think my father must have been influenced by those old war films which depicted airmen lounging about runways in armchairs and smoking pipes.

The medical subjected us to all manner of indignities so I shall pass over a more detailed account, suffice to say I was classed as Grade 3. Three – the magic number! Not healthy enough to be shot and not ill enough to be put down! Evidently they failed me on account of a nervous tic which wasn't at all surprising after the things they had done to me.

I left Acton at 3.30 and, with all the conditioned training of a laboratory rat, caught a train back to Kentish Town. Such was my state of bliss that not even the Salvador Dali-esque rubbish-scape at Willesden Junction depressed me. I realised then that I hadn't eaten since 7.30 that morning. Oblivious of the crowds of St Trinian-style schoolgirls who crowded onto the train, I gorged myself in ecstasy on my Marmite sandwiches, wolfed down the *Lyons* Individual Fruit Pie and practically swallowed my Penguin wafer whole. The nightmare was over! I could get on with my life, such as it was. I was stuck with Dunn's and Dunn's were stuck with me until one of us should decide otherwise.

I couldn't wait to get back to Kentish Town with my joyful news, and it was worth it to see Mr Banner actually smile, which proved that he was human after all and not a Martian.

'And I've got some more good news for you,' he told me when I had finished babbling. 'Mr Drew telephoned today to say that you are being transferred back to Harrow as from next Monday.'

My cup of happiness was certainly running over. I almost felt guilty at being so happy – but only almost. My one regret was that I could not get to see Mr Figgis again before I left. I did see him later on my half-day that year just before Christmas. Having spent the afternoon prowling round my usual West End shopping haunts I called in at Kentish Town to wish him well. I never saw him again. He died of a lung infection several years later. But I had enjoyed working with him and he had taught me a lot. Ironically enough, that lucrative business with the Russians died too. Evidently their trade legation at Highgate closed down as, or so I heard, it was discovered to be a spy centre.

But I was now returning to Harrow. Everything was going to be fine – which just goes to show how wrong you can be …!

THE HAPPY YEAR

Summer 1958 ~ Autumn 1959

It was Monday, glorious Monday 23rd June 1958 and I was making my triumphal return to Harrow. Radiating goodwill and joy up, down and in all directions, I breezed into the shop promptly at 8.50. Bertie Benson unfolded himself from his office stool and scrutinised me like a benevolent owl. 'Hello, laddie,' he greeted me. 'What are you doing here?'

'I've been transferred back,' I chirped, my cup of happiness filled to the brim. 'Mr Drew left a message at Kentish Town while I was failing my National Service medical.'

Bertie solemnly shook his head and some of my cup of happiness slopped into the saucer. 'I don't think so,' he murmured. 'I'll just phone him up and find out.'

Here we go again, I thought. Back to Kentish Town ... or where?

While Mr Benson was making his call I chatted with Mike Flynn, but I only half listened to his conversation. I was more interested in the telephonic mutterings drifting from the office. At last Bertie rang off and confronted me with an apologetic smile. 'It seems Mr Drew made a mistake,' he explained. 'He meant Wembley – not Harrow. He wants you to help out there for a fortnight while their junior is on holiday, and then you come back here.'

Oh, well, it could have been worse. Norman Hurst was the manager at Wembley and Lionel Parr the senior assistant didn't suffer from any attitude problems. Tall, fair and bespectacled, he had a tendency to be serious which was probably just as well as it counterbalanced Norman Hurst's madcap nature.

A mild ripple began as a rumour which gathered impetus and raged through the North London branches of Dunn's like the approach of the Angel of Death. It seemed that even Area Supervisors were not exempt from being transferred to other areas. Mr Drew had been moved to the Midlands and his replacement was said to be a bit of a firebrand. I was soon to find out.

On returning from my lunch break one day I found Mr Hurst in unusually serious conversation with a dapper, portly little chap. This was 'Jumping Jack' Flashman, our new Area Supervisor. I was duly introduced to him
and even though I had done nothing to incur his wrath I could tell this
wasn't the sort of man who would suffer fools gladly. In appearance he
was really immaculate. A curly-brimmed hat topped a round, olive-skinned
face and the piercing eyes and Hitleresque moustache were understandably
intimidating. His voice was pitched somewhere between a snap and a yelp
(a snelp?) as he fired question after question at me.

'So you're Keith Howard?' he began. 'Sounds like a film star's name.'

Naively I smiled and nodded, thinking this was going to be chummy.
'Yes, I suppose it does, Sir,' I agreed, beaming idiotically.

'You're not thinking of becoming one?' he demanded, his brow darkening.

I back-pedalled like mad and assured him that I would eat, drink and
sleep Dunn & Co until I was pensioned off to the knackers' yard, and that
seemed to mollify him. All very civil and pleasant but I realised that you
had to spit your words out and look at them before you said them. He
revelled in picking up the most trifling inconsistency. It was less of an
interview and more of an interrogation. I discovered later that during the
war he had been a corporal in the RAF Military Police, which explained a
lot.

But the encounter, as did the rest of the fortnight at Wembley, passed off
without trouble and I was back at Harrow again in high spirits. In three
weeks' time I would be taking my summer holidays which came and went
gloriously and I was happily settled back in my old stamping ground. It was
a very comfortable and satisfying feeling.

That alone should have warned me. One morning the phone rang and I
sensed it would be something concerning me. One develops a sixth sense
for that sort of thing. 'That was Mr Flashman, laddie,' Bertie informed me.
'He wants you to help out for a few weeks at Watford from next Monday.'

The pang of resentment was tempered by interest. I had heard about the
Watford branch. Those who had worked there reckoned it was one of the
best shops in the area, not so much because of the good trade but more
because of the 'ambience' of the place. That all sounded very grand but it
didn't tell me a lot. But on reflection I can say that my time spent at
Watford was as pleasant as it was unforgettable.

The shop was situated at the point where the High Street narrowed and
the pavement is even narrower. The building itself was four storeys high,
including the attic, the first floor being occupied by an optician, the second
by a jeweller and the attic – well I never did find out if that belonged to
anybody. As for the shop itself; one long window with the usual Dunn &

Co merchandise on display. But it differed inasmuch as it had little Persian carpets on the floor and a couple of small but ornately carved wooden tables on which the headwear was displayed. The entrance lobby was to the right of the window with a padlocked wooden gate which had to be taken off its hinges every morning and replaced when we closed. The shop's entrance was to the left at the end of the lobby, at right angles to the door leading up to the other floors.

The shop itself was square with built-in hat fixtures. The manager's office-coop was in the far corner behind the window and in the right-hand corner at the back of the shop was a staircase leading down to the basement sales floor. It was like a vault down there and the ceiling was so low it was possible to change the tube lights without standing on anything. It was creepy – all the more so for being L-shaped and the knowledge that just beyond the rear wall, separated by only a narrow public footpath, was a churchyard. In the corner below the staircase was the staff room, although it looked more like a ship's cabin. Its irregular shape was due to the staircase truncating the ceiling and wall in an indescribable geometric shape and a wooden pillar, obviously one of the building's interior supports, occupying a place dead centre. How they ever managed to get a table and two chairs wedged in there was something to wonder at.

Bill Humbert the manager was one of those personalities so much missed in recent years. In manner and appearance he had an uncanny resemblance to the late Sir Ralph Richardson. While he was certainly not the sort of man you would consider taking liberties with he had an impish – almost evil – sense of fun. Even so, he was a man to be treated with great respect and his philosophy was that when there was work to be done you worked, but when there wasn't – watch out. He was the very devil of a practical joker.

His senior assistant was Rupert Higgs whom I had worked with a few years earlier at Harrow, and the third member of staff, Frank Sherman, a tall, fair young man, thin to the point of emaciation with hooded eyes. He was the perfect foil 'straight man' to Rupert's sky-larking. Frank belonged to an amateur dramatic society and from the very first day at Watford it was one long laugh.

But I was to learn that there was sadness behind the laughter. Mr Humbert's only son was knocked off his bicycle one day by a lorry, and died. Ironically the accident happened right outside the shop. Mr Humbert (even in my mind I never thought of him as Bill) never mentioned this and the only company he and his wife had was Nelson, a very large, very black, one-eyed tomcat. Early every morning, Mr Humbert and Nelson would go for a walk across the fields at Kings Langley before work. He certainly never mentioned the tragedy to me and as far as I was concerned that was his own private cross.

Looking back it is easy to recall the good times but I am sure that there were 'off-days'. Mr Humbert was a very strict disciplinarian as far as work was concerned and I still had a lot to learn with regard to salesmanship. It was all too easy to grab the request order book when the required item was not available but the manager soon checked that little habit. 'Forget the request order book,' he told me. 'Pretend it doesn't exist. Try to get the customer onto something else that is a suitable alternative.'

I'm sure I silently cursed him at the time but he was right. After all, I was supposed to be a salesman.

The three weeks was soon up but nothing was said about me returning to Harrow. It seemed that I was now a permanent member of the Watford staff. Oddly enough I didn't mind as I had come to love the place. Watford was a far different town to what it is today. There were more individual shops and it had a rural air about it. There was a little coffee shop a few doors down from us where a diminutive little man used to stand on a box and grind the coffee in the window. The aroma of real coffee always brings recall of Watford in the Fifties.

My duties were much the same and I've always been at my best when I've had a routine to work to. The breaks could be eventful and I think that is when I learnt to watch out for myself with three jokers in the shop. Mr Humbert, like all other managers, took his tea in his office-coop and Rupert had his in the corner at the top of the stairs, his cup hidden in the wooden hat steamer bench. He never drank it until it was stone cold. Frank and I took our tea break in the pokey little staff room in the basement. One thing about that room which disturbed me was the way the back wall bowed out. That was the wall backing onto the church cemetery. 'We always keep an extra cup handy in case someone pops through unexpectedly,' Frank cheerfully informed me.

Occasionally as a treat I would buy a small packet of meringues from the local *Lyons* for my afternoon tea break. One day I returned with these goodies and took them down to the staff room where Frank had already taken his place at the rickety little table. He had an odd grin on his face and one hand was tucked behind his back. That grin should have warned me but it didn't. The next thing I knew was – crash, bang, wallop! A hammer had appeared and my meringues had been reduced to pink and lemon-coloured powder while still in their cellophane wrappings. And while I huffed and puffed with righteous indignation, he simply smiled and murmured in an almost confidential tone, 'I've always wanted to do that.'

Well I wasn't going to waste them so I spooned them out of the packet like sherbet powder.

Not that I was always the butt of their practical jokes. Frank had a favourite tie which he wore to work every day until it looked thoroughly warn and creased. 'If you wear that tie tomorrow,' Mr Humbert warned him, 'I'll cut it off.'

Frank did wear it the next day and, true to his word, Mr Humbert cut it off, just below the knot. After the initial outraged explosion Frank pleaded for someone to pop over to *Marks & Spencer's* opposite and buy a cheap tie. To no avail. Finally, he decided to go himself after carefully securing the severed length of material to the knot with a pin. But his ordeal had yet to run its course. Rupert followed him into the store and pulled the pin out.

On another occasion, a busy Saturday afternoon, Frank was serving a customer in the basement department when Rupert squeezed passed him, apparently intent on looking for some item on the customers' order rail. 'Sorry to push, Frank,' I heard him murmur.

Then Frank's voice hissed, 'Rupert, give me my bloody braces back!' whilst frantically clutching at his trouser waistband.

'What's that, Frank? Sorry – can't stop.' And Rupert had disappeared upstairs, holding a pair of twisted and frayed braces.

Rupert later told me that it was a trick he had learnt in the Army. He was in the tank corps for goodness' sake! It just didn't add up. Evidently it was an effective way to disable an enemy sentry. Well, I've seen plenty of war films but I've never come across that one.

Like all Dunn's shops we had a local tailor who did the alterations. He was a truculent little fellow called George Hobbs and I marvelled at how untidy some of these tailors were. He would slouch into the shop in a crumpled old jacket and trousers that had long been a stranger to an iron since the day they were made. An old check cap would be pulled down over his bespectacled, scowling goblin face and there was always about half an inch of hand-rolled ciggie dangling from his lip. He looked like the cartoon character, Andy Capp.

He didn't care a damn for anybody. On one occasion he had to see a customer about a query on an alteration to a waistcoat. The customer was complaining that the alteration had ruined the garment until George said that there was some crude stitching that he hadn't done and certainly didn't look like the manufacturer's work. 'Well my wife did attempt to make an adjustment,' the customer admitted stiffly.

'So how d'you think I'm going to put things right when bloody amateurs have been messing around with it?' George grunted.

I saw Mr Humbert shut his eyes and clasp a hand to his brow but the customer simply replied, 'all I want is the fitting to be corrected.' And that was the end of the matter.

I never knew George to laugh or smile but he was good at complaining. Every Monday morning I would take the alterations to his little shop in the back streets of Watford and he would pull open the bag and grumble. 'I suppose you want this lot for tomorrow. Blimey, 'ow d'you think I'm goin' to get three inches out of that? I can't work bloody miracles!'

With one final snort of fag ash over all and everything – me included – he would throw the whole lot into a corner of the workroom and I would be out on the pavement again, be-ashed, bothered and bewildered. But next day without fail George would slink into the shop with all the work completed and immaculately pressed.

Watford customers were very much upper crust in those days and many of them knew Mr Humbert personally. The shop often had the air of a country club. Considering only a few months before I had been working in Kentish Town this took some getting used to, but it was an enjoyable experience.

Every Saturday lunchtime, Mr Humburt would retire to the staff room with what was probably the most meagre fare I had ever seen; two slices of cold toast. But he always sent me out to get a small bottle of Guinness. The basement reeked like a brewery for the rest of the day but nobody ever complained about it. Watford was known for its pubs and breweries so the customers had probably become acclimatised to the smell of hops.

Stocktaking with our Area Supervisor Jack Flashman was a harrowing ordeal and woe betide any attempt to bamboozle him. He knew every trick in the book – except one. The tedious counting of clothing hangers could be a nightmare and, unlike other Supervisors, if the total wasn't right he wouldn't tell you if it was over or short, he would just snap, 'wrong. Count them again.'

But Mr Humbert had devised a scheme to get over this and the hanger totals were faintly pencilled on the back of a mirror in the basement department. But Jack would certainly have smelt a rat if anyone came up with the correct total on the first count so it was much more convincing to deliberately get the counts wrong the first time, endure 'Wrong. Count them again,' nip downstairs for a quiet smoke and then reappear ten minutes later, wide-eyed and innocent, with the correct totals. But I think if we had worked that trick more than a few times Jack would have become suspicious. Fortunately the situation never arose as, after a few months there was another reshuffle of Area Supervisors and Mr Drew was reinstated as our Area Supervisor.

I think we all appreciated Mr Drew's return as he was a lot more easy-going than Jack Flashman. Though to be fair to Jack, he wasn't a vindictive man. He was straight and utterly incorruptible, but too damned thorough for comfort. Anyway, Mr Drew didn't trouble us too much and his visits were quite infrequent. He usually made us his last call of the day as he lived in Boreham Wood, only a few miles away. By and large we seemed to be excluded from the urban rat race, existing in a blissful world of our own.

One particular visit of Mr Drew's springs to mind. He had broken his umbrella ferrule and rallied us round to help repair it. Mr Humbert stood aloof, spectacles held aloft and looking on with a critical eye while Mr Drew and Rupert held the umbrella firmly on the table. Then Frank took his meringue-crushing hammer while I stood by with a box of tacks.

While we wrestled with the gamp which kept rolling all over the place despite desperate attempts to hold it steady, Mr Drew remarked, 'All this industry reminds me of that item on *Panorama* last night. They filmed the birth of a baby.'

At which Rupert looked up, a whimsical smile on his Buddha-like features and said, 'Surely, S ir, not with a hammer and umbrella?'

As to our neighbours, those who occupied the floors above our shop, they also figured in my time at Watford. The optician on the first floor was an inoffensive little chap but his secretary was a bit of a dragon. Her name was Mary (just like the old song but there the resemblance ended!) although I never felt encouraged to address her as such if at all. She was a plump young lady with a most unsuitable pageboy hairstyle which looked like an ill-fitting black cap. For one so young she was inclined to be snappy and snooty and Mr Humbert used to refer to her as 'The Zephyr'. When I asked why, he said that a zephyr was a small breeze or puff of wind. Point taken.

The different floors above the shop were attained by several exhaustive flights of stairs; two to each floor with a landing in between where you could catch a breather. And I certainly needed it as the only available water tap in the building was on the second floor where the jewellery firm was located. Doubtless there were facilities in the optician's but I was never brave enough to beg for water there.

The jewellers on the second floor were a revelation. This was where the work was done. No smart velvet-lined display cases here. It was a scruffy hive of industry with the work-benches strewn with lumps of gold, Bunsen burners and saucepans on gas rings boiling deoxidising liquids. It was like a troll's kitchen.

The workforce was pretty impressive too. The business was run by Rex Prince, a very striking man of middle years with a leonine mane of silver hair and an all-year-round suntan. He looked more like a Hollywood star than a jeweller. He was very amiable and was not above passing the time of day with a lowly junior shop assistant like me. He was assisted and no doubt sometimes hindered by his two sons, Reggie and Brian. Reggie, the eldest was inclined to be of a more serious disposition than Brian who was a bit of a rip and forever skylarking about. Clive, the foreman, was a tall and quiet person, which is more than can be said for Paul and Denis the two apprentices. Finally, there were two young ladies on the team; Jane, a tall brunette with a tall brunette voice, and Valla, a very attractive blonde girl in her teens who had come over from Hungary as a refugee a couple of years earlier.

Life was never dull; what with Mr Humbert at the shop and those crazy off-the-wall types upstairs. Tea breaks meant a long trek upstairs to the second floor to get water. But if Reggie was ensconced inside the wash-room with a newspaper tea would be a little late that year. And even when access was gained one's life was imperilled by Paul or one of the others darting in to empty a saucepan of scalding acidic waste with which they had been purifying a small fortune of cloth of gold.

One lunchtime Clive, who was usually of a taciturn nature, called me into the workshop to show me a carriage clock they had been commissioned to make for Aristotle Onassis the Greek shipping millionaire. It was a truly beautiful object in solid gold with the hours and minutes picked out in diamonds and rubies. I said as much but Clive just smiled. 'The works only cost 17/6d,' he told me.

Rex Prince's two sons were quite capable of getting up to some really dastardly pranks. Luckily I was never at the sharp end of any of them but I have witnessed those who were. Like the tramp begging for money in the street, Brian threw some coins down from their upstairs window – after they had been heated over the Bunsen burner. Then there was the lorry which had stopped at the zebra crossing outside the shop. In the back, a workman clad only in a pair of jeans, lay stretched out in the hot sunshine, sound asleep. But as the lorry began to move off Reggie and Brian pitched a bucketful of icy cold water onto him from their window.

Wednesday half-day was a relaxed sort of day and to make it as such Mr Humbert would come to work in a pair of dark brown suede shoes and a bowtie. In fact, he got us all wearing bowties on Wednesdays – and not tacky-looking clip-on ones either. They had to be hand-tied or not at all. Once I had got used to the exposed area of shirt front I quite liked the effect. It looked cool, clean and comfortable. Oddly enough it didn't look the same when wearing a hat and the effect struck me as looking like a second-hand car salesman.

Every month we were required to complete detail sheets of all the ranges of headwear sold. The hat tickets were sacrosanct – well they would be – and after the sheets were completed all the tickets were carefully banded up in their various prices, placed in a special envelope marked 'Hat Tickets' and posted to Head Office. I can remember those paper tickets even now. Pink ones with rounded tops were 50/–, pink square 45/–, orange with rounded tops 28/6d, square grey and square blue were 16/6d and 21/– respectively and so on.

The cap tickets – white paper oblongs – were not afforded the same reverence. Once they had been listed they were thrown away. This head-wear listing was always done on a half-day and Rupert attended to the hat tickets upstairs while I was entrusted with the cap tickets in the staff room below decks. I always looked forward to this. It was half-day and I could plod along in peace and quiet. But one Wednesday ended up very differently.

All went as planned and at 1 o'clock we shut the shop and went our separate ways; Frank to the car park, Mr Humbert and Rupert to the bank with the morning's takings and me to the railway station. That is when I began to get what are now called 'bad vibes'. Something was wrong. I glanced over the road where Mr Humbert and Rupert were making their way to the bank and was sure of it. Those two smartly suited and hatted gentlemen were strutting along the road, smirking. Yes, something was definitely amiss! I paused and checked the back of my coat for a notice pinned on with 'kick me' written on it. There was nothing. That would have been too crude. But they had done something.

I then realised I would miss my train unless I put a spurt on and, forgetting about managerial pranks, I hurried on to the station. That was when I had my first mishap. The floor of the station booking hall could be slippery and I had metal tips on the heels of my shoes. The inevitable happened and I did a backward somersault, completely wrapping myself up in my unbuttoned overcoat. In my blinded state I was unable to see the following disaster but I heard it plainly enough.

It was an indignant screech from the ticket collector who, trapped in his little wooden sentry box, took the full impact of my case when it flew from my grasp. Highly embarrassed, I apologised, retrieved my case from his head and hurried down to the platform just as my train rolled in, thankfully staggering through the sliding doors and collapsing into a seat. The train rapidly filled up and, adopting the usual commuter practice to avoid staring at the person sitting opposite, I opened my newspaper – only to be covered in a deluge of paper cap tickets! That was it! That was what I had sensed! Those devils had deposited the entire month's cap tickets inside my newspaper!

Utterly mortified, I made a couple of despairing grabs at the paper heap that had cascaded from my lap to cover my shoes, conscious of the amused scrutiny of my fellow travellers. But any attempt to gather up the pile was futile and I spent the rest of the journey completely cowed and hunched in my seat with my eyes averted.

Another incident of pure slapstick of which I was the victim could not, in all fairness be attributed to the actions of my colleagues. It was purely 'just one of those things'. I was down in the basement cleaning the mirrors. This was before the advent of spray-on cleaners and the job had to be done with a bucket of water and a leather. Rupert had just finished his lunch and returned to the shop floor above when a customer asked to see some sports jackets. I heard the tread of the customer's foot on the stair and realised it would make a better impression if I made myself scarce. Picking up my bucket I quickly skipped into the staff room, not bothering to put the light on, and crouched behind the door, waiting for Rupert to take the customer around to where the sports jackets were.

But the unexpected always happens. Rupert remembered something he had left in the staff room and barged in. Now I have said that he was quite a chubby chap and heavy with it too. He hurled the door open, unaware of my presence, in the darkness and I was sent crashing backwards and ended up sitting in my bucket of water.

All Rupert knew was that I was swearing and splashing around in the gloom, giving voice to my predicament in the most strident tones. In any event he just couldn't attend to the customer for laughing and had to go upstairs and send Frank down.

My days at Watford were certainly not boring and I learnt a lot from Mr Humbert. Also he had the ability to command respect. It was the Christmas of 1958 that I was invited to join the senior staff in a convivial drink after we closed on Christmas Eve – the first time ever. I can see the five of us standing in the saloon bar of *The Bell* with our pints. Mr Humbert looking as solemn as a judge, quaffing his pint. Frank, Rupert, and George Hobbs the tailor sinking pint after pint, each one almost as big as himself.

As 1959 passed into Summer – one of the hottest to date in my working life – we took on a new junior which wasn't one of Mr Humbert's better ideas. Those busy Saturdays were sweltering for we had no air conditioning to cope with those 88° Fahrenheit Saturdays in the basement department. Doubtless it was the heat which finally deprived our junior's single brain cell of any form of rationality but he wasn't a very promising specimen to begin with. His name was Alan Betts and his only talent seemed to be an overdeveloped characteristic for self-interest. It certainly didn't embrace what he was getting paid for. Fortunately, he was only with us for a couple of weeks and what probably saw him off was a singularly dramatic incident which occurred one lunchtime in the shop.

Rupert was on holiday at the time, Frank was at lunch and Mr Humbert was in his recently-installed state-of-the-art office on the telephone to one of the other shops. As luck would have it he was looking away from the shop floor when the incident happened.

I was passing the time polishing the hat steamer with metal polish, vaguely fascinated by the way the liquid bubbled when poured onto the hot metal when I became aware of a faint drumming sound overhead. As the sound grew louder I realised that it was footsteps of someone descending the many short flights of stairs – and descending rapidly. But there was more than one person descending at a rate of knots.

Then Betts, wide-eyed and white of face, burst into the shop, heading for the stairs leading down to the basement. He was closely followed by Valla, the Hungarian girl from the jewellers and she did not look at all happy. Pushing up the sleeves of her blouse, she caught up with him at the top of the staircase and seized him by the throat. Well, I didn't like the fellow but I couldn't see him throttled. It would only lead to all manner of tiresome complications so I gently tapped her on the shoulder, murmuring words of a soothing nature to restore serenity. But all I got for my pains was her elbow at my throat and while I reeled around the hat steamer, gagging, she had thrown Betts down the basement staircase.

Recovering my breath, I croaked a tentative enquiry regarding her displeasure. She glared at me and for one awful moment I thought I was about to follow after Betts, but she had calmed down sufficiently to give me a very heated explanation for her actions. It seemed that she had been carrying a tray of tea things to the washroom when she had encountered Betts in the passageway. Seeing that she had both hands fully occupied he evidently laid his own hands on her person in a most ungentlemanly manner. What sort of reaction the idiot had expected, I don't know. He was self-opinionated enough to expect her to swoon in his arms but it didn't work out like that. She dropped the tray of crockery and went for him, thirsting for what passed as his blood. Yes, now I come to think of it, that is probably why he left.

But there was another danger which was evident during the Summer and that was manipulating the sunblind. This was before the modern push button electric blinds and we had to use a long wooden pole with a hook at the end. The hazard was the narrow pavement which meant I had to stand in the gutter. As it was a main road timing was vital and one day I got it wrong.

Mr Humbert was dressing the window and asked me to push the blind up. I was sure the road was clear and had just started operations when a great red double-decker bus came thundering up the High Street. I suppose I should have let go of the pole when I jumped back onto the pavement but self-preservation is a wonderfully overwhelming challenge to rational behaviour. The pole bent to an alarming degree at which I found time to marvel, dimly aware of the manager in the window, wide-eyed and clawing out what few hairs grew on his bullet head. The pole snapped just below the hook and I was in disgrace. I spent the rest of the day whittling the shattered end of the pole and ruined a perfectly good penknife in the process. But on the brighter side this meant that the pole was too short for me to use, and as he was the tallest, the task fell to Frank Sherman.

There was another kerbside occurrence at Watford which could have got me killed and this was during the most mundane of my duties. I was sweeping the narrow pavement in front of the shop, mentally miles away, when I was dimly aware of what sounded like a crash just behind me. I looked up and saw two policemen staring at me from over the road, open-mouthed with amazement.

I stared back at them owlishly, then peered behind me. Some fragments of white china were scattered on the pavement. Vaguely annoyed, I gazed at them. Now where had they come from? I distinctly remembered sweeping that area just a few moments beforehand.

Next instant I was assailed by a blonde whirlwind who seized my broom, trying to wrest it from my grasp. It was Valla. I resisted indignantly. It was my broom. Surely they had got one of their own upstairs? She jabbered at me in Magyar but I still hung on. A Hungarian broom thief! Thank heavens the police were on hand. But when I glared across at them they were both doubled up with laughter.

Gradually the light dawned. Valla had been carrying a tray of teacups into the workroom when she had tripped over and one teacup had flown out of the second floor window and come within an ace of braining me.

I relinquished the broom and, still rattling off what I took to be apologies, she swept up the broken crockery. I was touched. How thoughtful of her to be so concerned about me! Apart from my parents nobody had given a damn about me. I thought I might ask her out one evening as she apparently had a kind disposition when she wasn't strangling junior assistants, but alas, Fate intervened yet again.

The phone rang and Mr Humbert informed me that I was to be transferred back to Harrow. I was really choked. Despite being back on my old patch with kindly old Bertie Benson, I had really settled in at Watford and it seemed hard to credit that I had been there a whole year, for it was now the late Summer of 1959.

As it happened, Frank Sherman was driving through Harrow on my last day and gave me a lift home. I had learnt a lot at Watford, worked with a great team and had lots of fun. Dear, safe old Harrow would seem quite tame after all the thrills, spills and skylarking.

A PERSONNEL PROBLEM

Autumn 1959 ~ Summer 1960

It was a sunny Monday morning in late August when I returned to the Harrow branch of Dunn & Co, but not so jauntily as the previous year when I escaped the horrors of warfare by failing my National Service medical.

'Hello, laddie,' Bertie Benson greeted me, unfolding from his office stool like a benevolent spider. 'What are you doing here?'

'Mr Drew phoned last week to say that I had been transferred back,' I replied, uneasily aware that we had had virtually the same conversation just over a year ago.

Bertie smiled apologetically. 'I don't think so,' he murmured. 'I'll just give him a ring to make sure.'

Yes, it damn well was the same conversation. What sort of Area Supervisor was he? Couldn't he get anything right? Last year I ended up at Wembley. Where to now, I wondered?

As before I chattered with Mike Flynn while Bertie tried to locate the whereabouts of Mr Drew on the telephone. Mike introduced me to one of the two members of staff; Ron Pascoe and David Rollins. Ron came across as a very likeable chap; fair-haired, stocky and cheerful. There was something about him which reminded me of characters out of Charles Dickens. Maybe it was the double-breasted waistcoat which was really the wrong style for a rotund figure as it was cut straight across at the bottom without the usual points – that plus the fact that he was into hipster trousers – well only just into them – which meant that there was a two-inch gap of white shirting between waistcoat and waistband. He looked like a cream sponge.

David Rollins was something else. A year or so younger than me, tall, dark-suited and gangling. Everything about him gangled. Even his face gangled. His speech was punctuated with various snorts, giggles, grunts and other farmyard noises but he seemed harmless enough. But I was to learn differently.

'Mr Drew meant Edgware,' announced Bertie, emerging from his office.

Edgware! That shop had never crossed my mind. I had visited the shop in the past to collect or deliver something but otherwise it was new territory to me. It was one of our more 'modern' shops and had opened a year before I joined the firm. It still had the wooden fixtures but of a lighter oak, almost honey-coloured and – for those days – of a more modern and softer design.

Here we go again, I thought as I boarded the No 18 bus for Edgware. At least it wasn't a difficult journey. And it wasn't a slow one either. No 18 buses were renowned – or notorious – for their speed and reckless driving and I was there in no time.

Charlie Steele the manager stood at the door waiting for me. 'Enjoy your tour of Middlesex?' he greeted me amiably and without sarcasm. 'Stick your togs out the back room and put the kettle on.'

This was more like it. Charlie was well-known for his tea breaks and Edgware branch was known as 'The Shop Where The Kettle Is Never Cold'. The shop itself was squarish inside, bright and comfortable to work in with a large display window and a wide porch to the left of it. Up two steps at the back of the shop was what was called the packing room, resembling an unusually large prison cell. A doorway led off this to a yard which we shared with the builders' merchants next door and at the end of the packing room was the staff room. This was long and gloomy with a bench table running down one side and wooden shelves on the other where hats returned for cleaning were stacked.

Edgware seemed to be a sort of non-event shop in many respects. There were no departmental stores to bring the trade in although it was quite a wealthy area. It was certainly not a bustling hive of industry but good enough to jog along in. Trade was mainly on Saturday and it was something of a wonder just how we managed to pay our way.

Charlie Steele was quite a character. In appearance he looked most formidable with his bristling moustache, neatly trimmed under his aristocratic nose. His grey hair was brushed back and his light grey suite was immaculate. Two peculiarities about his dress were his shirt and tie. He nearly always wore a pale blue shirt with a white stiff collar and his ties were something of a shock. They tended to be light in colour with large red or blue spots. Also he never seemed to be able to tie them properly. The wide front piece was always too short while the narrow tail dangled down to his waist. It was only when he opened his mouth that any illusion was shattered. ''Ullo, cock. Let's 'ave a brew-up.'

We got on famously. He was a widower but courting a lady friend and paid me the compliment of asking me one day for my advice as to whether or not he should re-marry. I was flattered but it was not the sort of decision

I could make for him. I had never even met the lady. Indeed, I didn't know much about ladies at all then.

For the first few weeks there were just the two of us then one day Charlie told me they were sending a young man from our Golders Green branch. This is the point where Edgware ceased to be a 'non-event' shop. Billy Bailey was the oddest young person I had encountered to date. He looked and sounded like that immortal child of radio, Jimmy Clitheroe, and wore a black chalk-stripe suit that would have been old-fashioned on his grandfather. But to cap it all – an appropriate enough term! – he wore a bowler hat. Just imagine it. A diminutive eighteen year-old in a bowler hat!

But as to the person beneath the bowler hat and inside the ancestral suit, they could have done a TV comedy series about him. For one thing he was always late. We would see him hurtling down the street from Edgware Station, his lunch bag clutched in one hand while the other held his bowler hat in place. This became such a regular occurrence that the local newspaper took an interest in him and printed a spoof article, complete with photograph. Inevitably the manager had to be interviewed which didn't please him overmuch and his comments were very guarded and terse.

Two characteristics of Billy Bailey made it very difficult to work with him. He was accident-prone and a practical joker. It seemed that he had only to walk past some display fitting without even touching it for the whole thing to disintegrate into its component parts. But his practical joking was far from funny and inevitably got him into Mr Drew's bad books.

This occurred during stocktaking. Mr Drew and I were in the packing room when we heard the connecting door to the shop slam shut and Billy's strident Brummie voice raised in triumph. 'Ee, that's got you! You can't get out now! I've taken the door handle off!'

Mr Drew went pink. 'Bailey!' he exploded, rattling the door-knob which came away with its metal shank in his hand. 'Open the door this instant!'

'Ee, Mr Drew! I didn't know you were out there! I thought it were only Keith! I can't open the door! I've dropped the knob and I can't find the screws!'

Well it was obvious he couldn't open the door with Mr Drew holding the business end of the handle in his clenched fist. 'Well find them this instant!' he snapped back.

Billy Bailey couldn't find an elephant in a telephone box and he was in such a state as to be worse than useless. In the end we had to go out through the backyard, along the lane behind the shop, down the mews and in at the front door. It goes without saying that disciplinary words were uttered with threats of dismissal if Mr Bailey didn't buck his ideas up.

That was the beginning of the end for Billy Bailey. He finally upset poor old 'Long John' Neville the Staff Director by saying, when asked where he came from, Birmingham but didn't like to admit it as there wasn't a very nice class of person up there. It so happened that JN was from Birmingham and after a couple more blunders Billy left under a cloud. The last we heard was that he had joined another Gents' Outfitters and was causing just as much havoc there.

Another occasion when heated words were uttered it was Mr Drew who was on the sharp end of them. Charlie had had a very trying day dressing the window. With the last garment put in place he slammed the door shut at the back of the window and knocked the display stand over. I had never seen anything like it. I believe it is called the 'domino effect'. The whole display went and it just didn't stop. Coats and suits toppled down. Hats bounced up in the air. It was like watching the death throes of some strange organism. As for Charlie, Sir was blue with his fury. He leapt into the window, hurling display stands in all directions. I narrowly missed being decapitated by the base of a bronze coat stand with its coat streaming out behind it like a khaki pennant.

Just then Mr Drew walked in, his face like thunder and one hand dripping blood. He had fallen down the escalator at Camden Town. 'I've come to check the stock,' he announced.

'Not at bloody three o'clock you haven't!' snapped Charlie, still casting merchandise to the four winds.

For several seconds they glared at each other but Charlie Steele's wrath bested Mr Drew's annoyance and the latter replied, 'I can see you are busy, Mr Steele. I'll come back tomorrow morning.'

By the next day both of my superiors had calmed down and normality was restored, along with a freshly-dressed window.

Charlie and I managed quite well between us. I had got tea-making down to a fine art and we probably averaged about seven tea breaks a day. When the windows weren't collapsing Charlie could be quite a jovial character. For some reason he nicknamed me 'Bloggs' and regaled me with stories of his days in the RAF during the war which were as amusing as they were unrepeatable. And he had a splendid repertoire of service ballads in much the same vein.

Then just before Christmas we were told that one of the Harrow staff was being transferred to Edgware. 'That will be Ron Pascoe,' I told Charlie. 'He's a good bloke.'

'Anyone would be better than Bailey,' Charlie retorted.

But we were both wrong. I was wrong because it wasn't Ron Pascoe but David Rollins, and Charlie was wrong because he proved worse than Billy Bailey – infinitely worse.

To put it bluntly David Rollins was thick and if that had been all I would have felt sorry for him. But he was such an utter snob as well as being sly and deceitful. On his first day he asked me, 'What does your father do for a living?'

I told him that he was a foreman for a firm of local builders.

'Oh, works in the mud and filth, does he?' smirked our new addition. 'My father has an important job in Whitehall.'

I even had to endure his company part way on my homeward journey as he lived just outside Edgware at Canons Park. We were sitting upstairs one evening and as we approached his bus stop he got up and made his way down the stairs. Then I heard him talking to the bus conductor who had not yet collected our fares. 'I'll pay for the chap at the back upstairs. He's not very well off and his father only works on a scruffy building site.'

I over-reacted. Leaning over the stairwell I shouted out, 'You keep your bloody money, Rollins!' and threw a handful of coins down, much to the sympathetic amusement of the conductor. The wretched fellow got right under my skin. But he was as thick-headed as he was offensive, with a hide like an elephant.

My time at Edgware was not improved one Winter's afternoon when I discovered that someone had got into the staff room via the backyard and stolen my overcoat. The loss of the coat was bad enough on a cold and frosty night but the loss of the front door key in the pocket was a serious business entailing changing the lock.

Christmas Eve Rollins suggested that we go for a drink after work, so we went to *The Boot*, a pub in Edgware, but I didn't stay long. I had just one pint in the name of Peace on Earth and Goodwill to All Men and Rollins but my drinking companion, who had a lemonade shandy, began giggling and declared that he was getting tipsy. And a Happy Christmas to you, I thought as I slipped quietly away.

Somehow I tolerated this gangling albatross around my neck but it wasn't doing me any good. Virtually every evening I would arrive home trembling with anger and it was obviously going to erupt sooner or later. And it wasn't just me; Charlie Steele felt just the same. Some days Rollins would cycle to work – and I mean that in the most extreme literal sense. He would cycle right into the shop.

One day Charlie decided enough was enough. 'You do that once more, my lad,' he warned Rollins, 'and you'll regret it.'

Rollins just sniggered and wheeled his bike into the packing room.

He did it again the next day and discovered, most painfully, that the manager wasn't joking. As he cycled into the shop and across the carpet, Charlie picked up a broom and hurled it like a spear straight through the spokes of his front wheel. Rollins cartwheeled from the saddle and sprawled to the floor.

'I warned you,' Charlie told him. 'Now take that heap of rubbish you call a bike and get on with some work.'

Rollins spent the whole day in the packing room repairing his bike so we were left in peace. He was still at it at closing time. 'You can't go yet,' he protested. 'I haven't finished.'

'Tough,' Charlie growled, donning his snappy, roll-brimmed trilby. 'Then you'll have to finish your repairs outside.'

We left Rollins sitting on the pavement among the various detached sections of his bicycle with an interesting assortment of nuts and bolts on a newspaper. But if we had felt any pangs of conscience they were quite uncalled for. After we had gone he simply gathered up the various bits and pieces and went home by taxi. Well he could afford it. His father worked in Whitehall.

March 1960 marked my twenty-first birthday, and as the half-day in Edgware was on Thursday I decided to visit my old haunts at Watford where I had spent so many happy days. And the first person I ran into was Rex Prince who owned the jewellery business. He greeted me effusively and proudly announced that he had moved his firm to new premises across the road. He even insisted that I accompany him to see the place for myself. They were all there; his two sons, Clive and the others along with Jane and Valla the cup-throwing Hungarian strangless.

After the tour of inspection, I paid my respects to Mr Humbert, Rupert Higgs and Frank Sherman. It was a very happy meeting, reliving some of the hilarious moments during my time there.

As I was leaving the shop I saw Valla on her way home from work. Recalling her solicitude when she nearly brained me with a teacup I had, what I thought at the time, a brilliant idea. 'Hello again,' I greeted her. 'Look, tomorrow is my twenty-first birthday and I was wondering whether we could go for a drink to celebrate it before you go home.'

She studied me dispassionately with ice-blue eyes, then retorted, 'No, you are too old-fashioned. I don't want to be seen with you.'

Well that was that. I was too old-fashioned. Probably it was because of the hat. But it was no use crying over spilt Hungarians so I opted for Plan B and went to the pictures.

What with the social put-down and having to endure David Rollins at work I was feeling at a pretty low ebb. Then one day a splendid opportunity arrived which had distinct signs of easing the tension. Dunn's, after their abortive advert a few years previous of the 'Indestructible Hat', had decided to go public again. This time they were advertising in daily newspapers but only in the general sense. Black-and-white sketches of square-shouldered, military-moustached gentlemen in City suits or country tweeds could be seen with the usual phrase 'Dunn & Co – to be sure'.

During one of our many tea breaks Rollins seized upon a newspaper depicting a mature but impossibly tall drawing of a gentleman in a Harris Tweed jacket and matching cap. Just for effect the advert showed him holding a collie dog on a lead.

'Do we sell dogs now?' Rollins asked me.

I could hardly believe my ears but thought the situation worth playing along. 'Didn't you know?' I replied. 'Only top pedigree though. Dog Department has got a very wide range.'

I honestly expected him to guess that I was kidding, but no. 'I'd like an Alsatian puppy,' the idiot declared.

I finished my tea and made ready to return to the shop. 'Fair enough,' I told him. 'I'll phone Head Office while you are at the tailor's this afternoon and put in a staff order for one in your name.'

I thought that would be the end of it. Surely nobody could be that dense? But David Rollins could. It was Monday and it was his task that day to take any customers' alterations over to Joe Weiss at Kenton who also did Harrow's work. The general pattern was that Rollins would stop off at home for lunch on the way.

I had forgotten about the dog episode until the phone rang half an hour later. It was Rollins. 'Listen, Howard!' he snapped. 'My mummy says I can't have a dog. Get onto Head Office and cancel that staff order!'

That really got me on the raw. Not 'Keith' or even 'Mr Howard' – just plain 'Howard'. The dog subject ceased to be a joke and became a subject of retaliation. 'Now you listen to me, David,' I retorted. 'You are in deep trouble. Head Office sent your damn dog by special van and Mr Drew our Area Supervisor came with it as dog handler. Well the animal had rabies and bit him. He's now in Edgware General's Intensive Care section and the dog has been taken by the police to the dog pound – and you really are up the creek without a paddle. It's been registered in your name.'

I was blissfully rewarded by panic-stricken babblings issuing from the telephone receiver. I let him rave and gibber for a minute or so, then I decided to throw him a lifeline. 'There's two ways out,' I told him. 'You give yourself up at Edgware Police Station and ask for a yellow Bedlam form on your way back from the tailor's or call in at the Harrow shop. Mr

Benson has just received a stock of cocker spaniel puppies and may be able to arrange for your dog to be transferred to his stock.'

With a wordless yelp he hung up and I explained the whole business to the manager. Charlie was quite tickled about it but couldn't credit that anyone could be so stupid as to be kidded along like that. Then half an hour later the phone rang and proved my point. It was Bertie Benson at Harrow. 'Hello, laddie,' he greeted me in his usual mild and genial way. 'I've just had David in asking to see my dogs.'

Well a good laugh goes a long way to easing the pressure and it did help, if only for a little while. It seemed that even in my off-duty hours I was to be pestered by the fellow. One evening he turned up on my doorstep, blundering in, as was his usual style. The only good thing about his visit was that my parents could see that I had not been exaggerating about him. While we finished our meal he sat in a chair, still wearing his hat and raincoat, and fumbling to stir a cup of tea while still wearing his gloves.

I occasionally visited Watford to see Mr Humbert and the others, but kept well clear of the 'Hungarian Rhapsody'. Poor old Bill Humbert was feeling very bitter. Dunn's were opening up a new shop at the top of the town in Watford Parade. Quite understandably he had been expecting to be offered the position of manager but they brought in someone from a provincial shop. It was a slap in the face as he had managed the Watford High Street shop for fifteen years and had built up a very healthy trade. He was even known as 'Mr Watford'. But justice prevailed. Bill Humbert's shop knocked spots off the new one, despite the latter being four times the size. It was obvious that Dunn's had intended to close the High Street branch but they had to have a rethink. It was some years before the new shop became established and dear old Watford High Street held its own for many years before it closed, and Bill Humbert had long since retired by then. As to the other staff, Rupert Higgs had left to open up a grocery shop in Chatham and Frank Sherman had also departed to work for an electronics firm.

Meanwhile, back at the ranch – otherwise Edgware – things came to a head that Summer, regarding the Rollins Problem – violently so. Charlie was going to lunch and Rollins had gone to the bank. 'When "Horatio Dustbag" finally decides to come back,' said Charlie, 'get him to help you fold up those coats and store them away in the drawers.' Charlie had a very novel turn of phrase when it came to nicknames. I recall he once referred to Rollins as 'looking like a ruptured duck struck by lightning'.

So Charlie retired to the staff room to have some lunch and I began packing away the overcoats. About five minutes later Rollins breezed into the shop, a Mickey Mouse comic in one hand and a bag of cream buns in the other.

'Dave, would you give me a hand with these coats?' I asked.

His reply was as brief as it was crude. Then he shut himself in the fitting-room with his comic and buns.

'Dave you **are** going to help me with these coats,' I persisted, struggling to keep my voice low and steady. 'Now come on out and do some work.'

I got the same vulgar response. He wasn't even original.

There was nothing for it but to make him come out. I removed the padded seat from one of the shop chairs. It had no dangerous sharp corners and it was well-padded, but it was heavy. Deciding it would suit my purpose, I pitched it up and over into the fitting-room. There followed an angry squawk and the sound of tearing paper. That was Mickey Mouse gone for a burton. The door flew open and Rollins erupted forth, towing over me and snorting like an angry bull.

'Well that got you out,' I told him with no small glow of triumph. 'Now do some work and help me with these coats.'

And that is where I made my big mistake. I turned away from him to get on with my work and next thing I knew was an agonising pain in my kidneys as he kicked me in the back.

That did it. I got up and went for him, catching him a glorious crack on the jaw that sent him flying into the desk. He went sprawling, covered in red, blue and green ink and no small amount of gore.

'I'll get you sacked, Howard!' he screamed at me as he picked himself up. 'I'll get you for assault!'

Then he blundered past me, heading for the staff room to pour out his grievances to the manager. That's torn it, I thought, conscious of the raised but indistinct voices. I'm really in trouble now.

They seemed to be out there for ages and, feeling a bit ashamed of myself, I wondered on my possible fate. At the worst I would be charged with assault and, as I saw it, at the best I would be dismissed. And what about references? I wouldn't have any worth mentioning when it came to trying to find a worthwhile job.

Then Charlie Steele appeared at the packing room door, holding Rollins but the scruff of his jacket collar. 'Go on!' he barked. 'Go on! Apologise to Mr Howard for upsetting him!'

Then in an aside to me he murmured, 'about time you put one on him. He's had it coming for ages.'

Mercifully I was spared Rollins' presence in the workplace for a few days later Mr Drew telephoned to say that he was transferring me to Wembley. And this time he **had** got the shop right.

Strangely enough, just as the previous year when I had left Watford, I was given a lift home. Charlie's son was in the area and the manager was driving through Harrow to see him. He dropped me off near Harrow's town centre and wished me well. I never saw him again as he took early retirement on full pension. He was yet another fine man to work for and I hoped that he had settled down happily and remarried.

Thankfully I never saw David Rollins again either. All I know is that he left the firm and disappeared into oblivion.

THE WONDERS OF WEMBLEY

Summer 1960 ~ Winter 1962

In the early Sixties there was something peaceful about Wembley. The megastores and supermarkets had yet to hold towns in their thrall and individual stores still flourished. Although by no means possessing the rural air of Watford it had its own individuality with stores such as *Killips* who sold fancy goods, and all manner of things ideal for gifts. This store had two features which really gave it character. One was a sort of minstrel gallery running round the upper regions of the sales floor with elegant display cases. The other feature was that fascinating 'cable car' system they had for the money. Little metal rockets would whizz through the air on cables from the sales area to the cash desk and back again. Much more fun than watching credit cards being 'swiped'.

Another aspect about Wembley High Road was that a great portion of one side was only single-storey. Just the shops, and this made the place lighter and brighter.

Norman Hurst was still managing Wembley and as he drove through Harrow he would pick me up in the mornings, making a slight detour to drop his wife, June, off at North Wembley where she worked at British Oxygen. Norman was an early bird and by 8.30 we would be sitting in *Joe Lyons* opposite the Wembley shop, drinking an ivory-coloured beverage consisting of milk, sugar, some water and a few tea leaves.

There were two other staff members. The senior assistant was Bruce Wells, a very self-assured young man from Hull. The other was the junior, Robert Bates, skinny and 'knee-high to a grasshopper' but with all the 'side' of a seven-foot night-club bouncer.

Young Mr Bates was his very own fan club. Well, he had to be. I can never actually remember seeing him move though he must have done to get to the shop. The image that sticks in my mind most of all but sent Norman – usually of a cheery disposition – into a paroxysm of fury was that of Robert Bates standing at the bus stop. I suppose 'standing' is as good a word as any. His feet were in the gutter and he was leaning against the bus stop. His large horn-rimmed spectacles only just prevented his head from being completely enveloped by his violent green Tyrolean hat. A white shortie mac was draped around the shoulders of his hideous black-and-white check suit with trousers that seemed paradoxically narrower than his legs. But the final touch was the theatrically long cigarette holder. All this and only seventeen years old! I think it goes without saying that he wasn't with us long.

For most of the week there were only Norman and I as Bruce, more often than not, had to help out at our Liverpool Street store, with the exception of Saturday which was the half-day in the City. Wembley was a good shop to work in with an easy atmosphere – and a lift home in the evenings.

Promotion among assistants was never clearly defined. I was a sort of junior senior assistant rather than a senior junior assistant even though the more menial tasks fell to me. Not that I minded. In those days we all pitched in and got the job done.

Recalling Norman's ill-advised instructions regarding the doomed Drylon hat display of three years earlier, I was rather nervous when any special window displays were required but fortunately none of them were life-threatening. But there was one occasion when Norman's ingenuity had hilarious consequences. We were putting on a show of winter coats and he just couldn't get the sleeves right in one of the loose-fitting raglan coats. No matter how much tissue paper he crammed into the sleeves they hung limply at the sides in a dejected, almost apologetic attitude. Then Norman had a brainwave. From a street trader he purchased two sausage shaped balloons, already inflated, and inserted them in to the sleeves. And once the cuffs were pinned neatly to the sides of the coat the effect was perfect. An immaculate tweed coat with full shoulders that any man would envy and any woman admire.

But the next morning we were in for a shock. There was the coat, waiting to greet us with wide open arms! Evidently the pins had come out during the evening and the balloons had done the rest. This was later confirmed by a local customer who had been window shopping the previous evening when the metamorphosis occurred and the coat apparently sprang to life, flung its arms up and nearly gave the poor man a heart attack!

About that time, we took on a new member of staff. David Hopper was about seventeen years old but quite advanced for his age. Politely speaking he would have been termed a 'ladies' man' but that would have been putting it mildly. He was girl-mad and he must have been quite an optimist as he was not what would be termed 'beefcake' material. Pork would have been a more accurate description.

Florid and heavily bespectacled with a build more suited to comfort than speed, he was full of bounce and not very bright but at least he was nothing like the other David at Edgware. For a teenager he was suffering a premature hair loss and what hair he did have grew in a fair and curly coxcomb high up on his forehead.

Bruce Wells was moved permanently to the City and was replaced by Darren Pym, better known for some inexplicable reason as Ernie. If he had not been so unintentionally funny Ernie could have been one of the biggest bores in history. He was fanatically obsessed with traditional jazz and unless you were very careful he would lecture you for ages about it.

He was several years older than me, gaunt and long-jawed. His wavy hair was as pale as his complexion and with his Dunn's hat on he looked like the ghost of a dead gangster. 'Hey, Mister!' was his favourite opening gambit in virtually every discussion. He would rave about some jazz singer called Sister Rosetta Tharp, half-close his eyes and croon *The Old Rugged Cross* and was most indignant when I challenged him, declaring the song to be an old Salvation Army hymn.

The Salvation Army cropped up again when yet another youth joined our ranks. One Norris Chapman played the trumpet in the Salvation Army band. He certainly looked as if he had played the trumpet all his young life, angel-faced and chubby with wavy brown hair, he looked the picture of innocence.

I recall Norman haranguing us on the eve of our new recruit's arrival. 'Now listen to me, you blokes,' he said to Ernie, Dave and Yours Truly. 'I don't want any more swearing in this shop when the new lad starts. You've got to bloody well clean things up. He's Salvation Army and he won't be used to the way you lot bloody well go on.'

It turned out that Master Norris was the biggest villain of all with a truly wicked sense of humour and a most inventive gift for devilment. In short, he was a very amusing chap to work with.

Every Wednesday morning we had a cleaner lady, Mrs Wiggins. She was totally the opposite to the plump "allo ducks' Mrs Briggs who used to 'do' for Harrow. Mrs Wiggins was like a midget skeleton with greyish-fair hair screwed up in a bun, a shrill voice and a very delicate temperament which could easily be offended. She reminded me of Minnie Bannister from *The Goon Show*. One morning while she was cleaning the stairs I saw this small flickering ball of fire drift from behind one of the clothing fixtures like a miniature UFO. It dissipated but then another appeared. I watched, spellbound, as it soared towards the staircase and struck Mrs Wiggins in the rear as she was bending over the stairs. Fortunately it disappeared and no conflagration followed. She was not even aware of the fiery assault but

I deemed it wise to seek out the source of this phenomenon before any real damage could be done.

I soon found the answer to the mystery. Norris, holding a bronze metal tube which was part of the clothing fixtures, was squirting gas out of a plastic lighter refill bulb into the tube. Then using his powerful trumpeter's lungs he was blowing it out while David ignited it with a match at the other end. On my appearance they momentarily panicked. Norris dropped the bulb of fuel which somehow caught fire. David stamped on it but this only made matters worse. He was wearing Winkle-picker shoes and the half-melt-bulb fused to the point of his shoe and set fire to it. David hopped around in terror, waving his blazing Winkle-picker but Norris, displaying great initiative, extinguished the blaze by stamping on David's foot. It did the trick, even if it did half-cripple his partner in pyrotechnics.

The state of affairs at Wembley was fast approaching the wonderfully zany lifestyle of our Watford shop and working with that gang life at Wembley was never dull. But one day the joke really was on me and I had no one to blame but myself.

I had just sold an Austrian valour hat – the dearest hat in the shop. So rarely were they sold they were in danger of mummifying. Making a great show of steaming the hat into shape I thought that some civilised conversation was called for. Noting that the weather was blowing a gale and raining cats and dogs outside, I remarked to the customer, 'unbelievably tempestuous weather today, Sir.'

The customer seemed to start slightly. Norman, Ernie and the other two stared in astonishment. When the customer had left Ernie grinned and said, 'I suppose if he had only bought a cheap hat you'd have said, "bloody windy out there today, guv".'

All in all, I was enjoying Wembley. I felt that I was into things more. Apart from our ready-made clothing we also did made-to-measure. Not that we were bespoke tailors; we didn't do fittings. The various measurements were noted, sent to the makers and the completed suit was sent to the shop. Inevitably there would be instances where the garment did not fit correctly and would have to be returned to the makers. With so many different measurements involved this was bound to happen from time to time. But there was an easy way round this. If a customer was too long or too short for a stock size we would simply find the nearest size from stock, quote it on his order with specifications for example 'stock size long 40 with extra 2" on sleeves and legs'. More often than not the garment came in at stock price instead of the dearer made-to-measure price, so everyone was happy.

About this time, *Crombie*, who were well known for their top quality overcoats, produced a limited range of suits and jackets of extremely high quality fine wool. You could always spot them. The colours and the patterns were distinctive without being flashy. They could mix golds, mauves and greens in such a way that the colours blended in perfect harmony.

Towards the end of 1960 Dunn & Co really came into their own as Hatters when they launched a new style which soon became nationally popular. The 'Robin Hood'. This small crowned hat with a curled brim which dipped in front and was adorned with a highly decorative feather in the band was in green 'rough finish' fur felt. In simple layman's terms this meant that it had hairs all over it. Tony Hancock the comedian adopted it and it featured regularly in his TV show *Hancock's Half Hour* which doubtless boosted the sales.

This was followed by the 'Longbow', much the same as the 'Robin Hood' except that the front of the brim extended out almost to a point in such the same image as depicted in the illustrations of the Outlaws of Sherwood Forest. Unfortunately, this style crashed on take-off. This did not come as a great surprise as 'Long John' Neville, the dreaded Staff Director, tried one on during one of his visits. I had never seen JN without his hat before and what head that was uncovered seemed little more than a shallow slope with some black hair slicked across it. But when he put that stupid hat on and stared at himself in the mirror like a flatulent owl I just had to retreat out of sight to the upper regions of the shop or disgrace myself by laughing out loud. The 'Longbow' was most definitely a no-no and that was that. Norman wasn't really sorry. He was a bit wary of specialist style hats. He once got a rocket from Head Office for quite innocently putting a red Egyptian fez in the window during the Suez Crisis.

The fez in question was one of a range of novelty hats which Dunn's produced as 'lost leaders', the idea being that one placed in the window would stop a passer-by in his tracks and, hopefully, he would notice other more conventional merchandise on display. There were also various styles of cowboy hats, all made in the less expensive wool felt. These novelty hats were usually only stocked in the West End stores and they were quite saleable.

Our Harrow branch regularly each year received an order for a dozen or so tricorne hats with blue piping for the Herga Morrismen – Harrow's local Morris Dancers.

This calls to mind an unusual incident which took place in one of our West End stores. An African gentleman ordered a quantity of bowler hats to be sent out to some small African Republic which had recently been taken over by a new government and these hats were for the new Cabinet Ministers. But he stipulated that they should all be in different colours – red, blue, yellow, green etc – with all the individual's names printed on the hatband. He supplied the names plus a handsome deposit and said that he would send the balance as soon as the order was available to be shipped out.

The bowler hats duly arrived from the factory a few weeks later and an airmail letter sent informing the customer that the order was ready for despatch. There was no reply and it transpired that there had been a counter revolution and the Cabinet Ministers were probably wearing haloes instead of bowler hats. I can only speculate what happened to these hats but I could well believe that they were eventually sold to some pop group.

At Wembley there was one black rough finish horror which we just could not sell. It was an extremely small Tyrolean shape and what sealed its fate was when Norman Hurst tried it on. With his round face beneath it he looked like Toad of Toad Hall. It was virtually impossible to show the hat to a customer without getting a fit of giggles. It got to a stage when Norman said he would give five shillings to anyone who could sell one of those hats. There were no payouts.

A more successful style was the 'Maestro'. This was a porkpie style hat with a slightly higher and more tapered crown in rough finish felt. The brim was narrower than usual and the band wider. It caught on and sold well. Even forty years later, long after its demise, I saw an elderly gentleman wearing a dark grey 'Maestro'. He really must have looked after that hat with tender loving care.

I think 1961 could be said to be another of my happy years. That year saw all manner of innovations in all directions and it was definitely the Year of the Hat. There were new styles nearly every week and we were selling them like hot cakes. Yes, giving the hats a style name gave them an identity and a 'snappy' name could catch the public's imagination.

The most successful of these was the 'Atlantic' which came in two versions. The most popular one was similar to a style favoured by Frank Sinatra. Basically it was a porkpie shape but the crown was narrower and the hatband, often self-patterned, was wider. The felt had a lovely silken sheen in several dark but distinctive colours.

I personally opted for the alternative style. This was narrow-brimmed with a straight crease and no front dents. In my vanity I acquired a navy blue one with a purple lining and a bronze-coloured one with a welt-edged brim. They looked very James Bondish and I doubtless thought myself no end of a devil.

I really did myself proud sartorially that year. I bought a double breasted camel-coloured overcoat in the 'British Warm' style which had been knocked down to £5 because it was an oddment, and a tweed suit. The suit was what was called Border Twist, a Scottish Tweed but not as bulky as Harris Tweed and smoother than the indestructible Thornproof Tweeds. It was in green and brown Prince of Wales check and I liked it so much that I had a matching waistcoat made up. I wore that suit for many years until my waistline compelled me to pass it on to an uncle who was of a much slimmer build.

These days all suits are formal. But back in the Sixties men wore weekend suits, either in Scottish Tweed or of the softer all-wool West of England suits. A far cry from today's uniform of T-shirt and jeans.

In the bigger scene of things great changes were to take place that year. Changes of a revolutionary nature of such a conventional firm. We had a new Managing Director, formerly one of the departmental heads at Camden Town. This was how things were done. It was pretty much like the Feudal System. But our new MD was something of a surprise. George Fraser Pedrick was an elegant but unassuming man. He had never worked on the shop floor in his life yet he understood the needs of his employees better than many of his predecessors. On Saturdays the shop staff, if they so wished, could wear sports suits but they still had to wear black shoes. I never cottoned on to this. The word 'naff' had yet to be coined but I could not reconcile myself to the image of a green tweed suit and a pair of highly-polished black shoes. But at least it was a move in the right direction.

Also we were presented with Dunn & Co ties and cufflinks. Happily I still possess the cufflinks, shield-shaped in red enamel with GAD in gold. Unfortunately the ties did not enjoy the respect they deserved and ultimately went the way of all discarded ties. I think it was the colour which failed to endear me to them. A red, slightly darker than tomato ketchup and diagonal gold stripes interspersed with the ubiquitous GAD.

One highlight of 1961 was seeing the Royal Car going and returning from the Cup Final at Wembley Stadium. With the splendid view from our well-windowed upstairs department I was fortunate enough to catch a glimpse of Her Majesty and Prince Philip.

But the biggest event of 1961 was the Day Off! Mr Pedrick in his wisdom decreed that all staff – not only Head Office personnel who enjoyed a two-day weekend – should be treated the same. The system worked thus. Each of us had a certain day allotted to us a fortnight which meant, taking into account the half-day closing, over two weeks we would be working the hours equivalent to a couple of five day weeks. In some cases it was simplified where one member of staff had every early closing day off. It was as broad as it was long.

I was given Tuesday. A bit early in the week but I didn't look a gift horse in the mouth and I might well miss the window dressing which was usually done on Tuesday. It was a splendid step forward. But dear old Dunn's still had this hang-up about senior assistants not doing relief work in their own shops, even for a day. Well in some of our shops such as Kentish Town there just wasn't a senior assistant available. They got over the problem very neatly. There was a good number of middle-aged senior assistants in the West End who were quite capable of fulfilling the task. It was a nice little number for they would never be in the same shop two days running and could – and did – distance themselves from any irksome responsibilities beyond what they considered their call of duty. They had Monday as their day off and from Tuesday to Friday inclusive, managed different branches. On Saturdays they returned to their own shops as ordinary assistants.

Individually they were anything but ordinary. Our day relief manager, a bald, bespectacled, moustached little gentleman called George Barratt who, although married, still seemed confused as to his preferences regarding gender. But he gave me no cause for offence and he had a fantastic sense of humour. We would often spend a quiet day talking about food of all things! Well, I've always liked Tchaikovsky's music and look what has been said about him.

Dunn & Co made a splash of their 75th Anniversary in 1962. All branches were instructed to contact their local florists and buy vast amounts of red and white carnations to be given out to customers as button-holes. Okay for some customers but when you got a 'yeoman of England' – 'give us a clorf cap, mate' you thought twice. The place looked like a funeral parlour with bowlfuls of the blooms cluttering up the place and dark-suited assistants lurking behind them. Our reluctance to risk a fat lip by handing out the button-holes to someone who might think we were being funny resulted in an abundance of surplus blooms which inevitably were taken away that evening by the managers as gifts for their loved ones … or probably their wives.

Staff ebbed and flowed. We took on one Lyndon Melling, a tall, dark and handsome chap with the looks and bearing of a Regency buck but he left after a year or so to go into insurance. David Hopper was moved to our little shop in Fleet Street and Norris Chapman to Ealing Broadway. I never worked with him again and he left the firm a few years later.

Then the big move. Norman Hurst was transferred to our Ealing Broadway shop and we had a new manager, Chris Pringle. Chris was a likeable chap but utterly shambolic when it came to any sort of work system. His strong point was selling and everything else was a disaster. His bookwork was a mystery to everyone and more often than not poor old Ernie Pym had to sort that out. Window dressing was a nightmare. It took him practically the entire week to dress the window and during that time the shop was cluttered up with display stands, wads of tissue paper and various half-pressed garments.

Poor Chris lived on his nerves although first appearances belied this. He was very tall, pink-faced and bald, with a little blonde moustache. His suit – the sort of check design seen only on travelling rugs – always looked in need of a good press and his neat little curly-brimmed green hat was always tilted jauntily back on his pink skull, giving him a slightly inebriated look.

That was another thing about Chris. He liked his 'falling over water'. Nearly every evening after work he would try to coax Ernie and me down to the local pub. A pint or two after work on Saturday was all right but not every evening of the week. The trouble was that Chris lived on his own. He lived in digs in Wood Green and had no one to go back to.

Mr Drew had this thing about me helping out during the holiday period at Richmond. This was not received happily by me. It was a wretched journey involving a train to Willesden Junction, changing onto the High Level and waiting for ever and a day for the Richmond train.

In all fairness I must say that the manager, Paul Case, was a very nice gentleman; a younger version of Bertie Benson. But I didn't enjoy working there at all. The customers tended to be difficult, though I did see a couple of familiar faces during my time there. Two actors, Peter Arne, immaculate in blazer and bowler hat, wielding an umbrella like Excalibur, and Terence Alexander.

But the thing I didn't really care for at Richmond was the staff room. This was in the basement, gained by a narrow staircase at the back of the shop. A long and dark passage ran the length of the shop and beyond the pavement because light filtered down through small opaque panes of glass. It was very creepy down there. Doorways without doors were ranged along that passage, leading to huge dark rooms filled with building rubble. Also there was a staircase in the passage which led to nowhere but the passage ceiling and gave me the impression that I had wondered into *The Twilight Zone*.

One of these rooms, free of rubble, was the staff room. It was the biggest staff room I had ever seen with a tall and narrow window looking out onto a well formed by the adjacent buildings. Graveyard ivy and tombstone moss clung to the damp grey walls beyond the window and the staff room's interior was just as cheerless. What was particularly unnerving to an imaginative mind were two more of those dark doorless doorways leading into adjacent rooms and I once made the grave mistake – pun deliberately intended! – of reading a ghost story during my lunch break one gloomy, wet day. For some reason my eyes kept straying to those two black oblongs in the wall behind me …

By happier contrast that Summer I was called upon to help out at Harrow for one week. They didn't really need me; there were four staff excluding me. This left Wembley with Chris, Ernie and a junior called Ron who was as short as his name. But for some strange reason it was always the same with Harrow. They would be over-staffed rather than under-staffed – and the shop was only half the size of Wembley.

Bertie Benson was on holiday and that silver-tongued dandy Simon Delgado was in charge. The three assistants were all quite young and unknown to me. One of them lived in Harrow and one evening we all met up at his home for a game of cards. This was exciting. I was almost being wicked. Mind you, I didn't know any card games apart from Snap and Whist which we used to play on Boxing Day when my godparents visited.

The game that evening was Newmarket and they had to explain the rules to me. Call it beginner's luck but I cleaned them all out. I remember Simon leaning back in his chair, placing his fingertips together and murmuring, 'On Saturday evening, Keith, after work you can buy me a double brandy at *The Havelock*.'

That evening I bought the first round but Simon decided that he would settle for a half pint of ale as he didn't want to fall off his 'putt-putt' going home.

It had been a good week and sadly the last time we would work together. Poor Simon passed away two years later with a brain tumour. We all missed the colour he brought into our lives as well as the colour of his rainbow waistcoats.

However much I enjoyed working at Harrow the same could not be said for Chris Pringle at Wembley. Although he tried as hard as anyone to improve the sales figures with his meticulous windows – and they were meticulous despite his untidy method of preparation – 1962 was a bad year trade-wise. He had only been at Wembley six months when he was transferred to Aldgate and we had yet another new manager.

This was John Davis or 'Dickey' Davis as he was more generally known. Mr Davis (I never called him John and certainly not Dickey) was a good manager. Systematic in his work, unflappable and always quietly spoken. He was in his early thirties, not very tall but compactly built with dark bushy hair and a moustache to match. With him as manager order and serenity were restored.

The end of 1962 saw the start of the worst Winter since 1947. A Winter which lasted well into the Spring of 1963. But before then I had other worries and should have been warned that things were running too smoothly. Just before Christmas Mr Drew telephoned. I was on the move again to Ealing Broadway for 'an indefinite period'. Norman was no longer manager there. He had taken over at Watford when Bill Humbert retired. The Ealing Broadway manager was none other than Ronald-veal-and-ham-pie-Harvey!

GO WEST, YOUNG MAN

January ~ Winter 1963

'Now is the Winter of our discontent made glorious Summer by this sun of York'. Thus wrote Shakespeare in his opening lines of *Richard III*. Well he got the first part right as far as I was concerned. It certainly was a 'Winter of Discontent'! The weather was abominable; snowy and cold right through into the Spring. But it certainly wasn't 'made glorious Summer by this sun of York'. It was made sheer hell by Ronald Harvey, Manager of Ealing Broadway.

To start with the journey was horrendous, involving a train to Wembley Central where I had to wait for a No 83 bus to Ealing. It was crawl, crawl, crawl all the way through ice and snow, and Hangar Lane is a nightmare at the best of times to get through so I very rarely succeeded in getting to work on time. I couldn't face the same route home so just for some variation, caught a train from the Broadway to Ealing Common and from there to South Harrow where the rest of the journey was completed by the first bus that came along.

Dunn's had moved to new premises a few doors along in the Broadway since my first visit there several years earlier. Gone was the dark passage of a shop. Gone was the buoyantly flamboyant Nicholas Willoughby – to Hounslow I believe. A brand new shop with a central lobby faced me – with Ronald Harvey inside. The shop itself was single-storey and had a very elaborate skylight of blue-tinted glass. It gave the impression of working under the sea.

The staff area was a separate building across a narrow alleyway at the rear of the shop. It consisted of a large storage room with the staff room at the end. It was decent enough but the store room with its dusty wooden walls looked like an old barn.

It was quite a performance locking up every night. We had to make sure that the storeroom was securely locked – not that there was anything worth stealing – and then secure the back of the shop. This wasn't as straightforward as it initially seemed. The back lobby was about the size of a telephone box with a stone floor and when the inner door was closed it was quite claustrophobic. The outer door was like something out of the Tower of London with its two iron bars placed across it in brackets as well as the ordinary lock. One evening whilst locking up I dropped one of the bars onto the stone floor. In that enclosed space the noise was deafening. It was like being inside a bell. No wonder Quasimodo went deaf, I sympathised.

So much for the inorganic features of Ealing Broadway, but what of the organic? Apart from Mr Harvey who hadn't improved any there were two youngsters; Hawkins and Silver. I thought I had strayed into *Treasure Island*. Joe Silver was based at some other West End London branch and helped out at Ealing for odd days and Saturdays. Harry Hawkins was a sort of senior-junior. In that light I was what amounted to in the military sense a non-commissioned senior. Also helping us out on Saturdays was Bruce Wells from Liverpool Street whom I had worked with during my first several months at Wembley. I welcomed his company. His directness and no-nonsense attitude helped me through the days of whingeing from Mr Harvey.

One Saturday in particular stands out as a good example of this. Just as he used to at Harrow the Manager would say to me, 'make me a cup of tea, Keith.' No 'please' of course. That wouldn't have been Ronald.

'Next time he says that don't do it,' Bruce advised me.

I was aghast. 'But I can't refuse the Manager,' I protested.

'Look here,' came the retort with typical Northern candour. 'You're the senior assistant here. If anyone should be making him cups of tea it should be Joe.'

I knew he was right. I recalled those Saturdays at Harrow when we stayed behind after closing time booking up; Mr Harvey would go out to the washroom, spruce himself up then tell me to make a cup of tea. On one occasion when I pointed out that there was only a drop of milk left, he retorted, 'Well make **me** a cup of tea.' Yes, Bruce certainly had a point there.

With no small sense of trepidation I thought I would give it a try. I had never defied a manager before – and this was Ronald Harvey who virtually used to get me jumping through hoops in my younger days at Harrow.

The next Saturday morning it happened. 'Make me a cup of tea, Keith,' commanded Mr Harvey.

'No, Sir,' I replied in a quiet but steady voice. 'I think Joe should do that. After all, I am supposed to be on the sales floor.'

He glared at me in amazement. Then his expression changed to that old familiar look of a reproachful monkey, 'You'll make me a cup of tea, won't you, Joe?' he muttered, glancing at Joe Silver. 'You know how to make me a nice cup of tea.'

He didn't speak to me for the rest of the day but I didn't cry into my pillow over that. And the next week things were back to normal, but he never asked me again to make his tea.

The only day I didn't dread was Thursday as that was Mr Harvey's day off. The day relief man was Dickie Dixon, a dapper little fellow as chirpy as his name. But after a week of Ronald Harvey anyone would have seemed dapper and chirpy.

Harry Hawkins was a strange young man. He was very thin and his head looked like an extended neck with a fair quiff and large rimless glasses that gave him an American appearance. His speech was a series of yelps. It was like having a conversation with a Chihuahua dog. But one day he really had something to yelp about.

The bleak mid-Winter was still with us and all the pipes had frozen up. That was when Master Hawkins had his brilliant – but disastrous idea. 'We can unfreeze the pipes in the storeroom easily,' he yelped. He then proceeded to tear up several cardboard boxes and pile them with wads of tissue paper around the frozen pipes. Then he applied the match.

He unfroze the pipes all right but he had forgotten that the walls of the storeroom were wood. As the astronaut said, 'Huston, we have a problem.' We hadn't any water to hand to douse the flames and had to work like Trojans, beating them out with any non-inflammable object we could find. We finally succeeded but had to leave the door open all day for the smoke to clear. Fortunately Mr Harvey never knew about it for the storeroom was quite gloomy otherwise he couldn't have helped but notice that one wall was just a cracked and blackened panel of incinerated timber.

Another thing about Ealing that added insult to injury were the tremendous ice patches. I don't think there was a day when I didn't go skidding into the gutter and I'm sure that people must have thought I was some dysfunctional eccentric. That being the case I didn't venture around Ealing too much. All I can recall is the bleakness and the two massive church spires covered in snow. I am sure that it is a very nice and interesting town but at that time the weather and the presence of Mr Harvey overshadowed any appeal that the place might have held for me.

During this severe Winter Dunn's, with clever timing, introduced a new line in headwear: the fur hat. Only the top notch prices were real fur; the others were acrylic. They sold like hot cakes which was just as well as, owing to the arctic conditions, we had virtually sold out of all our other hats. The fur hat was the same shape as a forage cap with a deep cuff. We did another style called 'The Trapper' which looked like one of those

Canadian affairs with ear flaps which, when not in use, were folded across the crown and secured on top with a little ribbon bow. When the flaps were down the wearer was guaranteed warmth and comfort but rendered stone deaf.

As January progressed the weather improved slightly and one Saturday, instead of catching the train to work, Mr Harvey arrived by car. 'I'll give you a lift home this evening,' he told me, as if bestowing a great favour.

In a hollow, despairing murmur I thanked him very much as I recalled it had not been until his fifth test that he had been granted a driving licence and legally let loose among the traffic, and I spent the rest of Saturday wondering if I would live to see Sunday.

My fears were not unfounded. Having relinquished his smart trilby hat for a racy checked cap which looked like a pea on a drum, we set off that evening bound either for home or Heaven. Seat belts were not around in those days but I didn't need one. I was rigid with terror; totally immovable as he cursed other drivers, skidded on patches of black ice and generally acted as if he was driving at Brands Hatch. Then the windscreen misted up. This was probably due to condensation induced by my fear sweat. Mr Harvey was quite unperturbed. Without slowing down he whipped off his cap and mopped it vigorously across the windscreen, more or less holding the steering wheel with one hand, causing the car to sashay across the road in dramatic zig-zags.

I was going to die and we would both end either in Heaven or Hell. The latter would be bad enough but with Ronald Harvey grumbling at the demons, 'you blokes – sluck,' it would be infinitely worse.

Somehow we survived and the car began to slow down. We were at Sudbury Town. 'There's your bus stop over the road,' said Mr Harvey, 'See you on Monday – and don't be late.'

And then the old devil drove off and left me at the bus stop just as it began to snow again.

It was then I decided that 1963 just wasn't my year but then a light appeared at the end of the tunnel. On his next visit Mr Drew hinted that my 'indefinite period' at Ealing may soon be over and I would be returning to Wembley. He didn't elaborate but a few discreet enquiries soon filled in the jigsaw. Just before Christmas our manager at Slough had been taken ill and Bill Jellicoe, an assistant who 'floated' between the West London shops, had taken over. The Slough manager had recovered and Bill was being transferred to Ealing which would otherwise have happened before Christmas.

I was elated. It was only a matter of waiting a few more days and I would be free, free, FREE!

Sure enough, Bill Jellicoe appeared the next Monday morning, bright, bouncy and cheerful. Our paths had briefly crossed at Golders Green and Watford, and he was a pleasantly dopey sort of chap but easy-going and cheerful. I bade farewell to my Ealing colleagues and departed with almost indecent haste least fate should have a change of heart. Round the corner like a scalded cat and onto a bus, settling myself comfortably upstairs. Unfortunately, I had not noticed that the bus was only going as far as Alperton Garage and I was compelled to alight into the raging blizzard.

I wasn't really bothered. I was quite happy to walk the remainder of the journey. That was until I realised that I had left my briefcase upstairs on the bus. In panic I dashed back to the garage as the bus began driving into it. I was actually within a couple of feet of the platform when I received one of the biggest shocks of my life. My proximity to the large vehicle obscured my vision of where it was heading and I followed it blindly – right into the garage's equivalent of a car wash!

Within seconds I was scrubbed by huge brushes, soaked by water jets and smothered in foam. Choked by water and half-blinded by foam, I clambered onto the platform, struggled upstairs and retrieved my briefcase. I dimly recall the open-mouthed speechless garage staff as I squelched out of the garage but made my escape before any tiresome questions could be asked.

What with the snow and wind, the foam half-frozen on me from my hat and all down my long black overcoat, I must have looked like a giant Christmas cake decoration. After what seemed like hours I slithered into the Wembley shop to be greeted by Mr Davis, eyebrows and moustache raised in mild surprise and 'I thought you would be coming by bus, Keith, not swimming up the Grand Union Canal.'

I never saw Ronald Harvey again. He was given early retirement which he accepted with some resentment. Poor old Ronald even telephoned me at Wembley with the news and, reading between the lines, I got the impression that he believed the firm wouldn't survive six months if they dispensed with his services. I could almost see the reproachful monkey as I listened to his hurt, indignant voice. But he made a clean break and moved out to Holland-on-Sea in Essex where he always spent his Summer holidays.

Another face to disappear from my working life was our Area Supervisor, Mr Drew. He had been transferred to the Leicestershire area and remained there until he retired. His replacement was Raymond North, a genial enough man and easy to talk to – too easy, some said. It was claimed that he would shake you by the hand with one hand and stab you in the back with the other. Personally I never had any quarrel with him. He was always very civil and friendly towards me and he had to contend with pressure from his superiors if the shops in his area were not showing a profit. That plus the pressure he encountered from discontented staff in the shops. We all have an instinct for self-preservation and I am sure that he understandably looked after his own interests which would inevitably upset some members of the staff. But he never did me a bad turn or was guilty of any malicious act.

Mr North was a large man, well-built to the point of being fat. His thin moustache reminded me of the popular image of a circus ringmaster's moustache. My only grouse was that he had this tendency for moving me around to various shops for odd days at a moment's notice. I had hoped that having returned to Wembley I would be granted a nice long spell of predictable routine but I had learnt from past experience that this was a dangerous attitude to slip into. And as it happened my theory was to be proved correct.

This was the biggie. Mr North phoned up and said that I was to go Oxford Street for two weeks to cover for the Summer Holidays. I had never worked in the West End before and didn't relish the idea but orders were orders. It was a boiling hot Summer and London is the worst place to be in heat wave. I duly arrived the following Monday morning at our imposing emporium on the corner of Rathbone Place. It was all so different to what I was accustomed to; almost as daunting as my first day at Harrow nearly a decade ago.

Dark oak pervaded everywhere and around the upper regions of the shop ran a sort of minstrel gallery. In the centre of the floor a broad staircase led down to the clothing department which seemed to ramble off in all directions. There was even an ornately-tiled fireplace down there (not in use, of course, but just to assure the tourists that they were in 'Merrie Englande'). The staff area behind the scenes was spacious and untidy; the walls covered with pin-up photos. For a second I thought I had inadvertently wandered into a ladies' sauna.

There were staff everywhere; a bewildering number of them. On the final count I think there were about ten. Obviously, my first duty was to seek out Mr Baines the manager and make myself known. I had never met him and felt a bit foolish having to ask which of these well-dressed, urbane gentlemen was the boss-man. Then I noticed one person being greeted and deferred to in such a way that he must be an authoritative figure. He didn't look at all what I imagined a West End manager would look like. He was short, slim with thick, wavy hair of a fairish, gingery mixture brushed back and worn rather long. He was handsome enough in a suave, self-assured way and gave the impression that he knew it. His bearing was so laid back as to be almost horizontal.

'Mr Baines –' I began but he checked me with an amused smile. 'Good God, no!' he exclaimed in a mahogany brown voice. 'I'm just one of the serfs – Victor Buckingham. That's Mr Baines by the office.'

I was not to know it then but in the years to come Victor Buckingham was to feature prominently in my working life.

By comparison, Mr Baines was a tall, middle-aged gentleman, not unlike the American comedian, the late Jack Benny – even down to the poker-faced mannerisms. I didn't come into contact with him much as all staff instructions were passed along the line by Mr Preece the assistant manager, a genial man but very thin, resembling a human-size grasshopper.

I never took to the West End and much preferred what was called the 'home trade' where you got to know your customers and could 'tune' yourself in to their various personalities. Generally the West End customers were too aloof. Not that I had any complaints about my colleagues at Oxford Street. We all got on well enough but the place somehow lacked the personality of the smaller shops.

Two of the staff in particular I recall; Ron Jennings and Bert Saunders. During their lunch and tea breaks they would play cards with such intensity you would have thought their lives depended on it. Bert was the resident window dresser and that was all he did. Very rarely would you see him serving a customer. But I can still see those two, hunched over their cards and quietly swearing at each other.

In those days Oxford Street was more up-market than it is today and we had a few of the toffs in but also a fair number of customers from the North London suburbs. As for the tourists, a few of our transatlantic cousins strayed through our portals but most of them patronised our Piccadilly and Regent Street branches.

One American couple were treated to a floor show when I darted downstairs to the clothing department, trod on a dollop of floor polish that one of the juniors had left on one of the stair treads and went cartwheeling across the shop in front of them. I hit 'ye olde oake table' with a hell of a crack, pivoted over it and landed in the 'Merrie Englande' fireplace. 'It's all free, folks!' was all I could think of to gasp as I scuttled away from their astonished gaze and Ron Jennings' poker-faced stare of disapproval. Then I skulked off and hid in a fitting-room until they had departed.

Two things I definitely did not like about the West End were the lunch hours and the enforced inactivity when trade was quiet. All menial tasks were done by the two juniors and an elderly porter. As for the lunch break, any temporary member of staff was put on 'first party' which meant from 11.30 until 12.30. And on Thursdays when we opened until 7pm this could make a very long afternoon indeed.

The Thursday of the second week was very trying as my mother had gone to the doctor after finding a lump in her stomach and we weren't on the telephone at the time so I was unable to find out how she had got on. And that morning I was sent to our Islington branch until the afternoon when they closed for half-day. Then it was back to Oxford Street for the afternoon – a very long afternoon. Things were not made easier by another temporary assistant from Liverpool Street. He was a pleasant enough chap but not what you would call cheerful company. He kept moaning about the wardrobe in his lodgings. I couldn't have cared less about his wretched wardrobe. I was too busy watching the clock slowly moving around towards closing time. I wanted to get home to find out how my mother had got on but at the same time I was dreading it. Even the trains seemed to be against me that evening and it was turned 8pm by the time I reached home. Fortunately, the lump turned out to be a hernia. Serious enough in its own right but not half as bad as the score of things I had been imagining.

Strange as it may seem in these days of shops being open all hours the West End half-day was Saturday. The first week I had Tuesday as my normal fortnightly day off and then the Saturday afternoon. Oddly enough I didn't enjoy the Saturday afternoon. I had become used to mid-week half-days and there seemed too many people about. The second week I had a Thursday off to maintain the status quo and, along with several others, was farmed out to one of the suburban shops for the Saturday afternoon.

I had been logged for our Kilburn shop and at 1pm that afternoon we all left Oxford Street – but not to disperse to our allotted branches. I think it was Victor Buckingham's idea and we visited an interesting little pub around the corner in Rathbone Place for lunch. That lunch turned out to be what is known as a 'liquid lunch' and I can't actually recall any food. In fact I can't recall much about it at all except that it was getting on for 3 o'clock as we staggered out into the bright afternoon sunshine and went our separate ways.

We were all in very good spirits, no doubt due to the very good spirits in us and it is something of a miracle that I managed to find my way to Kilburn. Not that I cared a damn. I had done my West End stint and would be back at Wembley on Monday. Somehow I negotiated the escalators and rabbit warrens at Tottenham Court Road and fell into a train bound for Kilburn Park. The shop was just around the corner from there in Kilburn High Road. With some difficulty I found it as they had moved to new premises on the other side of the road. Even then there was a slight problem. A rival firm of Gents' Outfitters called *Meakers* had two shops next door but one to each other and somehow Dunn's had taken the central property.

Eventually I found the right door and made my triumphal entry in high good humour and a condition which, in polite words, referred to the rear end of a rodent. My old buddy from Harrow, Mike Flynn, was the Kilburn manager and being fond of 'grown-up lemonade' himself, wasn't unduly put out. 'Not much trade about today,' he told me, steering me towards the stairs that led to the staff room. 'Everyone must be on holiday. You have a rest upstairs. I've got a couple of staff here, so just come down when you feel like it.'

I didn't feel ill; I felt fine but somewhat drowsy. Anyway, just for the look of the thing when I found I could coordinate my movements I put in an appearance about 4.45.

Mr North left me alone for a while after that and I fell into the usual routine at Wembley with Mr Davis, Ernie Pym and Ron, our diminutive junior. The weeks passed pleasantly through the remainder of Summer and into Autumn.

Then during the last week of September something very strange happened, and in a way it was quite eerie. The phone rang one afternoon just as I was reflecting that I had been at Wembley virtually three years – not counting that tiresome interlude at Ealing. It was Mr North. I was to be transferred to the Harlesden branch the following Monday. And as Mr Davis passed on this most unwelcome news two things occurred. I suddenly realised that the Harlesden manager was none other than Hubert Harvey, the brother of the recently retired Ronald. Then the picture cord supporting the large sepia photograph of our founder snapped and George Arthur Dunn's stern image crashed to the floor. If that wasn't an omen, what was?

THE UNQUIET YEAR

September 1963 ~ October 1964

Our Harlesden branch was located on a corner of a mews not far from the Jubilee Clock Tower. From the outside it was quite unremarkable with its two large windows; the main one in the High Street and the other facing the mews. The narrow entrance lobby diagonally separated them, angled in from the corner.

It was the interior of the shop that struck me as strange. Quite roomy with the usual headwear and clothing fixtures and the ubiquitous office-coop located halfway down on the right. No, it was the rear section of the sales floor which struck me as odd. This area was a raised section of floor, not very big and gained by three steps. Oaken banisters flanked the steps with wooden rails along the top, giving the impression of a poop deck on an old fashioned sailing ship. This was the coat department with a small rack for customers' orders and a pokey fitting-room right at the back.

The staff precincts were meagre in the extreme being a triangle formed by one of the coat rails pulled out at an angle, behind which a member of staff could have his lunch break at a flap table. It was a dangerous dining area as the chair just fitted where the floor opened up to the cellar stairwell. An after lunch siesta could prove fatal for you could easily tumble down into that hellish abyss and break your neck.

The cellar itself was a glory hole of unused and rusted display stands. With an effort a strong man could fight his way through the junk to the toilet in one of three brick alcoves. A wash basin occupied another alcove and the third was adorned with pin-up pictures from the *Reveille* magazine.

If the shop was like an old sailing ship then its captain was a bit of a Captain Bligh. Not that he whipped me if I lost a sale but he had made petulance into a fine art. Hubert Harvey — younger brother of Ronald — could be extremely irritating. He had very odd mood swings. When he was in good humour he would prance about the shop, twanging his braces and singing peculiar ditties such as *Polly in the Garden* and *I'm Looking for my Ogo-Pogo*. This was not a pretty sight as he was inclined to rotundity. 'Porky' is a word that springs to mind. In appearances he was something like his brother but shorter, plumper and not so swarthy. Like Ronald his hair had a centre parting but in Hubert's case the parting was ten inches wide. Also, just above his snout – yes, his nose was quite like a snout – he had a cross-shaped scar. I never did find out how he came by it but wondered if at some time in his life a priest had hit him with a crucifix.

After I had worked with him for a while I stumbled on a very useful ploy to draw him out of any fretful or petulant mood. During the Second World War he was in the Royal Artillery out East. All I had to do was drop some word in the conversation about the war. I know a lot of people would get bored but I had fortunately been blessed with the ability to be a good listener. Also, and I think I must have inherited this trick from my father, I could mentally switch off and nod and grunt automatically in the right places.

Not that all his reminiscences were boring; far from it. In his shoes I do not think I would have owned up to them – but I wasn't Hubert. For instance, in Italy at the Battle of Monte Cassino, he was sent on a recce up to the hills with a radio set strapped to a donkey. Honestly we could easily have lost the war if his brother had been on active service too instead of a pay clerk at Portsmouth. Hubert saw what he thought was gunsmoke and radioed down to base that the enemy were attacking. It was ground mist. Later in Damascus, while on sentry duty one night he was knocked out by a bat which had lost its sense of direction. He could go on for hours with yarns like this.

During my first week there was another assistant, Peter Parker, tall and thin with a Beatle hair-do. On the Saturday he had a blazing row with Hubert. I don't know what it was about but I suspect it was just the culmination of Hubert's fads and fancies building up until Peter finally snapped. Hubert ordered him out of the shop. Peter said he would leave when he was good and ready. I think if Hubert had told him to stay Peter would have left. It was that sort of argument.

At that point Hubert turned to me and snapped, 'Mr Howard, throw him out!'

I looked up at this six foot plus youth and he looked down at me, who was endeavouring to smile reassuringly and convey that I would be gentle with him. Then we both burst out laughing. Peter then left and had himself transferred to our shop in High Holborn.

There were two flats above our shop and they were occupied by Mike Flynn and Bruce Wells. This was the usual procedure for Dunn & Co. Where there was living accommodation they would let it out to married members of staff for a peppercorn rent.

I didn't know how long I would be working with Hubert but I thought it best to keep on the right side of him and not do anything stupid. That is always fatal because the very next thing you do is stupid. A parcel had to be sent to one of our provincial shops. I wrote out the invoice carefully. After three years at Wembley it would be easy to write 'from Wembley' instead of 'from Harlesden'. Harlesden, Harlesden, I kept telling myself. I must think Harlesden. Next day a parcel arrived at the shop. Hubert was in an exuberant mood. You would have thought it was a Christmas present. 'Someone's sent us a parcel!' he exclaimed, twanging his braces in excitement. His mood soon changed when he opened it. It was the self-same one I had posted the previous day. So intent had I been to erase Wembley from my mind and think Harlesden, I had written the Harlesden address on the label! It took me the best part of two hours to bring the conversation round to the Army and how a brown-eyed beauty in Damascus had tried to lure him down an alley with the intention of cutting his throat and selling his papers to the Germans.

Even at closing time I couldn't get away from Hubert. He lived in Harrow too, only a few streets from me. He would buy an evening paper to read on the train which I decided to do as well. I don't think either of us wanted to spend the fifteen minute journey in conversation. Oddly enough I very rarely saw him in the mornings and I suspect he caught an earlier train to avoid me.

Another little ritual which occurred every Saturday night was just before we closed. He would send me out to buy an ounce of tobacco and a box of chocolates. I suspect the chocolates were for his wife but I could have been wrong. He might have given her the tobacco. I only met her once and she was quite a formidable lady. As was the case with his brother I strongly believed she was the ruling force at home.

Mr North had not forgotten me during the weeks that followed and I made several excursions to the West End for odd days and also Liverpool Street. I even was sent to the holy of holies, the Piccadilly shop, managed by Mr Lawton, a frail and gentlemanly character who was as much part of the venerable old place as the oak fixtures. Mr Payne, the assistant manager, was renowned for his impeccable book-keeping. His copperplate handwriting in 'real' ink was so neat as to be of exhibition quality. How many can boast that today!

As Christmas approached we took on a new junior, John Braden. He was a very strange young man and quite small. He looked like a ventriloquist's dummy. His skin was a peculiar orange-fawn colour and his hair, which was brushed straight back from his forehead, had a similar pigment. He even smelt of oranges. At any rate it was another pair of hands to help out during the Christmas trade.

The customers were a bit on the rough and ready side and shoplifting almost an established custom but fortunately we weren't hit too severely. Hubert's day off was every other Friday and the 'Orange Wonder' had alternate Tuesdays. As Thursday was Harlesden's early closing day it simplified things to give me every Thursday morning off which suited me very well as it meant that every other week I wouldn't see Hubert for a couple of days.

The Christmas of 1963 was one that I would rather forget. I had arranged to meet the Wembley staff for a drink on Christmas Eve. Leaving Hubert on the train at Wembley Central, I met Mr Davis, Ernie Pym and David Hopper who had travelled up from our Fleet Street shop and we went for a few drinks at a pub not far from the Wembley shop.

Mr Davis, being a sensible man, decided to call it a night and left. He had a long journey home to Enfield and if I had had any sense I would have followed his example. But hindsight is a wonderful thing. Ernie was enthusing about a new pub which had just opened in Sudbury and what a good idea it would be to give it a try. Like a fool I went along with the idea. It was only a few minutes' walk down the road and I could get a bus home outside the pub and anyway I would only have one drink.

It was a very nice pub called *The Fusilier* with lots of pretty Christmas lights outside. Everyone was in a very festive mood to such a degree that my one pint turned into two. But I'm sure that at some stage someone – most likely Dave Hopper – spiked my drink with a large dose of vodka.

A veil is best drawn over the rest. I dimly recall getting home and staring at a plate of egg and chips until it cooled and congealed into an inedible mess. Then my mother growling as she took the plate away, 'You obviously don't want that – and your face has gone green.' Then oblivion.

I awoke early on Christmas Day aware of two things. I had a splitting headache and I had yet to wrap up my mother's Christmas present. Now a folding umbrella isn't an easy thing to deal with when you've got a clear head but I managed it in the end. My parents, God bless them, never mentioned my embarrassing fall from grace and I made a vow to be more careful at future convivial get-togethers.

The New Year began calmly enough and I hoped it was going to prove better than 1963. Mr North visited us each fortnight, as affable as ever. 'My ideal, Mr Howard,' he said to me on one visit, 'is to get all my assistants working in branches as close to their homes as possible.'

This from the man who moved me from Wembley, even further out to Harlesden!

One morning in February on Hubert's day off the Archie Andrews look-alike engaged me in conversation during the tea break. We were perched in our precarious staff area atop the cellar steps while George Barratt, the day relief manager, quaffed his beverage in his office-coop.

'Do you like working here?' was young Mr Braden's opening gambit.

'Not much,' I grunted through a mouthful of Mars Bar, 'but it's better than some places; Golders Green for instance.'

Braden fixed me with an intense state. He often did this and I found the habit somewhat disturbing. 'Do you like working up town?' was his next question.

'No,' I retorted flatly. 'I can't stand the West End.'

'What about the City?'

'What about the City?' I challenged, deciding to become the questioner instead of the questionee.

'Holborn for instance.'

I shrugged and turned my attention to my strangely orange-smelling tea. It must be the washing up liquid I decided. He probably doesn't rinse the cups out properly. 'Don't know anything about Holborn,' I replied off-handed, becoming fed-up with what I considered to be a boring conversation. 'Why do you ask?'

'Because Mr North was here on your day off yesterday,' came the bombshell, 'and he's transferring you to Holborn from next Monday.'

I blew up. I raved, ranted and generally kicked up the devil of a fuss. He'd done it again! The fat fool was moving me even further away! Was this his idea of moving me nearer to home – via Luton, the North Pole, Asia and so forth? And what was worse he hadn't the decency to tell me to my face – I had to hear it from the junior!

I confronted Hubert about it on Saturday. Evidently it was only for three weeks while the senior man was on a staff training course. And as Holborn, like other London shops, closed on Saturday afternoons, I would be back at Harlesden for that day.

My wrath was undiminished despite the knowledge that it was only a temporary transfer. It was the sneaky way it was done on my day off that rattled me. My temper was not at all improved by the train journey on Monday morning. Harrow to Baker Street, a tube to Oxford Circus and another change to Holborn. I must admit to being impressed by the shop itself with its two long windows and central doorway. The interior seemed vast, with the suits hung in glass cabinets. It was subtly different to the West End shops as was the City trade. You could almost say it was more sedate.

There were only two staff; Mr Rivers the manager and a junior who had the genetic make-up of a sloth. He hardly seemed to work, speak, move or do anything at all. Mr Rivers was a very pleasant man, not unlike Bertie Benson at Harrow and he thanked me very graciously for helping out. I confess to admit that despite his courtesy I was not to be put off and said that they should at least have had the decency to tell me about the move first-hand – and what day off would I be having?

Poor Mr Rivers looked even more embarrassed at this. 'Well, Mr North wondered if you would agree to bank your days off for the next three weeks and have the time off when you were back at Harlesden,' he ventured mildly.

I hooted like a demented owl at this. No, non, nein, nyet, nada and any other foreign negative! I was having my day off and that was that! I had things to do, places to go and people to meet! My, my, wasn't I a little fibber! Anyway, I got Thursdays off.

Holborn proved to be amazing. On that first day, after I had got over my churlish outburst, I suggested making a cup of tea. 'Oh, thanks,' smiled Mr Rivers, obviously glad that hostilities were over. 'Just up the stairs. The door is behind the mirror.'

He indicated the usual battered wing mirror in the corner. Behind it I could see an equally battered door trying to hide. Armed with kettle and electric lead I opened the door and stepped through. I had expected to find the usual dusty and grotty uncarpeted staircase but I suddenly felt giddy at my new surroundings.

This was a few years before the film *2001: A Space Odyssey* but I realise now how David Bowman the astronaut must have felt after his terrifying journey through the kaleidoscopic dimensions when he found himself standing in that strange, bright but eerie room.

The ceiling seemed to be miles above me and I was surrounded on all sides by gleaming glass, chrome and veined marble. Underfoot tiles like black mirrors and a broad staircase which would not have disgraced Buckingham Palace led to the stratospheric upper regions. Of course, this was not Dunn & Co property. These were facilities shared with the offices that conducted their business in the same building.

Clutching my kettle and lead I humbly ascended this superb stairway and found myself at the entrance of a vast room, one flanked by dazzling white basins. As I filled the kettle from a strangely shaped state-of-the-art tap I noticed that there was no soap in the basins. Instead each basin had a little container like a vinegar bottle over it on a pivot bracket, filled with liquid soap. This was different from the usual brass taps and cracked sinks.

As the days progressed I came to like the place. The customers, mostly suit customers, were no trouble and the trading times seemed to be regulated by office hours; busy first thing in the morning, a lull until lunch time and a final burst around five o'clock. An old acquaintance of mine from the Kentish Town days stood in for Mr Rivers on his day off. Mr Banner, the spikey-tempered, spikey-nosed and pointy-eared little man who looked even more like a Martian in that ultra-modern glass and chrome office. At lunch time I would wander around *Gamages* Departmental store and poke around the interesting little shops around Chancery Lane. I found a quaint little tobacconist shop and bought a pipe and bowl shaped like an owl's head. Yes, I smoked a pipe and wore a trilby hat. You don't see much of either these days and it conjures up a whimsical image. But in those days we were legion.

By the time my spell at Holborn had finished I was almost sorry to leave the place. Apart from the messy train journey, I had enjoyed it. But I had made such a song and dance about having to go there I had to save face and keep a still tongue and never mind the mixed metaphors!

Neither Harlesden or Hubert had improved in my absence. We had a new junior, Sean Flynn, younger brother of Mike, and I must say it; he was as thick as two short planks. He was affable enough but his brogue was very thick and difficult to understand. One day Hubert asked him to repeat what he had just said. Sean beamed at him and replied, 'D'you know, Sorr, Oi hardly understood a word of it m'self.'

Another time Hubert told him to replace the light bulb in the cellar and I spotted him just in time, descending the cellar steps with the new bulb in one hand a hammer in the other! At least these incidents took the heat off me and I found I had developed a shell to Hubert's grumbling, and a semi-comfortable routine took over.

By this time George Barratt had retired and the new day relief man was one Harry Coppins alias 'The Spangles Kid' because he was always sucking boiled sweets. All these day relief bods looked uncannily alike. All late middle-age, slim, slightly under average height and bespectacled. They also had a taste for yellow check waistcoats with their dark business suits and I began to wonder if the firm was secretly breeding this species in some dark and dank laboratory cellar in Camden Town.

In the Summer I did have a fortnight's respite when Hubert was on holiday and Bruce Wells did the relief. It was like a breath of fresh air and it suited him admirably as he lived over the shop. But what I remember most of the Summer of 1964 is Dave Hopper's wedding. Ernie Pym and Norris Chapman had also been invited but obviously we were unable to attend the actual wedding due to work. However, we arranged to meet that evening outside the Wembley shop and attend what was left of the reception which was being held in a hall a short distance away in Sudbury.

We had bought a large gilt-framed wall mirror as a wedding gift, all nicely wrapped in pastel-coloured paper infested with fat little cupids and, looking more like political delegates from the Eastern Bloc with our hats and dark suits, marched into the hall which was full of music and merriment.

A sweaty-faced young man with glazed eyes and a hot-looking morning suit intercepted us. He was obviously the Best Man, but judging by the state of him this title could only apply to his official function. Ernie thrust the parcel at him, grim-faced and solemn. You would have thought he was surrendering the Elgin Marbles rather than a wedding present.

'Come and meet the happy couple,' burbled the Best Man, shepherding us through the crowd of guests to where the newly-betrothed sat at the far end of the hall, gazing into each other's eyes, fit enough to turn your stomach.

But the 'happy couple' seemed to metamorphosis into the 'bewildered couple' as we were presented, and we were no less bewildered. The groom most certainly was not David Hopper! We had somehow arrived at someone else's nuptials.

'Sorry – wrong wedding,' Ernie announced, snatching the mirror back from the astonished Best Man. 'It must be in the hall next door.' And we made our dignified exit.

This proved to be the case. In an adjoining hall Dave's wedding celebrations were in full swing. We were greeted cordially and the wine flowed freely.

Apart from one little mishap all went well. This mishap occurred during that strange and primitive ritual when we all had to dance the Conga. This idea of forming a chain and prancing around the hall, holding the waist of the person in front of you and chanting 'hi-yi-yi-yi-conga!' does not come easily to those of us who have led sheltered lives. And as the chain is made up of males and females alternately one is a little hesitant of where to place one's hands. All was going well, or not as bad as I thought, when the procession decided to vacate the hall and progress up various passages.

Unfortunately, there was a step which I did not see but managed to stumble over. One of the bridesmaids was in front of me and as I fell, with the natural instinct of saving myself, I desperately clutched at something substantial. Then came a blood-curdling twang of sundered elastic accompanied by a scream and I fell flat on my face with the rest of the Conga piling up on top of me.

I forebore to ascertain the resultant damage to the bridesmaid's personal attire and made myself scarce. It was quite obvious that such social occasions were too rich for my blood.

Thankfully the Summer passed without any further dramatic event until one day in September when Mr North made his usual fortnightly visit. He had some good news for me. At least he thought it was good news. Not Harrow, I thought. That would be too much to hope for. No, this was a positive advancement in my career. I was to go to our new Watford shop in October on a training course which would entail instruction in management, salesmanship, display and administrative work. I would emerge after three weeks a completely fully-trained new person. Well, that was the theory ...

THE FIFTH FORM AT ST DUNN's

October 1964

I had never been inside the Watford Parade shop even though it had been in existence for five years. The frontage was really splendid. Located at the end of a row, it had a very long side window but it was the upper regions of the building which caught the eye. An ornate balcony featured in the centre of the second storey with mullion windows and ornamental brick-work reminiscent of the Tudor style. Watford featured many such build-ings in those days but, alas, most of them have fallen victim to the modern day equivalent of the Four Horsemen of the Apocalypse – Profit, Progress, Development and Modernity.

One Cecil Short was the manager; a twitchy, gnomish little man of the Harvey breed but thinner. I only saw him once on that course as we trainees were told to use the fire escape at the rear of the shop to gain access to the training school and not thunder to and fro through the sales floor like a herd of elephants.

The training school area was like some devilish maze only encountered in a bad dream. A bewildering complexity of little passages and empty storerooms. Some of the passages ran parallel with each other with the central storeroom in between which seemed utterly pointless as they both emerged into the same room which was our 'schoolroom' over the front half of the shop. I was told that these upper regions originally were very high class tea rooms which would account for the elaborate fascia and the decorative metal balcony at the front of the building.

The terms of the course were remarkably generous but at that time Dunn & Co were sailing in golden waters. We were granted excess fares, commis-sion allowance, lunch allowance and days off banked, to be taken when we returned to our respective branches. The course spanned from Monday to Friday inclusive and on Saturdays we each returned to our own shops. I'm not sure what the arrangements were for those who were roped in from the provinces but nobody had any complaints. And the hours were easy. The course started each morning at 9.30 and broke at 10.30 for a half hour's tea or coffee. Then at 12 noon we packed up for lunch which went a full hour and a half until 1.30. Then another afternoon break from 3 o'clock until 3.30, after which we put our 'toys' away at about 4.40.

There were twelve of us on that course, nine being from the provinces, boarded at the Malden Hotel just opposite Watford Junction Station. Apart from myself there were only two others from the London area; Ron Edwards and Joe Whitman, both from West London. I only have vague recollections of the others. There was a suave and dangerous-looking fellow called Kessler who kept falcons – happily he didn't bring them with him, Morrison from our Aberdeen shop, Mickey Morgan, a roly-poly little fellow from Cardiff with the looks and disposition of a miniature Harry Secombe, Hebworth, a ginger-haired chap with worry-lines, Barry Tyler from Bolton, and a podgy, bespectacled chap called John Frayne. Sadly the others have passed from my memory.

Now with any assembled group of chaps it is always a sure thing that there is a fly in the ointment and John Frayne was the biggest bluebottle going. As a creep and a crawler he filled the bill perfectly. I thought I had left that sort of rubbish behind in the classrooms of my schooldays.

Our instructor was Eric Mitchell, one of the directors who had drawn the short straw and been designated as Display Director which meant that the remaining years of his working life were condemned to be spent instructing an ill-assorted bunch of idiots and misfits in the arts of window dressing and administration.

Although we were not dealing with the public there were definite instructions regarding our attire. We were graciously permitted to wear casual clothes but we still had to wear the Sacred Hat. To my mind this posed a problem. How casual was casual? It didn't seem right to turn up in a zipper jacket and a natty trilby; the two items just didn't gel. I settled for my favourite three-piece brown and green check sports suit and my bronze snap-brim 'Atlantic' trilby. I felt like a gentleman pig farmer from the Yorkshire Dales.

The mornings were occupied with the practical side of window dressing. We were teamed off in pairs – I was teamed with Barry Tyler the Bolton wanderer – and each pair presented with a table-top model of a display floor, marked off in squares and a set of model items of clothing. The trousers were simply cardboard rectangles but the other items – hats, coats and jackets – were made from a strange, evil-smelling substance resembling petrified plasticine. They were coloured a sickly greyish-green though some were greenish-grey. There were umbrellas too but they were far from scale size. Bearing in mind that a model overcoat was about six inches high the umbrella was longer to such an extent that in real life it would be about seven feet long. There were miniature stands as well, as we were left to vent our creative talents upon these toys and see what we could come up with.

Barry was about as good as I was, which wasn't all that good. He looked at me lugubriously and sighed. He had that sort of face. He reminded me of a sad horse.

We fiddled around with no real idea of what we were trying to do until the break. Some of our group had gone to a little teashop which specialised in delicious toasted teacakes dripping with butter. It was opportune that the rest of us should appear when we did as the 'hat rule' which meant that even venturing out for a tea break hats had to be worn, was about to break out into an ugly scene. Several of the local lads were making sport of four of our group and it showed all the signs of escalating into one of those 'let's step outside and clear the air' situations. The arrival of the rest of us, numbering eight, poured cold water on the problem and the tormentors left the scene with the usual snarled but ineffectual insults.

Our table-top display was a bit hit-or-miss and we were thankful when we broke for lunch at noon. But not all of us galloped off at once and it wasn't until about the third day that I became aware of it. John Frayne, the class toady, would linger behind with Mr Mitchell and criticise our efforts along the lines of, 'I don't think he's got that quite right, do you, Sir? I would have done ...' and so forth.

Needless to say this did not endear him to the rest of us and Mickey Morgan, the normally cheerful little Welshman, went ballistic. It really must have got to him for he was such a genial chap. But he was after Frayne's blood as well as any vital organs he could get his hands on. We managed to calm him down to dark and vague threats that he would get his own back before the three weeks was up which we had to be content with.

Over the three weeks this happened to all of us and we all reacted pretty much the same way as Mickey. But Brother Frayne was oblivious to this and persisted in his whispering campaign. To be fair to Mr Mitchell I don't think this cut any ice. He didn't have any favourites – I know I certainly wasn't one. Barry and I had a long road ahead of us before we could be considered proficient window dressers.

Those lunch time breaks were great fun. The whole crowd of us would race down the High Street to *The Robert Peel* and for the next hour and a half recharge our batteries. How well I remember those lunches! Two pints of Worthington and three rounds of cheese and tomato 'doorstep' sandwiches. Life was good. By the end of the course, rather than resembling a gentleman pig farmer I more resembled one of the pigs!

The afternoons were given over to lectures. We would amble, stagger or stumble our way back depending on how much we had imbibed. Then for the rest of the afternoon we would sit in a semi-circle while Mr Mitchell expounded on the theories of display, salesmanship and administration. The latter was dealt with on the first afternoon. Mr Mitchell indicated a stack of ledgers, invoice books and forms on his table and said, 'You've got all these in your branches. Your managers will explain them to you.' And that was the beginning and the end of the administration course. Being of a fairly innocent disposition in those days it did not occur to me that he probably didn't know the first thing about them.

I doubt if any of us could recall those afternoon talks; we were too tanked up. The window behind Mr Mitchell caught the full rays of the sun in the afternoon and that droning voice didn't help much either. To be fair to him he doubtless had to say the same things over and over again to previous groups so it came out parrot fashion. But it was difficult to stay awake. Occasionally a discreetly suppressed hiccough could be heard, or a belch, and once even a gentle snore. Fortunately, the afternoon break helped to split the session up and restore a degree of our senses and wits otherwise we all would have succumbed to slumber.

About the only thing I can (partially) recall through my alcoholic haze was Dunn's equivalent of the Ten Commandments, 'The Nine Steps of Salesmanship'. I admit to having only a vague memory of them as I must at some time have nodded off. As for what I can recall they went thus: 1: Welcome the Customer; 2: Discover the Customer's purpose; 3: Decide what to show; 4: Ascertain Customer's size; 5: Mention the garment's selling points; 6: Clinch the sale; 7: Suggest something else; 8: Final courtesies; 9: Kick the Customer out. Or something like that.

Like many theoretical rules though, I found that you cannot adhere rigidly when the human factor is involved and the simplest rule is to treat each customer as you would wish to be treated yourself.

Really the three weeks could have been condensed into one week and we just had to move more slowly to stretch things out.

Then the day came when each pair of our happy little team had to dress a life-size window from our table-top efforts. There were two full-size display windows in the classroom but they had no glass which meant that they were easy to dress as you could just step in the front of them. This in itself didn't really give us a working knowledge of window dressing as it is more difficult in a shop where you have to start with the front and work backwards.

Barry and I had a crack at it and I don't think either of us was relishing the exercise. All garments had to be immaculately ironed or steam-pressed.

The steaming was done with a Martianesque-looking machine called a Jiffy Steamer. This device consisted of a water-filled glass container atop a mental base on casters which housed the electric motor. From this a flexible tube reared up, supported on a metal pole fixed to the base. The end of the tube terminated in what looked like an attachment of a floor sweeper but instead of sucking up dust it blew out jets of scalding hot steam.

Barry and I finished our window and the rest of the class gathered round to give their verdict. It really came as no surprise to me when Mr Mitchell's first words were, 'if you dressed the window of your shop like that your manager would have my full permission to shoot you.'

Oh well, back to the drawing-board – or rather the table-top models.

One afternoon we touched on made-to-measure – the operative word being 'touched'. 'Do you all know how to measure someone for a bespoke suit?' Mr Mitchell asked us.

A few beery grunts responded non-commitally.

'Well, let's see how good you are,' decided our mentor. 'I'll want a volunteer to be the customer and the rest of you can take turns in measuring him.' He cast an eye around the intoxicated crescent of human-ity before him. Unfortunately, his eye fixed on me. 'Mr Howard, you can be the lucky lad.'

That's a matter of opinion, I sourly observed as I hauled myself out of my chair. Just my rotten luck.

A few ribald and derisive comments were uttered as I was subjected to the indignity of being measured by each of the eleven in turn. Comments such as, 'blimey, Keith, you'll have to be dusted for fingerprints,' or 'watch out for Mickey. I think he's bi-centennial.' All in all, it was horribly reminiscent of my National Service medical.

The last week of the course was a complete waste of time. We were simply rehashing what we had already done. The only thing I didn't mind continuing were the pub lunches. That Tuesday morning we were idling around chatting when Mr Mitchell said, 'Mr Neville has just arrived. He'll be taking you all over the road for coffee. He always takes the group out during the last week – but only for coffee.'

'And by the way,' he added, 'he'll want to look at your window models.'

Barry and I had just put ours away. 'What'll we do?' he whispered, his face lengthening about ten inches with concern.

'Get the things out of the box quickly,' I told him. 'We'll set up a repetition display.'

A repetition display is the easiest of all. You simply arrange three of everything across the window in a line; tallest at the back and shortest at the front. In the few minutes that it took 'Long John' to appear we had finished. A line of three coats at the back with three suits in front of them and three hats and umbrellas, the latter tastefully angled diagonally to give a touch of interest. Well, I thought so anyway.

'Long John' buzzed a general greeting to us all and stalked around the worktables, imposing in his bowler hat and black overcoat, but obliviously knowing nothing about what he was looking at. You could tell by the glazed, faraway look in his eyes. Occasionally he would stop at a table, grunt behind his moustache then buzz a murmur of criticism at the two-man team responsible.

When he got to our table he grunted in surprise. 'A repetition window,' he buzzed. It was a suspicious-sounding buzz.

Full marks, I thought but I said, 'Yes, Sir.' Well I wasn't looking for an argument.

'We don't do repetition windows now, Mr Howard,' he buzzed.

'I know, Sir,' I replied, thinking on my feet, 'but as we have been doing pyramid and triangle groups I thought it would be a good idea if we kept our hand in and did a repetition display – just for a change.'

Barry and I were favoured with another suspicious grunt but he decided to let the matter drop. 'Get your hats, gentlemen,' he told us. 'I am taking you all out for morning coffee – and only morning coffee.'

'What was all that about?' Barry asked me. 'What's he mean "only morning coffee"? Mitchell said the same thing.'

I hadn't a clue but we were to find out later. Evidently 'Long John' had taken a group out for coffee and the whole lot of them had ordered a full English breakfast and left him holding the tab.

There was definitely a holiday air pervading from then onwards. Wednesday we simply went through the motions of display and covering old ground. But we did have one diversion that afternoon. We were to have our photograph taken. This was the usual thing for each course and it was just like those group photos of classes at school. Six in front on chairs and six standing behind them. We waited with fixed grins while Eric Mitchell fiddled with the camera. Then just as he pressed the button we all presented what was then known as the 'Harvey Smith' salute. As far as I know none of us ever received a copy of the photograph.

Thursday was the penultimate day and there was only one ordeal to face. Dinner with the directors at the hotel where the provincial staff were staying. 'You will all wear your Dunn & Co ties and decent suits,' Eric Mitchell told us. 'We are to be there by twelve o'clock.'

The outcome of these instructions turned out to be pure farce. Earlier that year a special suit pattern bunch had been sent to all branches exclusively for the staff. They were inexpensive materials but durable enough for requirements. The only problem was that all of them except one were utterly diabolical in both pattern and colour. And that one, by a seemingly impossible coincidence had been selected by all twelve of us. It was a nice enough pattern, dark blue-grey with a bronze shadow check, but seeing us Thursday morning all with identical Dunn & Co ties, identical suits and almost identical grey curly-brimmed hats was bizarre in the extreme.

Poor old Eric Mitchell had the grace to look embarrassed. 'I've got to march all twelve of you through the High Street,' he declared. 'You look like something off an assembly line.'

At least he was dressed differently in a light grey suit and green hat. We were the ones who should be embarrassed.

With our Course Instructor leading the way we formed a crocodile, two abreast, and followed him along Watford High Street and down Clarendon Broad, much to the amusement of the passers-by. I'm not sure if the advertisement with the 'Home Pride Flour Graders' was in existence then. If not, we probably gave someone the idea for it.

'I reckon we'll be in for a heavy day,' Barry muttered as we progressed towards the hotel.

I knew what he meant. The Dunn & Co Head Office staff were renowned – or notorious! – for their convivial sessions. The ale wouldn't just be flowing – it would be gushing! Rumour forewarned. An old friend had given me some very sound advice.

'They'll try to get you drunk,' he cautioned me. 'Mozart and Liszt,' he added using rhyming slang with an indelicate translation. 'They'll try to get you talking about your shop and how the manager runs it. Be careful what you drink. Stick to brown and mild. It'll keep you going to the Gents all night but you won't get sozzled.'

I took this advice seriously. Not for one moment did I suspect that our masters would employ such underhanded tactics but rather because I didn't want to make an exhibition of myself.

We arrived at the Malden Hotel and were duly presented to the directors. Mr Pedrick the Managing Director was there and so was the Chairman Mr Butterworth. Also in attendance were Ron Hale of the Staff Department, a grey and gentle man, Mr Armstrong the Chief Cashier and Mr Brooke the Buyer.

Mr Armstrong met us as we filed in. We all had adhesive paper name tags on the lapels of our cloned suits with our branch on for easy identification. Mine said 'Howard Harlesden'. I quite liked the sound of it and thought it would be a good non de plume should the occasion ever arise.

'What are you drinking, Mr Howard?' Mr Armstrong asked me.

'Brown and mild, please,' I mumbled, overwhelmed by the illustrious company.

He curled his lip at my choice and thrust a foaming pint glass into my palsied hand and I tottered off in the wake of my companions.

The dinner itself had a baronial air about it. Table wine was treated with scorn. We all had our tankards of ale to wash down the lukewarm chicken and veg. Ever faithful to good advice I stuck to my advised poison. I was seated between Mr Hale and Mr Brooks but there was no sign of 'Long John' Neville. He couldn't help being a bit of a snob and he didn't fit in very well with the social circle at Head Office. Well, he never did me a bad turn and I felt a bit sorry for him.

Dinner over, we formed two discussion groups. Six round each table and each group presided over by Mr Pedrick and Mr Butterworth with the minions in attendance. Eric Mitchell acted as potman. As soon as a glass emptied it was filled. I may have been doing him an injustice but I began to suspect his motives when Mr Mitchell scorned my brown and mild requests, urging me to try something stronger. But I stuck to my guns, even if I did have to keep on being excused.

I cannot recall what was being discussed as everyone was talking very loudly but I did add a few intelligent-sounding grunts to let them know that I was still with them. Then after a while – it could have been a couple of hours – Mr Pedrick swapped with Mr Butterworth and came to our table and the conversation became easier and more relaxed. While I didn't say anything compromising about Hubert Harvey or any other member of staff, I did drop my guard a bit. Well it was getting on for 6.30 and we all had been drinking since noon. I hate to think how many pints had wended their way through me in that time. And while I didn't get too garrulous or paralytic the alcoholic intake inevitably had to have its way.

Mr Pedrick had a very relaxed and friendly manner and it got to the joke-telling stage. It happens at all these sorts of meetings; the boss tells his joke and everyone laughs wildly. Mr Pedrick told his joke which was very funny and everybody dutifully laughed. John Frayne, who was in fine toad-eating form and crawling for all he was worth, may well have clapped. I confess my reaction was different. Barely before the accolade had died away I chipped in with, 'I know a better one than that,' and went on to tell it. On reflection it was a terrible joke and received as such.

It was greeted with a deathly hush and a few faint smiles. Whoops! I thought. I've really shot my bolt this time. I'll be on the delivery vans this time next week, but at least they can't say I'm a crawler.

Then an unexpected diversion thankfully came from Morrison from the Aberdeen branch. For a Scot he was really foxed, having started on beer and graduating to malt whiskies. He had reached the 'I love everybody' stage and, gazing fondly at our Managing Director, announced, 'Mr Pedrick, you really are a fine gentleman. You remind me of my father-in-law.'

'Thank you, Mr Morrison,' replied Mr Pedrick with a slightly embarrassed smile, 'That's very nice of you.'

'Yes,' murmured Morrison, gazing into his glass of finest malt, 'he'll be ninety-two next week.'

Uproar all around the table! Even Mr Butterworth with the other group of inquisitees fell silent and stared across the room at us. But Mr Pedrick took it all in good part. 'Eric,' he called out to our instructor-turned-potman, 'it's getting on for seven. Fetch my bathchair. It's time old gentlemen were home in bed.'

The rest of the evening was a series of montages. Well we had been drinking for six hours and I hadn't fallen over once. I was very grateful for my friend's advice, even if I did put my foot in it, trying to cap the MD's joke. With the departure of Mr Pedrick and his minions my thoughts were also straying in a homeward direction. There's no place like it, especially after that sort of evening. But Ron Edwards and John Whitman had other ideas.

'They're setting the evening meal for the inmates,' Ron told me, referring to our provincial colleagues.

To which John added, 'It's T-bone steak.'

That settled it. The three of us suddenly became provincials and took our place at the long table.

I can remember Mickey Morgan the Cardiff assistant, sitting almost opposite me, his round, ruddy, bespectacled face aglow with sheer happiness. Knife and fork clenched and ready for action and his napkin tucked underneath his chin. He looked like someone from a Charles Dickens Christmas story.

The next thing I remember is buying a cigar of almost Churchillian proportions at the bar and savouring its fragrance and the night air on the steps of the hotel. I felt content and replete. Then a voice spoke out of the shadows behind me. 'Well, Mr Howard, you seem to be doing very well for yourself. Dunn & Co must really be looking after you.'

It was Mr Butterworth the Chairman. And I thought he had left with the other directors!

I made some polite but non-committal response, wondering apprehensively if he was aware that I had just treated myself to an illicit dinner at the firm's expense. But he made no reference to it and sauntered off to the bar.

Then I found myself on the train with Ron and John. We were all in high spirits which is quite understandable, singing and joking. Then things got a bit lively — I think it is referred to as 'horseplay' — and my 'posh' curly-brimmed grey hat disappeared through the carriage window (I nearly went with it) somewhere between Carpenders Park and Hatch End. I didn't miss it at the time and it was several weeks before I found out what had happened to it. During that time I was sure I had left it behind at Church one Sunday morning. Not that I was bothered. I never really liked it and snap-brims looked much more mysterious.

But there was an interesting climax to the three weeks on the last day. There wasn't much to do and Eric Mitchell was just skimming over a few points concerning display technique to fill in time. Everyone looked weary after the previous night's celebrations but that was to be expected. But John Frayne, the team creep, looked positively disastrous. His face was whiter than his shirt and he looked scared. Over morning coffee Ron Edwards told me what he had heard had happened at the hotel after we left.

It seemed that Mr Frayne had taken too much drink on board and made a pass at one of the waitresses. She was a pert little blonde (almost) in a uniform which earned her the nickname 'Nell Gwynne'. All the Dunn & Co boarders had noticed and approved of her but never overstepped the mark of decorum. Evidently that oaf Frayne did and was firmly and properly put in his place by the lady concerned.

Then the night took a sinister turn. Frayne was by then utterly legless and insensible so the other boarders took him to his room. Then a person or persons unknown undressed him and, with fiendish Machiavellian cunning, paid him back for his un-comradely behaviour of the past three weeks of trying to score over the rest of us. A set of false teeth were applied to the fleshier parts of his anatomy and clenched firmly enough to bruise but not break the skin.

In the morning Frayne could recall nothing of the night before and was alarmed when he found his person infested with purple bruises in the form of teeth marks. He was even more alarmed when the others told him that he had spent the night with 'Nell Gwynne'.

He just kept muttering, 'Whatever will my wife say?'

'Quite a lot,' Mickey Morgan cheerfully retorted.

That is as far as the story went and the identities of those perpetrators of rough justice were never revealed. But I had my own ideas about that when I saw the beatific smile on Mickey's face, even more beatific than it had been when presented with the T-bone steak. Yes, I am certain it was a case of Welshman's Revenge.

BACK TO THE SALT MINES

November 1964 ~ September 1966

Rupert Harvey was unbearable as far as window displays were concerned. I knew I wasn't the world's best window dresser but his criticism was so negative that it destroyed any trace of confidence I possessed. I knew I had no flair for display work but he wasn't the sort of manager who would work with you to get things right, and I came to dread Tuesdays when a new show had to be put in.

'I don't know what good that training course did you,' he would say. 'I'll have to dress the window myself completely.'

But there is always a little ray of sunshine among the darkest clouds. The firm used background screens consisting of a wooden frame covered with coloured felt and some piece of decoration nailed or screwed to it. One day I was struggling with a screen on the 'poop deck' area at the back of the shop. I had the screen flat on the floor and was attacking it with screwdriver and hammer, determined to get something right.

'How much longer are you going to be?' a querulous voice rang out.

'Nearly finished, Sir,' I replied.

'You said that five minutes ago,' came the grumbling response.

Finally, I was able to announce, with no small measure of triumph, that I had completed the job.

'About time, too,' Hubert snapped, seizing hold of the screen to put in the back of the window. But that was as far as he got. The screen wouldn't budge. I had done such a thorough job of assembling it that I had screwed the whole thing to the floor.

I couldn't stop laughing but honestly you would have thought I had committed a murder. The way he carried on, huffing and puffing, almost dancing with fury. It took me a long while to calm him down with my applied psychology method, somehow dovetailing into the conversation a mention of the Army which set him on the track of his favourite reminiscences. Just to keep the change of mood sustained I asked him about the incident when he was knocked out by a bat while on sentry duty in Damascus. I genuinely wanted to hear it again as it prompted a memory of something his brother Ronald had told me at Harrow some years earlier, concerning an incident which happened on his honeymoon.

That was pretty unbelievable too. The thought of Ronald Harvey on honeymoon did not rest easily between my ears and I certainly would have thought twice before relating it to a junior member of staff. Evidently Ronald and his bride went to a very up-market country hotel for their honeymoon but were disturbed during the night by something tugging at the bedclothes. Switching on the bedside light Ronald saw that the intruder was a large owl which had flown in through the open window and was clawing at the eiderdown with its talons. Mrs Harvey screamed and Ronald bravely leapt to her defence. Hurling himself from the bed, he seized his furled umbrella and did battle with the owl. One can imagine him in his winceyette pyjamas, prancing about, thrusting and parrying like Douglas Fairbanks. He finally drove the owl off which had probably become bored with the whole business and flapped out of the window and into the night from whence it came. But it gave me interesting food for thought. The brothers Harvey were definitely unlucky where nocturnal creatures were concerned.

During the Spring of 1965 we had a new shop front fitted. It was a much lighter and brighter design and afforded me a few perks. To get the job done quickly the shop-fitters worked through the week from Monday to Saturday. This meant a member of staff staying behind on the Thursday half-day, which meant a day off in lieu and overtime pay. I really enjoyed that Thursday. The shop-fitters were a cheerful bunch and I kept them well supplied with tea. One of them, a gnarled and moustached little man in a flat cap, had the unlikely name of James Bond!

Occasionally I had to do the odd day at one or other of the West End shops but the big milestone was my first ever experience of relief management. I was to manage the Southall branch for two weeks while the regular manager was on holiday. Southall was the 'jumping off' ground for all first-time relief managers in the London area. It was a small, dark shop with modest takings and a manager who must have had the patience of a saint. Dave Manson, uncle of Ray Manson who had left the firm some years ago to become a bus inspector, was very much in the Bertie Benson mould. How he could enjoy his holidays is beyond me when he must have been wondering all the time what the new sprog was doing to his shop. But there were two intelligent young assistants to help me through so I didn't make a hash of it. Also it was a quiet shop and the manager had a stack of Western paperbacks in his office to pass the hours with.

I did struggle with the book-keeping as I had never been fully instructed in clerical matters, and it was only due to the kindly and helpful advice of my colleagues at other shops that I managed to win through. I must have sent the shop's telephone bill through the roof during that fortnight.

But a couple of things did stand out memorably during that period. I became almost paranoid about security. At the end of the first day I went to the bank, deposited the takings in the night safe and then on to the bus stop. I had a long journey down the Uxbridge Road and an even longer one when I changed buses at Hillingdon to finally get to Harrow.

As I stood in the bus queue at Southall I was struck by the thought that I hadn't turned out the shop lights. Leaving the queue, I returned to the shop, un-padlocked the wooden gate at the lobby entrance, unlocked the door and peered into the shop. Yes, all the lights were out. Reassured, I returned to the bus stop and resumed my vigil. Then another thought occurred to me. Had I locked the shop door when I checked the lights? Leaving the queue a second time, I made my way back to the shop, un-padlocked the gate and checked the shop door. Yes, it was securely locked. Breathing a sigh of relief, I returned to the bus stop and joined the end of the queue. Then just as my bus appeared I was seized with terrible doubts. Had I re-padlocked the gate? There was nothing for it but to relinquish my place in the queue yet again and make sure. Of course, the gate was as secure as Fort Knox. After that I shut my mind to the whole thing and managed to get home about seven in the evening.

The second incident was one I knew I would have to tackle – and I dreaded it. It was mandatory that every relief manager had to dress a window at least once during his sojourn at another branch. This was made even more daunting as it was to be a special Summer Holiday display, which meant that I had to strip out the existing display completely and start from scratch. Surprisingly enough I managed that side of it well enough, even if the display groups looked lost in that very large window. But what confounded me were the 'special effects' for the Summer Holiday show. These consisted of a fishing net draped over and around the display blocks and stands and plastic crabs and starfish dropped in at strategic intervals.

It sounded easy enough and it should have been – but it wasn't. Somehow I got myself hopelessly entangled in the net with crabs and starfish rolling all over the place. The public seemed to enjoy the spectacle and I don't suppose the shop ever had so many people staring in the window before. I really should have sold tickets; I would have made a fortune.

A few weeks after I returned to Harlesden it was Hubert's turn for a holiday. That in itself was as good as a holiday for me. The relief manager, Ted Warren, was quite small and looked as if he had been dead for a long while but he was easy to get on with and possessed a dry if indelicate sense of humour. His deadpan manner was pure Buster Keaton.

But one incident during his fortnight really did upset him. Some weeks previous Hubert had decided to use a new alteration tailor. The new man had a lock-up shop just by Willesden Junction Station where we could drop the work in on the way home and collect it on the way to work in the mornings. Previously our alterations had been done by a Mrs Josephs, a frail and elderly widow whose work was impeccable. Also her charges were remarkably low considering the high standard of her work. Half-a-crown – the equivalent of 12½p in today's money – for shortening a pair of trousers.

The fly in the ointment was that she lived in Craven Park and I had a pleasant break from the shop (and Hubert) when it came to delivering and collecting the items to be altered. This didn't suit our Hubert and it was because of this that he changed tailors. What we were unaware of was that he didn't even have the decency to tell Mrs Josephs. One Saturday she phoned Ted up at the shop and asked why we hadn't sent any work round. It was altogether a very embarrassing situation and echoed a similar occasion during my early years at Harrow.

Joe Weiss, who was our alteration tailor, decided to go into business with his brother so we took our alterations to a Mrs Davies, a charming lady who lived in West Harrow. After several months Joe came back, cap in had so to speak, asking us to take him on again. Ronald Harvey agreed and as far as I knew at the time, had informed Mrs Davies accordingly.

One day we had an alteration which was required urgently. Joe was unable to do it so Ronald sent me – all innocent and unknowing – to Mrs Davies. The reception was cool and very embarrassing to say the least. But she was very decent to me about the matter as she realised that I was unaware of the facts and agreed to do the alteration for the customer's sake – but no more. She never wanted to hear from Ronald Harvey again.

Of course, he blustered and grumbled about it. 'Who does she think she is?' and so forth but it showed up the two brothers in a most unfavourable light.

By the end of the year Sean Flynn, our unorthodox electrician, had left and we had a steady succession of junior staff of all shapes and sizes into 1966. The New Year had an optimistic feel about it. Hubert Harvey continued to mutter and whinge but I found that I was able to tune him out and get on with my work. Even the knowledge that I was to be given two more sessions of relief work at West Ealing – two weeks in the Summer and one in the Autumn – didn't bother me.

I enjoyed the West Ealing relief. Considering it was only a mile or so from Ealing Broadway the difference in clientele was remarkable. Whereas the Broadway customers were generally difficult to please, the West Ealing customers were a dream. They were straightforward ordinary folk; what we termed as the 'Mums and Dads'.

I must have enjoyed it because I didn't even grumble about the journey – and that was anything but straightforward. There were two ways of getting to West Ealing from Harrow. One was to catch a bus to South Harrow and travel on the Piccadilly Line to Ealing Common and pray for a 207 bus to come along to complete the final stage of the journey. The other way was travel by bus to Northolt and catch a diesel train to West Ealing. I enjoyed this alternative, especially on a Summer's evening. The train would pass by golf links, glowing a soft green in the setting sun and we would go through somewhere called Castle Bar. The name intrigued me as there wasn't a castle to be seen anywhere amid those mellow emerald expanses. But England is like that; simply another example of our national mysticism, much the same as calling bowler hats 'stiffs'.

The West Ealing manager was Lionel Parr whom I had worked with at Wembley just after my National Service medical. He was comparatively young for a Dunn & Co manager, somewhere in his mid-thirties. Promotion in those days was a slow and steady process.

There was one assistant, Johnny O'Toole, and we got on well with no 'attitude' problems at all. He even asked me to help with a poem to his girlfriend but as it turned out I wrote the whole thing. But first I needed to know a few details about the lady in question.

Johnny supplied the salient details. Her name was Susan Evans and she was in an amateur dramatic group. The current show she was in was based on *Hiawatha* and she was a bit miffed because her mother preferred to spend her evenings at the local Bingo Hall rather than see her daughter decked up as Minihaha. Anyway I managed to rattle off something which seemed to fit the bill. It was something on the lines of …

An Indian fishing? Good gracious! Good heavens!
It's not Minihaha, it's little Susan Evans.
And while she narrates in Red Indian lingo
Her mum and her neighbours have gone to play Bingo.
With make-believe paddles she canoes on the stage.
This lady's performance is the greatest rage.
Should someone get fresh with her, the reckless fool
May well have to reckon with Johnny O'Toole!

He was thrilled to bits with it and copied it out in his own handwriting. Next day he looked as happy as a cat which had been locked in a dairy. I was quite amused about the whole thing as I never visualised myself as Cupid – stupid maybe.

Johnny proved to be one of the most obliging people I had ever worked with on relief. We worked together on the obligatory window display – an elaborate affair with the clothing stands placed on columns of what looked like yellow plastic chicken wire instead of the usual felt-covered wooden blocks. But next morning disaster struck. As I approached the shop I noticed something odd about the window display. The garments were all at very strange angles. The heat from the window lights had melted the plastic columns and the whole lot had collapsed. Evidently this had happened in quite a few of the branches and we had to redress the display with the good old dependable blocks.

But there was one occasion involving West Ealing which I could have done without. Dickie Dyson, another dapper, waist-coated and bespectacled day relief look-alike, had suffered a fall and broken his hip. He was supposed to be at West Ealing that Friday to cover the manager's day off so I was asked to do it. But how was I to get the shop keys? Mr North, the Area Supervisor, would get them to me beforehand. But I was starting my Summer holidays on the Saturday so how could I get the keys back to him? No problem, he said. When I had locked the shop and deposited the takings in the night safe at the bank, all I had to do was put the keys in an envelope and 'post' them through the shop letterbox.

On the face of it, it seemed straightforward enough so I set out in my new steel grey suit and matching trilby hat, feeling no end of a killer. The day went swimmingly with no hitches. I locked the shop at 5.30 and Johnny and I went our separate ways; Johnny homewards or Sue-wards and me to the bank.

That is when things, to use modern parlance, began to go pear-shaped. It was a good fifteen minutes walk to the bank and storm clouds were gathering. Then the first heavy raindrops began to fall as I reached the bank. I still had to return to the shop, return the keys through the letterbox and retrace my steps to catch the bus to Ealing Common.

By this time the rain was pelting down and I was soaked to the skin. I caught my bus and train to South Harrow where I joined the tail end of a very long bus queue for the last part of my journey. Buses came trundling along, chock-full of saturated humanity and only a few were fortunate enough to find a place. Slowly but surely the bus queue shuffled a few feet forward every several minutes along until I was at the head of it and – glory be! – an empty bus came along.

As I squelched aboard the conductress said, 'We're only going to the station, luv.'

'That's good enough,' I replied, thinking she meant Harrow.

But she didn't. She meant South Harrow Station, just across the road. I was forced to suffer the indignity of being transported across the road in full view of a sniggering bus queue where I was compelled to alight and rejoin the queue at the end. I finally arrived home at 7.15, wetter than a drowned rat.

That Summer had not been all wine and roses. My mother's hernia, diagnosed three years earlier strangulated and she was rushed to hospital for an emergency operation. Hospital visits when working at Harlesden were not easy. I had to get off the train at Kenton, dash to the Metropolitan line half a mile away to catch a train from Northwick Park to Northwood Hills where I had to wait four evers and a day for a bus to Harefield Hospital. And did Hubert ever let me off early? Not a chance.

But the Summer holiday was with us and I looked forward to lazy days on the beach. Two weeks of glorious sun, sea and sand. My emergency meals during my mother's hospitalisation had trimmed me down and I felt sharper; fitter to cope with things.

I returned to work revived, alert, refreshed as the advertisements proclaimed for a popular bed-time nightcap, and soon settled back into the routine. Hubert definitely seemed to have improved but I think I had got used to his Harveyesque ways. Whatever it was I felt quite buoyant and I was looking forward to my week at West Ealing in the Autumn.

There had been a change of management. Mike Flynn, my old chum from the Harrow days, was now managing West Ealing, having swapped over with Lionel Parr who was now lording it up at Kilburn. The week's relief went like clockwork. Johnny O'Toole was still there and we had a very profitable week's trade. But West Ealing was that sort of shop. All in all, Mother's hernia excepted, 1966 was proving to be a better year.

A CHANGE FOR THE BETTER

September ~ October 1966

I had been at Harlesden for three years. Usually this was the allotted span of my existence in most of our branches. It had been so at Harrow and also at Wembley. I was prepared for anything and wondered, without much concern, where the next move would take me. Just as long as it wasn't the West End. I just wasn't cut out for the passing trade; it was too impersonal.

We were never really very busy in the Autumn months and the retail trade doesn't get fired up again until the latter part of November as Christmas looms up on the horizon. Sales were not so rife in those days. There were January Sales and Summer Sales but Dunn's didn't go in for them at all in the halcyon Sixties. They held themselves aloof from such things and, it must be admitted, probably considered such things as beneath them.

But there were rumours that we would be making retail history in the New Year by having our very first January Sale. How the dear old firm would cope with such an enterprise was a matter for speculation, and doubtless circumstances had forced this upon them. I sincerely hoped that I would not be working with Hubert Harvey when the time came to embark on our new venture.

One Monday morning Mr North paid a visit and said that I was being transferred. Harrow? I thought. On the back of a flying pig. It was Kilburn. That was just as good as far as I was concerned. Three years of Hubert Harvey was more than enough for me and Lionel Parr was the Kilburn manager and we had always got on well together.

This wasn't just a random move; there was an ulterior motive. Each week stock had gone missing at Kilburn and the senior assistant was suspected. Dunn's didn't bother with sales receipts in those days unless the customer requested one. Much was done on trust and it worked well both sides of the counter. How the pilfering was being done was all too easy. A customer would pay cash and the assistant simply destroyed the sales ticket so there was no record of the transaction at all. How this came to light I do not know but Mr North was no fool and he was sending the Kilburn assistant to Harlesden and I was to take his place. It was a clever move. Should the stock losses cease at Kilburn it would be strong proof, albeit circumstantial, and the suspect would be a complete idiot if he tried to work the same scam on Horrible Hubert.

So there I was, actually on my final week with the last of the dreaded Harvey brothers. And after all of three years of biting my tongue we had a blazing row on the very last day.

A customer called in that Saturday morning, saying that he had come about his overcoat. I checked the customers' rail but couldn't find it, so I looked through the recent request orders. Not there either. It must be an alteration. But nothing there either.

'I left it here on Thursday,' explained the customer, which was why I didn't remember him as Thursday was my day off.

I asked Hubert about it and he exploded. 'It's a complaint coat and I posted it to Head Office for examination!' he snapped. 'Why don't you keep on top of the job instead of wasting the customer's time?'

He then turned to the customer, apologising for my 'stupidity' and said that he would be in touch as soon as he heard from the makers about the faulty garment.

When the customer had gone he turned on me again but I got in first. 'How the hell am I supposed to know about something that happened on my day off?' I told him. 'And furthermore, don't you ever dare to speak to me again like that in front of a customer!'

Hubert went as white as a sheet but he didn't reply. In fact he never spoke to me again for the rest of the day. We went home in the rain with our evening papers in an even more intense silence and when we parted at Harrow there wasn't even a handshake or the decency to wish me luck at Kilburn. That was Hubert Harvey for you. I don't think even his brother Ronald would have been as mean-spirited as that.

I settled into Kilburn on the first day. It was a roomy and comfortable shop to work in. At one time the original building must have been a private residence as there were two floors above the shop as well as an attic. Access to these upper floors could only be gained by a staircase next to the cash desk so they were useless as living accommodation. The first floor was used as storage space for display material and cardboard boxes used for posting items to other branches, but at the front there was a spacious staff room which afforded a splendid view along Kilburn High Road. The second floor was used as a training area for junior staff who met there every Monday and Tuesday.

Apart from Lionel Parr the manager there was only one other member of staff, a youngster called Colin Jones. Colin really was a fantastic character. Nearly every morning he was late, but it was worth it just to hear his excuses. 'I'm sorry I was late, Mr Parr,' he would begin his excuse in his usual hangdog manner. 'I caught an early bus but the engine blew up and we had to get off and wait for another one. Well, that came along and we were just coming through Cricklewood when there was this smash and grab robbery at a jeweller's shop and the getaway car collided with the bus. The police made us all wait and took our names and addresses and said that we might be called as witnesses if the robbers were caught. By then I had missed three buses but I got here as quickly as I could.'

It was well worth him being late to hear his excuses, each one more preposterous than ever. But to give him his due, when he did get to work, he worked. I have never seen anyone work harder, no matter how menial or messy the task might be. If he thought the shop front might need washing down, Colin would get a bucket of water and cloth, roll up his sleeves and get on with it.

Not only was his fertile mind always ready with excuses, he could make up poetry at the drop of a hat – a Dunn & Co hat, of course. All you had to do was suggest a subject and he would go off for a few minutes, muttering to himself, and then present you with half a dozen verses of doggerel on the chosen theme. Not that much of his inspiration would bear quoting in mixed company but Colin could certainly deliver the goods. Just to give an example of his genius I can recall the last verse – but most likely the only repeatable one – about an encounter with a leper in 'Israeli Road'.

He threw his arms and legs at me
And then he threw his head.
And when he'd nothing left to throw,
The poor sod fell down dead.

Colin puzzled me when he mentioned that he had gone to *The Gog* with his girlfriend at the weekend. I thought that it must be a disco club but I found out later that he meant the Synagogue. No, Colin was okay and he gave us plenty of laughs, often unintentionally.

Mondays and Tuesdays could be a bit of a headache on account of the Junior Staff Training School on the second floor. Monday was presided over by Raymond North but as it didn't start until 10 o'clock he took over the shop telephone as soon as we opened to ring round all the branches in his area. And as the telephone was situated in the cash office it seriously curtailed the usual Monday bookwork.

But Tuesdays were a different matter. 'Jumping Jack' Flashman, that hawk-eyed and too-clever-for-our-own-good Area Supervisor was in charge then. It was eight years since I had last seen him at Watford and he hadn't changed a bit. Still the same sharp and waspish character as before.

That first Tuesday morning was a disaster. It happened that Tuesday was Lionel Parr's day off and the day relief manager was a chap called Arthur Hall. I had heard of him but never before met him. He was always an early bird and got to the shop in good time. I arrived just on nine and by some miracle Colin did too, which was just as well as Mr Flashman came strutting into the shop.

Now it was Arthur Hall's first day at Kilburn and he had never met any of us before. I had just entered the shop as 'Jumping Jack' marched in behind Colin who was struggling to bring in the wooden gates which were locked across the shop lobby every night. Then the catastrophe happened. Colin tripped over and dropped one of the gateposts against the shop counter, hitting the end of a box containing the soft little metal hat initials. These were black and silver ovals which could be clipped inside the leathers of a customer's hat for identification. The upshot of this was, well, the upshot of the initial box. The whole lot cascaded over Mr Flashman like a swarm of metallic flies. And to add insult to injury Colin tripped over his own feet, fell backwards, giggling, and head-batted our fearsome visitor in the stomach.

It would be wrong to say that the air was blue and unfair to Mr Flashman because I never once heard him swear. He didn't need to; he had a good command of the English language and used it with great eloquence, loudly and at length. Then, his wrath spent, he disappeared upstairs.

'You must be Keith Howard,' Arthur greeted me in a softened Northern accent. 'I wasn't sure which of you was Mr Flashman. After that outburst,' he added with a wry smile, 'I think I know who's who now.'

Arthur Hall was something of a loner. Some ten years older than me, he lived in very comfortable 'digs' in Bushey. He was one of the smartest people I had ever seen in the firm. Thin-faced, with a well-groomed quiff of black hair and an immaculate stiff collar and well-pressed suit. He looked as if he had just stepped out of a bandbox. It transpired that we had much in common as regards to music, both having a taste for Classical and that, along with his sense of humour, cemented a friendship that has lasted to this day.

An added bonus to working at Kilburn was that I got a lift part way home. Lionel lived in South Harrow and after work we would cross over to Brondesbury Road where his car was parked. All around the back-doubles we would go. I can still recall some of their names. Mortimer Road, Harvist Road, Bathurst Gardens, all flanked by houses that had once seen better days, doubtless with domestic staff living 'below stairs' but now had been broken up into separate units of individual flats. Through Harlesden we would go and across the North Circular Road to Wembley High Road where I would catch a train from Wembley Central for the seven-minute journey to Harrow and Wealdstone. Yes, Kilburn suited me very much indeed.

Just for the record, on checking our stock the first week I was there, we were one item short, but that was the last shortage. The culprit, who had taken my place at Harlesden, was challenged on these stock losses and freely admitted his guilt. A divorce and other domestic crises resulted in him going through a bad patch and he foolishly was unable to resist the temptation to bolster his slender funds.

Through the 'grapevine' I learned the outcome of this. Mr North placed a full report before Mr Pedrick the Managing Director. The assistant was not sacked. Instead a set sum was deducted from his wages until the losses were made good. Is there any wonder that most of us were content to spend our working lives with such a firm?

One very favourable aspect of working at Kilburn was that Lionel hated window dressing which meant that I was obliged to do it. After my negative experiences with Hubert Harvey I didn't relish the idea, but it couldn't have worked out better. 'Yes, that looks fine, Keith,' Lionel would say. And those few words of encouragement – however placatory they may have been – helped me much more than any training course could ever have done. So much so that I actually came to enjoy the display work.

One window display which was all my own idea proved to be a great success. With James Bond films and books much in evidence I dressed the small window by the shop doorway with a navy blue raglan raincoat and two narrow-brimmed 'Atlantic' style hats of the same colour. The result was most gratifying. Young James Bond wannabees poured in and we were compelled to submit a special request order for another supply of navy hats and raincoats.

Lionel also gave me a free hand with the interior displays. Along each side of the back half of the shop – the front area was still sacrosanct to headwear – were 'bays' as they were called. For example, every other one was a 'double-decker' with two clothing rails, and those in between had just the one with a deep display shelf above. This enabled me to design displays with a theme which I was able to enhance with the abundant supply of coloured felt from the stock room. A raincoat display with a snappy gabardine-covered 'Wethergard' trilby, backed by swathes of rainy blue and storm grey felt backdrops. Oh, the little artist in me ran riot. It's a wonder I didn't end up in the Tate or National Gallery.

I was enjoying my work more than I had done for years. I worked with a good staff in a comfortable shop and getting a lift part way home most evenings. Trade was brisk and profitable; in particular the overcoat trade was proving to be our most lucrative source. In those days Kilburn had its fair share of barrow-boys and these husky types would swagger into the shop, rubbing their chapped hands together with a 'gimme a *Crombie* overcoat, mate.' This was the most expensive coat in the shop but they would just peel off the required amount from a thick roll of fivers and we would part company, each perfectly satisfied with the transaction.

But they weren't all barrow-boys; far from it. Our shop was more towards the Hampstead end of Kilburn where the more theatrical element lived. One afternoon two elderly and tubby gentlemen entered the shop. They looked like the grandfathers of Tweedledum and Tweedledee. One of them wanted a hat. 'What do you think of this one, darling?' asked the prospective customer of his companion in a plummy voice.

'Quite nice, dear, but do try the beige one on again. I think you look quite lovely in that.'

Yes, I was still learning about people and they weren't all barrow-boys. I will admit that I was glad when they finally made their selection and left the shop.

But there was one occasion which I will never forget and was hilarious, although at the time I wanted the ground to open and swallow me up. It was all due to Lionel Parr's knack of saying the right thing the wrong way in his loud and distinct voice.

In those pre-computer days much of our stock was coded by names instead of numbers which was a much easier system to remember them by. For example, some of our suits were supplied by Sumries and all their ranges began with the letter 'S'; Sandown, Selsey etc. Another of our suppliers was Hammersley's with suit ranges such as Hastings, Heston and even – I say this in all modesty – Howard.

I had sold one of the Hammersley suits from their Hawes range but the trousers needed shortening. With alterations the usual arrangement was that I would leave work at five o'clock and drop them off at the alteration tailor at Willesden Junction, the very same one who did the alterations for our Harlesden branch.

About 4.30 that afternoon a young lady came in and asked to see some gloves which she wanted to buy for her boyfriend. As we had a very extensive range she was hard put to choose and the time was ticking away. I noticed Lionel glance at his watch, then at the trousers and then at me. He repeated this series of actions several times, becoming more agitated as the time passed. Finally, just before five o'clock he could stand it no longer. 'Excuse me, madam,' he politely announced to the young lady. Then turning to me he said loudly and clearly, 'Keith, I think it's about time you took that Hawes trousers down!'

THE CIRCLE COMPLETED

October 1966 ~ October 1967

There is something special about a week's holiday in the Autumn. Not that I felt in great need of it; I was quite happy at Kilburn. It is the psychological break in what can be a dreary spell of gloomy days in the run-up to Christmas. The only memorable event of that week concerned a young lady I met while working at Harlesden. I wanted to impress her and, knowing that she liked Classical music, booked tickets for the Albert Hall. I really should have checked on the programme, but I assumed it would be something highbrow that Thursday evening. It wasn't; it was a Wrestling Tournament. Fortunately she had a sense of humour!

Back to work and the pre-Christmas trade and preparations for Dunn's first ever January Sale to deal with. All in all it was fun. I even decided to change my image by growing a moustache and combing my hair in a fringe. The Christmas trade was brisk and then there were all those little red sale tickets to make out and the ready reckoner forms we were given to work out the discounts. And the January Sale actually began on New Year's Day (it wasn't a Bank Holiday in England then), not Christmas Eve like it does now. The days immediately after Christmas before the New Year were busy enough for us. It was inevitable that Christmas gifts would be returned for exchange or refund and that week was invaluable for getting such things sorted out and clearing the decks.

The Sale went well but early in 1967 Colin Jones left the firm and was replaced by an ever-changing succession of what are now known as 'twits'. One twit in particular caused me some grief. He had been polishing the floor with liquid traffic wax in preparation for going over it with the electric floor polisher. Typically he had left the can of traffic wax standing in the middle of the floor without replacing the cap. I picked the can up and spotted the cap on the counter. Really I should have put the can down when I went across to retrieve the cap as I trod on a dollop of polish that the twit had neglected to rub in. Backwards and over I went, executing the finest somersault ever. Old 'Monty', my PE teacher at Whitefriars, would have been proud of me. I landed flat on my back but the unsealed can of polish went spinning up into the air, spraying the horrible, orange, syrupy stuff over all and everything. Then the can came down on my chest and spent the remainder of its contents all over me.

'Blimey!' exclaimed Lionel Parr from his managerial office. 'Are you all right?'

I appreciated his concern. My well-being was his first thought. I am sure that the reaction from the brothers Harvey would have been considerably less sympathetic. True, I was covered from head to foot with highly-scented traffic wax but no bones were broken. I felt more concerned about the stock. A liberal amount of polish had splashed over several coats.

Lionel frowned slightly. 'I'll send Dave (the current twit) along to the chemist to get some carbon tetrachloride. That should get the marks off.'

Well I'm glad he didn't ask me to go. My nerves were all of a jangle and I doubt whether I would have been in a fit state to say carbon tetrachloride.

'You'd better go home and get changed,' Lionel told me. 'Take your time. We'll have this cleared up by the time you get back.'

It isn't funny going home by train and smelling like a well-kept piece of furniture. Furthermore, the sun had come out and dried the wretched stuff into a high gloss so that I was light reflective. I eventually reached my station, thankful that my mother was out. Unbeknown to me I was seen by an aunt who thought I had been in a road accident. Why a road accident? I cleaned myself up, effected a change of suits and returned to work. On arriving back at Kilburn I found that Lionel had worked a miracle with the carbon tetrachloride and removed every trace of polish from the afflicted garments.

I am not superstitious but the suit I had been wearing was what I called my 'James Bond' suit; a natty navy-blue two piece, and it had proved to be an unlucky suit in the past so I should have been warned. I originally purchased it in my Wembley days and decided to wear it home instead of creasing it up in a bag. Unfortunately I had left my doorkey behind that morning and, as nobody was in, it being Wednesday half-day, I had to climb in through the top half of the kitchen window. Not the best way to treat a new suit. Then on August Bank Holiday 1966 I was caught in a terrific thunderstorm atop Invinghoe Beacon in that same suit which was utterly drenched. But what worried me at the time was the metal trouser zip as the lightening was frightening. So you can see I cannot really blame the junior assistant for leaving the cap off the tin of polish. It was my fault for wearing that unlucky suit.

The moustache fringe hairstyle only lasted a couple of months but I was particularly aggrieved about the moustache. For weeks my parents had complained about it and when I shaved it off they didn't even notice.

During the Spring and Summer I had to do relief work at Acton. Not one of my favourite shops which that accursed High Level at Willesden Junction involved. My time there wasn't much helped by the one and only assistant there – another young twit – who seemed to be asleep on his feet most of the time. At any rate I knew how long I would be there and that I would be returning to Kilburn, so that afforded a light at the end of the tunnel.

But that light was to be extinguished after my Summer holiday. Raymond North phoned up one morning in August to say that Mr Black, the manager of our Twickenham branch, had had a heart attack and I was to go there at once and take over. Oh, great, I thought, I love surprises – I don't think, was my reaction. The trouble with 'sick relief' is that you never know how long they are going to last.

Twickenham was quite a 'round the houses' place to get to. I had to catch a train from Kilburn High Road to Willesden Junction, then up to the inevitable High Level and all the way to Richmond where I eventually caught a bus to Twickenham.

If I expected to see an ambulance and paramedics swarming around our shop and around a heart-attacked manager I was to be disappointed. Mr Black stood in the shop doorway, puffing on a cigarette and demanding to know why I hadn't got there sooner. 'The stock's been checked,' he told me as he slammed on his hat, handed me the shop keys and lit up another ciggie. 'I'll be off work for about eight or nine weeks. Doctor's orders.'

Thanks a bunch, I thought as he sauntered off down the road. I hope this turns out better than Acton.

The shop looked very much like the Harrow branch from the outside; two square windows and a central lobby, but the interior was bigger. It was a square shop with the office-coop located halfway down on the right and the minuscule staff room beyond a door in the back left-hand corner. There wasn't much stock and the clothing racks seemed so sparse after Kilburn that I could virtually count the stock from the office.

There was one young assistant; half Chinese – I don't know which half – and thankfully he was of cheerful disposition and a helpful nature. As to Twickenham, it was a nice area and we should have done well there but we were between Richmond and Kingston and these branches took the lion's share of the trade. What trade we did get was good quality but lacking in volume; Twickenham was what was called a 'Cinderella branch'.

Nearly every morning there was one problem which cropped up. It was a rule that every night the cash float should be hidden somewhere in the shop as in those days we didn't have safes. The usual idea was to put it in one of the hat buckets which I duly did. The only trouble was that almost every morning I would have forgotten which one I had hidden it in. There would follow a frantic ten minute search until I found the missing money.

The day relief manager was yet another dapper little clone, Fred Ballard from Balham. Like many of his contemporaries he had an easy-going, laid back attitude. He was only a few years away from retirement and 'shop-hopping' was an ideal way of getting through the last few years of his employment, never being in one place long enough to incur any responsibilities.

It was my foul luck to fall for the Autumn window display. It consisted of stiff tubular card supports instead of the usual chipboard blocks, patterned to look like green-veined marble and the background screens were covered with dark red patterned flock wallpaper which reminded me of pubs. I had no idea what the theme was supposed to represent. It certainly didn't look Autumnal. I dressed the display but wasn't too happy with it. I just didn't seem able to get the heights right.

Just for good measure I dressed the other window, using the existing window blocks and colours, and felt a lot happier with the end result. That would do until old Blackie had got over his heart attack. I just wanted my spell at Twickenham to coast along gently without any complications.

Imagine my surprise when, returning from my day off, I received a phone call from Fred Ballard to say that 'Long John' Neville, our Staff Director, had paid a visit. 'He liked the Autumn window,' Fred told me, 'but he wasn't too happy with the other one.'

'The man's an idiot,' I replied. 'I wasn't too happy with the Autumn window but I thought the other one was okay.'

'Well he didn't think so,' Fred retorted. 'He wanted me to alter the height of that coat stand at the back and I told him that I couldn't go messing with Mr Howard's windows.'

'What did he say to that?' I prompted.

'He said, "you're not messing about with it, Mr Ballard, you're correcting it".'

Well, that sums up old JN. He didn't know a thing about displays but he just had to say something to justify his existence. I wasn't sorry I had missed him.

Twickenham was one of those shops that had flats above it which were generally let out to members of staff. The one over Twickenham was let out to Ernie Pym from my Wembley days. 'You'll have to stay overnight sometime,' he kept urging me. 'It will make a change from that long drag home on the train.'

I wasn't over-enthusiastic about the idea. In a way I wouldn't be getting away from the shop. It also may mean I would have to share a bedroom with their precocious five year old son who – to add insult to injury – was also called Keith.

I decided to agree and get it over with. Anyway, old Blackie should be back soon and I could escape back to Kilburn. Ernie's wife, Joy, was as fat as he was thin and when they stood side by side they looked like the number ten. For dinner we had baked beans on toast with undercooked 'albino' sausages. I ruefully remembered from my Wembley days when they lived at Rayners Lane they seemed to have baked beans for every meal and I just cannot abide the things.

As feared I was obliged to share a room with my infant namesake, an arrangement I didn't much relish as I have never liked sharing rooms or sleeping in strange beds. I always preferred to crawl into my 'pit'. And in the morning I had to suffer the ordeal of the child watching me shave. It was one of those families where privacy was a low priority and I was glad to get downstairs to the shop and normality.

The days dragged on, thankfully without event or mishap and a fully-refreshed but no better-tempered Mr Black finally returned in late September. Mr North was at the shop on the day of his return to officiate in the Ceremony of Checking the Stock which went off without any real problems. Back to Kilburn, I wondered hopefully?

Mr North put on his 'old pals' smile – or rather smirk. 'Just a couple of weeks at Ealing Broadway,' he cajoled.

Well that's all it would be as I was booked for a week's holiday in October, I tactfully pointed out.

No problem, was his response. He would be visiting Ealing while I was there and we would get things sorted out.

It was to be said that my two weeks at Ealing Broadway were a great improvement on the first session there some four years earlier with Ronald Harvey. The current manager was a very tall young man called Smith. We simply called him 'Tall' Smith. Then as promised, Raymond North paid a visit. When he had finished laughing at my interior display efforts he brought up the matter of my posting after my week's holiday.

'No, not Kilburn,' he told me. 'I did promise you this and although it seems to have taken longer than I thought it would at first, you are returning as permanent Senior Assistant at Harrow.'

At last, after ten years almost to the day, the circle was complete!

'GOODBYE, MR CHIPS'

Autumn 1967 ~ Spring 1970

Yes, it was true! At long last I was back at Harrow, and as Senior Assistant! The same dear old manager, Bertie Benson, as placid as ever and the last ten years since I had been winkled out and moved to Kentish Town were almost like a dream.

There were two junior assistants; Mike Reynolds, who looked like a somnambulistic Norman Wisdom, and Martin Tibbs. Mart was a sharp young man with a dry sense of humour. He was a 'Mod', one of the current species which had succeeded the Teddy Boys. Very smart with a slim-cut Mohair suit and a neat haircut which looked as if his head had been sharpened.

Christmas Eve at Harrow was memorable. After we closed the shop Bertie took us to *The Havelock* for our festive convivialities. 'Now, laddies,' he said in his avuncular manner, 'you keep your pennies in your pockets. I'm buying the drinks and you've got to have something to eat first.'

Three rounds of beef sandwiches and a pint of beer each. Bertie really looked after us well. And he looked after himself well with three double scotches, but he was as steady as a rock the entire evening.

During our session we were joined by Mr Boulter who managed our Edgware branch. Eddie Boulter was one of those people who just had to 'talk shop' throughout the whole evening. Fortunately he didn't stay long as he had to get back home to Isleworth and I occupied the time, not listening to him, but watching the contortions of his very thick and bushy eyebrows which looked like a couple of prawns.

Mr Boulter was accident-prone. While managing Harlesden branch he suffered a nasty experience when the cellar steps collapsed under him and he had to be rescued by the local Undertaker who lowered a ladder down to him. On another occasion at our Ealing Broadway shop, whilst bidding goodbye to a customer he stepped backwards and fell through the trap-door to the store cellar which had been left open by one of the junior staff. He managed to save himself by catching the sides of the trap with his elbows and while one member of staff struggled to pull him up another went after the customer who happened to be a doctor. As it turned out, he was a doctor of leprosy which wasn't much help in the circumstances.

But that was poor old Eddie for you. I never had the luck – good or bad – to work with him. Half an hour at the pub on Christmas Eve was long enough.

It was an easy-going atmosphere at Harrow as I expected it would be. Mike and Mart didn't exactly work themselves to death, especially Mike, but the work got done. But I was to see another side of our esteemed manager. As well as a kind and fatherly disposition, he had a quietly mischievous sense of humour. We had been dismantling the Christmas display and one of the placards was a white plastic oval, about four feet long with adhesive tape on one side. This had been split in half longways for its final trip to the dustbin. I was serving a customer and was utterly unaware of Bertie hovering behind me with the two halves of display. Without me feeling a thing he gently attached them each side of my shoulders so that they hung down like a pair of wings. It wasn't until I was putting on my coat at lunchtime that I discovered them.

But Bertie was quite impartial with these little pranks. One morning when Mike was hoovering the floor Bertie crept up behind him, unscrewed the suction tube from the cylinder and left Mike blithely working his way the whole length of the shop while the cylinder remained at the other end. We really should have been on our guard as he had already surprised us when he let it be known that he was a great fan of radio's *The Goon Show*.

Mart, who was very well up in the Pop scene, was always warbling the latest hit, and one in particular was a great favourite of his. It was called *Fire* with appropriately fierce lyrics. *Fire – you're gonna burn, burn, burn!* After a few minutes' silence we would hear murmurings from the managerial office, quite soft and even mild. 'Fire – you're gonna burn – you're gonna burn, laddie ...' At least Bertie had his finger on the pulse of the modern scene.

During my ten year absence the shop had been given a makeover. Gone were the two square windows with the central lobby. Now there was a square lobby with the main L-shaped window on the left and a narrower window on the right. The wood was lighter too, as it was inside the shop with built in fixtures with a more modern cash office on the left at the front of the shop. Gone, too, was that terrible redstone floor and in its stead attractively patterned linoleum, industrial grade which would last for years. But the one thing which hadn't been replaced, I am happy to say, was the wonderfully friendly atmosphere.

But it wasn't all fun and games and I couldn't expect it to be. Raymond North seemed to have earmarked me for holiday relief at Twickenham for

Spring, Summer and Autumn. About this time, my mother had to go into hospital for another hernia operation. Happily it was not so serious and as I was working at Harrow the visiting would be easier. Bertie promised that he would let me off early which was something that never once occurred to Hubert Harvey during my Harlesden days.

That is when Murphy's Law took over. The date for my Mother's operation was changed to coincide with my two weeks in Twickenham in the Summer. No rest for the wicked but it all worked out right in the end.

With regard to my leisure time, I had always preferred to keep it separate from work and, apart from Christmas drinkies and the odd wedding (and some of them were very odd!), I rarely socialised with my workmates out of hours. An exception cropped up when Mike, who had acquired a cine camera – the forerunner of the video camera in case you are too young to remember – suggested we should make a short comedy film about fishing one Sunday afternoon over West Drayton near some river or canal. The upshot of it was that I fell in but I should have realised the peril. I was wearing my 'unlucky' navy blue suit. I returned home, a fuming, stinking creature with slime baked on me by the sun from head to foot. That was the final indignity as far as that suit was concerned. It was beyond even *Oxfam* and passed out of my life and into the dustbin.

Life was exciting enough without Master Michael's flights of filmic fancy. In a fit of whimsy Mr North decided that I should manage our Putney branch for one day. 'You can get the shop keys from Mrs Hooper upstairs,' he told me.

Her husband was one of our West End staff so it seemed straightforward enough. I arrived at Putney and found that I had to go up an alley at the side of the shop to get the keys. As bad luck would have it a van parked in the alley, completely blocking any egress, and the only way I could get back to the shop was by crawling underneath the van and emerging from under the radiator before the astonished gaze of the shop staff who were waiting in the shop doorway.

Another one-day trip involved managing our shop in Tooting Broadway. Nice enough shop with a decent junior who kept telling me I looked like a film star. An elderly gentleman came in for a pair of trousers. I showed him into what I thought was the fitting-room but belatedly realised, on hearing feminine screams of outrage, that it was a connecting door to the upstairs flat.

Mr North seemed to enjoy trying me out in different shops. North Finchley was not all that far away as the crow flies but not being a crow I had to rely on public transport. Then there was Fulham – and that was a three-week spell where I nearly frightened an old lady to death.

'Long John' Neville decided to pay his Summer visit to Fulham during my relief and complained that a coat in the window needed redressing. 'Long John' knew nothing about displays. He knew nothing about anything but just had to say something to justify his position of authority. When he had gone I thought it just as well to do something to the display in case he might come back to try to catch me out.

Now Fulham was one of our old shops and you had to step over a ledge at the window-back to get in. The trouble was that the window was so crowded it was almost impossible to turn around and you had to come out backwards. Also, it was quite easy to forget the ledge behind you ... which is what I did.

Imagine the scene. Joe Biggs, the senior assistant, is serving a nice old lady and gentleman with a tweed cap when suddenly, and seemingly out of nowhere, a screaming body plunges out of the window-back and crashes to the floor right at the old lady's feet. The screaming body then scuttles off, covered in confusion and skulks in the office-coop until the customers have departed.

Joe was tickled pink. 'I didn't know you were given to strong language like that,' he chortled. 'Right in front of the old lady, too.'

I asked him what I had said and he told me. Well I was in an extremity of terror at the time; what one might class as 'mitigating circumstances'.

The days, weeks and months passed pleasantly enough but poor old Bertie didn't enjoy good health. He suffered from varicose eczema and even the walk from the station was all that he could manage. He even had an aerosol spray for his face which had to be applied during the day. One morning he asked me to spray his face with it while he sat on the office stool with two wads of cotton wool protecting his eyes.

At that moment a customer came in. 'Blimey!' he gasped. 'What's going on?'

'Nothing to be alarmed about, Sir,' replied Bertie, calmly removing his eye pads. 'It's not an embalming parlour. I'm just having my daily "fix".'

New staff came and went. One youngster I recall was a timid little chap. He had very curly black hair and wanted it 'mod-style' with a parting but his hair just wasn't compatible with that form of styling. One day, in desperation, when he had just dated a girl and was taking her to the cinema in the evening, he tried to carve a parting in his hair with a razor. It is a miracle that he never drew blood but he made an awful mess of his hair. There were white zig-zags of bare scalp all over the left side of his head like streaks of lightening.

Mike and Mart were moved to help him, more out of a sense of challenge than pity. They took him out to the staff room and boot-blacked his head.

He had quite a distinctive gloss when he emerged and went off on his date, full of confidence. Alas, the outcome was not a happy ending. Cinemas are warm places and during a romantic moment in the back row of the stalls the boot polish melted all over his beloved.

He wasn't with us long and moved on to other spheres of employment but I was to see something of him again several years later in the most unexpected circumstances. I was serving a customer who had just purchased a record at a nearby music shop. I happened to glance at the LP album he had just placed on the counter and did a double-take. 'He used to work here!' I croaked in amazement.

'What – this chap?' the customer replied. 'Their song is at number one on the charts.'

So he had made the big time after all despite the boot polish. Good luck to him, I thought. He deserved it.

Inevitably there were other changes. Mart left and emigrated to Australia, Mike got married and I – well I was logged for another relief at Twickenham. This was in the early Spring of 1970 and we were snowed under.

Late one afternoon at Twickenham I was about to lock the shop and take the day's cash over to the bank when the special security lock jammed. It had worse than jammed; I had heard a spring inside it give up the ghost. That lock was a highly complicated affair and the metal tongue had jammed in the 'out' position, making it impossible to shut the door. Also the key was trapped in the lock and refused to be withdrawn.

Trying not to panic, I phoned the Shopfitting Department at Head Office. Not to worry, they said. Their locksmith was at the Strand shop and he would be straight round to sort things out. There was nothing for it but to wait. The snow had begun to fall again heavily and the only heating in the shop was a small bar electric fire. I donned my overcoat and phoned my home so that my parents wouldn't be unduly worried by any delay. In fact I had to phone them at least twice before I left the shop.

At 6.30 the locksmith turned up. He was not what you would call a precision worker. He banged the metal tongue back in the door with his hammer and wrenched the key piecemeal out of the lock with a pair of pliers. 'That's okay now,' he told me. 'You'll be able to lock up with your spare key.'

'What spare key?' was my bleak reply.

'Oh, well, you'll have to stay here all night until we can fit another lock tomorrow,' came the response.

I wasn't having that. Then I remembered the locks and bolts on the back door and suggested that he remove the mortise lock from there and fix it on the front door. There were enough bolts on the back door to keep an army at bay.

Thankfully he did this but it was a long job and turned 7.30 by the time I could consider leaving. The snow had ceased and everything was covered in a picturesque white mantle, even though the silence was eerie. The bus crawled to Richmond but I caught the High Level train without difficulty and made my connection for the final stage of my journey to Harrow and Wealdstone.

I first smelt a rat when the train left North Wembley. It was travelling at walking pace. We eventually trickled into South Kenton and even more eventually Kenton. Then after an unnaturally long wait the train shook itself like a dying beast and creaked and groaned its way on the last lap of my journey. Then it stopped. We all sat reading our newspapers, even the adverts. I looked at my watch. We had been stationary between stations for forty-five minutes. It had been a hell of a day and enough was enough.

'What are you doing?' asked a fellow-traveller as I opened the carriage door.

'I'm getting out,' I retorted. Thankfully it was before the days of controlled sliding doors or I would probably have been there still, and skeletonised. Although it was dark I could see well enough where we were. The train had stopped over the tunnel at the end of Elmgrove Road; an old haunt of mine in my childhood. I had often scrambled along the narrow, blue-black brick mouth of that tunnel.

'You can't do that,' my fellow-traveller protested. 'We aren't in a station.'

'Just watch,' I told him, and hopped out and down the embankment and scrambled over the railings without impaling myself. I finally arrived home, covered with indignation and snow. It was what you would have called the end of a very long day.

The next morning I found out what had happened. The heavy snow had caused a landfall further up the line near Carpenders Park, but why the trains couldn't have been stopped at the earlier stations so that the passengers could disembark instead of being stuck between stations was never explained.

Evidently there had been several trains stranded. Arthur Hall, the day relief manager, was on one of those trains. Like me, he had climbed down to the embankment when a stout lady who had been in his carriage called down to him, 'It's no good, young man. You'll have to help me.' And before he had a chance to reply, she jumped, landing heavily on his chest, knocking him flat on his back and tobogganing down the embankment on him. Poor Arthur! Such things should not happen to such a smart and sedate gentleman. The memory of that experience probably scarred him psychologically for life.

One day at Harrow Mr North took me aside and I, knowing Raymond and suspecting another transfer, probably to one of the outer moons of Jupiter, was understandably on my guard.

'It's about Mr Benson,' he confided. 'I've seen him hobbling to work from the station in the morning and he can hardly put one foot in front of the other. We are going to retire him on full pension this Spring.'

I was grateful for the shared confidence but very sorry to lose a manager who had been like a second father to me. I also wondered, with no small measure of trepidation, who his successor would be. As the news of the retirement became official it was generally thought that Norman Hurst, who was managing our Watford High Street branch, would take over. But no; it was John Karswell, the manager of our Hounslow shop. I had worked with Mr Karswell in the past and the only way to describe him is as a fusspot. Oddly enough he and Bertie were great friends yet they were as alike as chalk and cheese.

I was very pleased when my mother called in the shop to see Bertie and wish him well in his retirement. He told her that he would miss 'the laddies at the shop' and he had really enjoyed his fourteen-plus years at Harrow. Mum said there were tears in his eyes. We were all more than a little choked, too. He reminded me of the title character in that wonderful old Robert Donat film *Goodbye, Mr Chips*, the teacher who was so beloved by his pupils. Bertie could have been a role model for that film.

On the actual day of his retirement Raymond North took him to *The Havelock* and deliberately got him squiffy to soften the blow. But we hadn't seen the last of Bertie. For several years afterwards he would invite us over to his home in Chesham for a drink down at his local then back home where his wife, Doris, had prepared a banquet of a supper. Eventually they moved down to Devon and we never saw Bertie again. But we never ever forgot him.

THE RETURN OF 'JUMPING JACK'

Spring 1970 ~ Autumn 1973

John Karswell our new manager most certainly wasn't one of my most favourite people. He was a nit-picker with very fussy fads and fancies and always had his lunch in the office instead of the staff room so that he could keep his beady eye on the shop. He invariably had tomatoes with his lunch and clearing up afterwards was a messy business as he always left the skins hanging over the edge of his plate. He also had his own little teapot because he would only drink Darjeeling tea.

In appearance he somehow reminded me of a snake. I think it was because he had a very narrow head on a very thick neck. As the rest of him was skinny this probably added to the effect. He also had more than the usual amount of teeth. Actually they were dentures but when he smiled – though sneered would be more accurate – those teeth seemed to go halfway round his head.

Two mornings a week we were spared his company as he attended a special clinic for traction and had to wear a special corset. This earned him the nickname 'Tinribs' and, surprisingly enough, this was coined by my mother. He was a fanatical bowls player and had even coached one of the local teams. This was very useful to know as I could always head off one of his more querulous days by getting him on his pet subject, much the same as I did with Hubert Harvey at Harlesden with his wartime reminiscences.

But it wasn't a happy shop. He was a competent enough manager, Dunn & Co through and through, but he was a fusspot and a whinger and always lurking behind you, watching and listening when you were serving a customer. Now this is the worst thing anyone can do as it puts you on edge and the tension can easily communicate to the customer. And if you lost a sale it was almost like a drum-head court martial. He also tried to instigate starting work at 8.30 on Saturday mornings. Tried to, but staff solidarity beat him down.

It was a great relief when his fortnight's Summer holiday came round and Nicholas Willoughby, who used to work at the old Ealing Broadway shop, stood in for him. I well remember his arrival at Harrow. A rotund, theatrical figure, he swept into the shop, doffed his wide-brimmed velour hat with a flourish and bowed. 'Nicholas Willoughby at your service, gentlemen,' he announced himself.

Needless to say it was a very jolly fortnight. The three of us – Nick, Mike and I – worked as a good team and the two weeks passed all too quickly. But I was destined not to be present on the Monday morning when 'Tinribs' returned from his holiday. Sadly I never saw Nicholas Willoughby again. His mother died soon afterwards and poor Nick suffered acute depression which finally drove him to suicide. He was found in his garage with the car engine running.

The Sunday before 'Tinribs' returned I suffered a terrible pain and sickness which was diagnosed as a kidney stone. I was fortunate and only off work for a week as the stone dispersed. When I was signed off by the doctor at his surgery he asked if I had found the stone and if so, bring it to him, sellotaped to a piece of card. Morbid lot, doctors. Always wanting anatomical souvenirs. Though what he could possibly want with my kidney stones baffled me completely. Probably he was building a rockery in his garden.

But when I returned from the doctor's I found the nice things were still happening. My mother had just had a visitor. 'Mr Parr, who you worked with at Kilburn,' she told me. It seemed that all the North London shops thought that I was in the intensive care unit and, knowing how mercenary some of my colleagues could be, no doubt had placed bets on how long I would last. It's funny how these rumours get exaggerated; almost like Chinese Whispers.

But there was a real surprise to come. Lionel Parr had called to let me know that 'Tinribs' had been moved back to Hounslow and that he would be managing Harrow instead. How my cup runneth over! Having worked with Lionel at Kilburn I knew that everything would be plain sailing.

And it was. We acquired another assistant from Watford; Mick Preen, a young man with a great sense of fun – almost too great sometimes. Mike Reynolds was moved to our Golders Green branch but the rest of us could run little old Harrow easily enough.

Mick seemed to attract a bevy of nubile young ladies. I could never understand it but nearly every day one of them would appear in the shop and ask, 'Is Mickey going to lunch soon?' It was altogether too much for me one day when a lady customer peered around the shop and enquired, 'Where's the good-looking one?'

'Madam,' I coldly retorted, 'there's nobody here who fits that description. We're all ugly.'

But there was a lot on the credit side for Mick. For a while we had a junior, David Meredith, who was a very strict Baptist. Needless to say he didn't approve of Mick and also complained about any 'strong language' used among the staff. He doubtless believed himself to be a good little Christian but one day something happened to see him and Mick in a different light.

An elderly lady slipped and fell outside the shop. Mick was out there instantly and helping her up. 'David,' he called out, 'bring a chair for this lady. She's badly shaken up.'

David Meredith merely looked down his nose, turned away and said, 'I don't want to be involved.'

I think that is the only time I saw Mick go ballistic. But it does give you food for thought. Happily Master David wasn't with us for long.

Yes, Mick was full of surprises. 'I just can't stand confrontation,' he confessed to me one day. 'No matter how rude a customer was to me, I wouldn't be able to stand up for myself.'

No doubt I murmured some vague words of consolation and went up to the bank to get some change for the till. And what did I see on my return? Mick standing in the shop doorway shouting, 'Get out! Get out and don't come back until you learn some manners!'

The object of his displeasure was an elderly, disgruntled, white-bearded man in a fur hat who slunk away, muttering.

'He used filthy language in front of a lady customer,' Mick explained, 'and I certainly wasn't going to stand for that!'

Saturday evening after work Lionel and I would 'lay the dust' with a quick drink at *The Havelock*. It was never a drinking session; neither of us wanted that. But it rounded the week off nicely and helped us to unwind.

From then on the months passed almost blissfully. We had another young assistant, Reggie Fowler, an amiable 'silly ass' type with an appetite equal to ten starving men. I've never seen anyone who could tuck away so much food as Reggie.

In the Autumn our day relief manager, Harry Coppins alias 'The Spangles Kid', retired. On his last day at Harrow we bought him a very elaborate table lighter as a retirement present. And just to make the occasion special we persuaded a young lady who worked in a nearby shoe shop to make the presentation which we photographed. The young lady – Coco we called her on account of her pale make-up and very red lipstick – was one of Mick's entourage. She entered into the spirit of the thing with great enthusiasm and planted a real smacker on Harry which pleased him no end. You don't see that sort of thing happen very often in a Dunn & Co shop, I mused. I hope he remembered to wipe the lipstick off before he went home to Mrs Coppins.

Sadly, only a few days later, my father passed away with a heart attack. It was quite unexpected and a terrible shock. Dunn's were very good about it and gave me the whole week off to sort out the funeral arrangements. No talk of lost work hours. They were a very compassionate firm. Lionel Parr and Mick Preen took time off to attend the funeral, a thoughtful gesture which I have never forgotten, and Arthur Hall, who had replaced Harry Coppins as our day relief manager, looked after the shop with Reggie Fowler. Dunn's were quite happy with this arrangement; they were that sort of firm.

I slid into 1973 almost without realising it. By then our annual holiday quota had been increased to four weeks and I would take a week in the Spring and Autumn and the other two in the Summer.

That Autumn Raymond North retired and we had a new Area Supervisor. Well, a new old one would be more appropriate. 'Jumping Jack' Flashman no less – and he hadn't changed a bit. Within weeks he had me jumping all over the West End.

'You have a choice, Mr Howard,' he informed me as if bestowing a great favour. 'Hounslow for a month or three weeks at Regent Street. Which is it to be?'

I opted for the latter. The journey to and from Hounslow by public transport would be horrendous. Mr Baines, whom I had first met at Oxford Street, was the manager and, as expected, there seemed to be staff everywhere, like myself, requisitioned from the suburban branches.

It sounds odd unless you have experienced it but in the heat of London's West End our best selling items were Harris Tweed jackets. American tourists loved them and they wouldn't just buy one; they would cough up for three or four. The basement stock room was packed solid with them. These Americans really made an occasion of shopping. One gentleman who had just purchased three dazzling checked jackets insisted that his wife should photograph me packing them up for him. So somewhere in Texas there is a snapshot of Yours Truly, much slimmer and darker-haired, wondering if this could lead to a summons to Hollywood.

Apart from this incident my time at Regent Street was uneventful except for an occurrence, which thankfully, did not involve me. 'Your neon sign's on fire!' a brightly-garbed American customer told us with that transatlantic touch of melodrama which we see so often in 'disaster' movies. 'Looks like the power's shorted and set fire to the wooden fascia!'

Thank goodness someone with intelligence had the sense to out the power but there was still the fire to worry about. Billy Boston, one of the senior staff, decided to take charge. He was a very camp, middle-aged little fellow with a blonde 'Beatle-style' toupee which did nothing for him but highlight his wrinkles. He obviously saw this crisis as his finest hour. With a junior helping, they seized the fire extinguisher and ladder and dashed outside to deal with the conflagration. Fortunately the fire was of no great consequence; just a bit of smouldering oak which would have died out on its own. But our intrepid heroes were not to be outdone. Billy scrambled up the ladder but the junior fumbled the extinguisher and set it off prematurely. The jet of foam hit Billy dead centre on his forehead and carried his toupee clean off his head, right over to *Swann and Edgar*'s on the other side of Regent Street.

'Gee!' gasped our American customer, almost reverently. 'I've heard of scalping back home but I bet it's never been done like that before!'

During my third week at Regent Street 'Jumping Jack' paid a visit. 'Still here, Mr Howard?' he squawked. Well that was a stupid thing to say as I was standing right in front of him and he had sent me to Regent Street in the first place. 'I'll telephone in the afternoon,' he added.

Good, I thought. Back to Harrow and no more packed lunches.

He did telephone in the afternoon – to send me to Oxford Street for two weeks before returning to Harrow. As it turned out Oxford Street wasn't so bad. The shop had been refitted since my last visit several years earlier and the basement was used for staff and storage areas. The regular manager was on jury service and a very laid-back relief manager was in charge. Also an old crony of mine from Harrow was on the staff there, Mike Reynolds from the Bertie Benson days.

Every lunchtime Mike and I would slope off down towards Tottenham Court Road and descend into one of those sub-surface, seedy little pubs which seemed delightfully wicked. There in the gloom we would sink a couple of pints and amble wearily back to the shop and try to stay awake until closing time.

On Thursday of the second week 'Jumping Jack' appeared in the shop. He didn't just walk in; that was too mundane. He was suddenly there as if teleported in. By the leery way he was looking at me while he was on the telephone I had a gut feeling that I was going to hear something not to my liking.

'Mr Howard,' he squawked, endeavouring to sound amicable which was quite a novel experience for me. 'I know I said you would be returning to Harrow next week but I would be grateful if you would do just one more favour for me.'

'Where to?' I challenged. I was beyond being intimidated. Probably my post prandial pints had given me Dutch courage.

'Piccadilly.'

'No,' I firmly replied. 'You said Regent Street and I've done that and ended up here at Oxford Street. Now you want me to go to Piccadilly.'

'Only for a week,' he temporised. This was a novelty; Jack Flashman actually wheedling. 'It will only be for the one week.' Then a new approach came to him. 'Is there any particular reason why you don't want to go to Piccadilly?'

This threw me; I had expected an argument. The old devil had learnt the art of subtlety. He took shrewd advantage of my hesitation. 'Is it Mr Miles, the manager?'

Goodness, he knew his men well. Yes it was Mr Miles, the manager. I had worked with Derek Miles before and he was one of those high-pressure, live-wire salesmen, forever chivvying his staff all the time. A favourite ploy of his was when you had just gone to lunch he would burst into the staff room, stare as if surprised at seeing you there and say, 'Oh, are you still at lunch? We're getting rather busy.'

The first time this happened I packed away my untouched sandwiches and went up to the shop floor and found it almost devoid of customers. This was just one of his little tricks. Another was to sneak down to the basement department via the interior spiral staircase which was an emergency fire exit to watch and listen while you were serving a customer. As with 'Tinribs' Karswell during his mercifully short sojourn at Harrow this practice is distinctly off-putting for both the customer and the salesman.

'Yes, it is the manager,' I reluctantly admitted in answer to Jack's question, 'but I don't want to make an issue of it. Just call it a clash of personalities.'

Somehow I knew I had lost the argument. Jack smiled, and a terrifying sight it was, too. 'Just leave it to me, Mr Howard. I'll telephone Mr Miles and tell him you've agreed to help him out for one week – and one week only. I promise you there will be no trouble. I well know the meaning of tact and discretion.'

And the next thing I heard him on the phone to Piccadilly demanding, 'Mr Miles, have you been browbeating Mr Howard?'

Oh, great! Thanks a bundle, Jack, I thought. You've really stitched me up good and proper. If that's your idea of tact and discretion, Heaven help us!

As it happened I didn't walk into a frosty reception the following Monday at Piccadilly. Derek Miles had the hide of a rhinoceros and there was very little that could offend him. But it wasn't an enjoyable week. The customers were mostly Scandinavians and all they seemed to buy were herringbone Harris Tweed jackets. Very boring. And what is more they were nearly all the same size; Long 44.

Thursday morning 'Jumping Jack' materialised. He didn't actually speak to me but I saw him talking to the manager and glancing in my direction a few times. I was quite 'shop-wise' by this time and guessed that there was something in the wind. And I was right.

'Mr Flashman mentioned your name,' Mr Miles said later that morning. 'He thought it might be worth considering that you stay here for the Christmas trade and the January Sale.'

At that point I went ape. I told him that the original arrangement had been for me to help out at Regent Street for three weeks but I had been coerced into following this up with two weeks at Oxford Street. Furthermore I had been hoodwinked into agreeing to a week at Piccadilly on the firm understanding that I would be returning to Harrow afterwards.

'What do you want to go back to that pokey little kiosk for?' sneered Mr Miles.

I told him. I told him in no uncertain terms that I'd had enough and I told him equally bluntly what he could do with his precious Piccadilly shop.

'Calm down, Mr Howard, calm down,' he replied. 'Look take an early lunch break. In fact, take an extra hour to cool off. Have a walk around the town and we'll discuss it further when you get back.'

A double lunch hour – from Derek Miles no less! This was definitely one for the book. I grunted an acknowledgement and descended to the nether regions of the shop and savaged my sandwiches. Then, taking the manager at his word, I escaped for the 'happy hour' and enjoyed a leisurely stroll around Regent Street and Piccadilly.

On my return to the shop, far from cooling down, I had another blazing row with the manager – and actually won it. I returned to Harrow the follow Monday. But all this fuss didn't seem to worry Derek Miles; he actually seemed to thrive on it. He certainly never bore me any grudge and you would have thought that we were the best of friends. He was one of those strange people who flourished and worked better under pressure and in an atmosphere of friction, and I wondered what planet he came from.

DEPARTURES AND ARRIVALS

Autumn 1973 ~ Spring 1974

Working locally at Harrow I found the beneficial factor of getting to know my customers – the nice ones as well as the awkward ones. Happily there weren't any really bad ones and the awkward ones fell into two categories; awkward/nice and awkward/nasty. But as I said we didn't have many of them.

I recall one family in the awkward/nice category where the mother used to make the first visit on behalf of her husband and son just to do a recce of our stock. This might take up to half an hour. A couple of days later the three of them would come in and spend an hour trying various garments on then go home and think about it. They would come in again the next day and, after another hour, make their selection. I was quite happy with this and they were charming people. After all, they were spending their money and had every right to take their time. I had the patience and I wasn't going anywhere until 5.30. Rudeness was another matter and thankfully rare. As one of our Area Supervisors commented some years later, nobody is paid enough to put up with outright rudeness.

I recall some of the nice/nice customers such as Mr Bailey. A young businessman who always had his suits made-to-measure. This was easy as he only needed a normal long fitting but with an extra two inches on the sleeves and trouser length. This was made up at the normal stock price because we quoted a standard stock size with minor adjustments, which pleased all parties concerned. Also, once you had his measurements on record it was simply a matter of 'the mixture as before'. And he would pay the full price on his first visit instead of leaving a deposit.

Another good customer was an aptly named Mr Friend. He lived out at Amersham and would come in once a year and restock his entire wardrobe. Apart from the business point of view the good thing about these customers was that you got to know them and – more importantly – they got to know you, and that way you could win their confidence. If we couldn't find them anything suitable we would never try to push them into something which they didn't really want. That isn't good salesmanship;

certainly not in the long term for a small shop with a limited catchment area. Trade had to be cultivated. Most of those books on sales psychology could be thrown out. These days every business is obsessed with targets – at any cost. I've always gone along with one golden rule; treat your customer as you would like to be treated yourself.

Another repeat order was for a Mr McMahon. Each year his wife would come in and order a repeat of the same hat and pay a deposit. All we had to do was look in the special order book for the previous order and simply send in a form stating, for example, please repeat Request Order No 12345. But one day it went all pear-shaped.

Head Office, on receiving one such order, telephoned us. 'Which particular hat is it?' they asked. Obviously they had lost the original details at their end and weren't going to admit it. Well it shouldn't have been too difficult. We would simply check backwards through our order book until we found the original one. It was quite a thick book and went back several years – and still we could only find back references. He must have been ordering the same hat for years!

There was nothing for it but to search through the archives which meant getting out the ladder and scrambling through a wooden hatchway above the shop's windows. The space there could be described as a very flat attic. I suppose 'flattic' would fit the bill pretty well. There was only about two feet of height to wriggle around in, well one foot eleven inches as the other inch was dust. With no little difficulty I wormed my way around clusters of dusty cardboard boxes, all containing ledgers and order books, probably dating back to the Battle of Hastings. I encountered several extremely polite spiders who got out of the way without a murmur of complaint regarding my invasion of their privacy and finally found the book I was looking for with the original details in it. After that it was simply a matter of notifying Head Office and updating the current order book with the required information. Of course, we could have contacted the customer and asked her to bring her husband's hat in for identification but it was a matter of professional pride. The wheels of retail had to be seen to run smoothly and without a hitch.

In the early Seventies credit cards were unheard of here and customers either paid by cash or cheque. Considering the lack of facilities for guaranteeing a cheque which we now have – an authorisation number to clear it – we had very few 'bouncers'. If a large sum of money was involved the customer usually had to wait for the cheque to be cleared.

But I came unstuck with one customer. One Saturday this middle-aged and quite respectable-looking man paid by cheque for a £6.00 cap. A few days later the bank returned the cheque. It had been stolen and this clever but naughty gentleman had made a killing in one afternoon using up the entire cheque book on a great number of modest purchases. We duly notified the police and an officer called at the shop for details and a possible description of the man. He then asked me if I would recognise him again and like a fool I said yes.

'Fair enough,' he announced, pocketing his notebook. 'We've got a young chap from a shoe shop up the road who thinks he can identify him, too. We'll be sending a car to take you both to Scotland Yard this afternoon.'

Well that was that. Me and my big mouth. I don't remember much about the other chap; he was quite unmemorable. We were driven up to Scotland Yard, led through a labyrinth of passages and offices and finally shown into what looked like a derelict classroom with a big table in the centre. My heart sank at the sight of a huge stack of photograph books. This would be even worse than looking at someone else's holiday snaps – and it was.

Putting myself in a more positive frame of mind I began to plough through book after book, the other chap doing likewise opposite me. I never realised there were so may villains in the realm. After a while my mental image of the man became vague. I had looked at so many faces that might – just might – have been him I could not be certain. 'Red-facing with protruding eyes' was all I could remember. But as the photos were monochrome that was fifty percent of my identification kicked into touch.

My companion handled the situation differently. Every so often he would yelp, 'This is the man!' and an officer would peer over his shoulder, shake his head and murmur, 'No, he's still inside' or 'No, he's dead.'

After a while they said he could go. He had obviously voiced so many false alarms that they realised his process of identification would be unreliable to say the least. That was where I had been going wrong. I had been too diligent. I knew that I had reached a stage where I could never put my hand on my heart and declare 'that's the man, officer.'

Nevertheless I decided to play the game right through to the last book. Then right at the last page I said, 'I'm pretty sure this could be him,' pointing to a blurred grey and black head-shape.

'No, it wouldn't be him,' replied the officer on duty after a brief scrutiny of my choice.

I was on the point of rising from my chair when he said, 'Never mind, I've got some more books you can look through.'

Thereupon he deposited half a dozen more sinister black tomes in front of me.

It was just over an hour later when they finally said I could go – needless to say without any success. I felt utterly mugshot-lagged. I had, in a manner of speaking, been face to face with every thief, murderer, conman and pervert in Britain. But on the credit side they did lay on a car to take me all the way back to Harrow, which is more than what they did for the shoe salesman who had to get a train back. I wonder if he managed to claim travelling expenses from his shop?

However securely entrenched I was at Harrow didn't apply to all of us. Mick Preen was moved back to Watford High Street and replaced by Gwyn Roberts from Edgware. Gwyn was a real joy to work with. Part Welsh, part Cornish, he looked like a Hobbit with his curly dark hair which seemed to start just above his bushy eyebrows. There was definitely a love-hate relationship between Gwyn and our Area Supervisor 'Jumping Jack' Flashman. They loved to hate each other but also there was a grudging mutual respect. Whenever there was a confrontation between them I'd swear I actually saw the hackles on Gwyn's neck bristle angrily, and his piercing gimlet eyes could look positively lethal.

That was the dark side of Gwyn but he had a more dominant lighter side. He was something of a clown and didn't know his own strength and on several occasions his skylarking had left me with the bruises to prove it. In stature he was short, but stocky and compact with it. He also had an eye for the fairer sex and would gaze through the glass shop door and mutter to himself – usually 'cor!' I even saw him steam the glass up in front of his face one day. He had a slight speech impediment which caused his voice to sound husky, as if it was just breaking. It would start off as a growl and finish almost castrato. The other embarrassing characteristic was when he got worked up. Not only would his speech go all over the sonic scale but he had a tendency to, well, dribble. One day when he was enthusiastically trying to sell a lady a raincoat for her husband, she asked, 'Is it waterproof?' Whereupon Gwyn, in his fervour to promote the selling points of the coat, gave a practical but accidental demonstration of its proofing qualities …

But his most endearing quality was his way with children. Tough rough Gwyn was truly an old softie and he would chat and play with any little kiddies who came into the shop with their parents.

The day before Christmas Eve 1973 the telephone rang. Instinctively I knew it was 'Jumping Jack' Flashman and just as instinctively I knew it would be something involving me. And I was right.

Lionel put the phone down, pointed at me and said, 'Keith – Wembley.'

I reacted at once with a knee-jerk response. 'Mr Parr – no!'

Poor old Lionel. His face dropped a mile. 'D'you mean it?' he murmured. 'Mr Flashman wants you to go there for the afternoon.'

I blew up. Who did he think I was? It was the day before Christmas Eve and I had my own shopping and a hundred and one other things to do. What really annoyed me was the short notice. If it had been put to me the day before I would have gone. I didn't blame Lionel but I thought it just as well to make a stand occasionally, if only to let them know that I wasn't simply switched off with the lights when the shop closed.

Lionel had the unenviable job of ringing Mr Flashman back and telling him that I refused to go and then I had to say my piece, but got away with just a few mildly reproachful words. In hindsight I think 'Jumping Jack' respected people who stood up to him. He had no time for 'yes men'.

Rolling into 1974 with no effort, Lionel, Gwyn and I worked together as a very happy team. Unfortunately as far as trade was concerned the year did not start off very well. After enjoying a profitable run for several years we found ourselves in a recession. Pressure finally got to Lionel and one day he took me aside and said that he was going to hand in his notice. He had applied for a job at Heathrow Airport and had been accepted, so that was that. I was sorry to hear this. Lionel, although some ten years older than me, had joined the firm on the very same day as I had twenty years previous.

The next thing we set our minds to was who would be the new manager of Harrow. Norman Hurst was favourite. Funny how we always put odds on old Norman. But as before it was not to be.

Our Golders Green shop had ceased trading and the manager, Victor Buckingham, was installed as the new manager of Harrow. I had worked with him before on my very first visit to Oxford Street and had been somewhat in awe of him. I think it was his grand manner and he gave the impression that he was the 'black sheep' of an upper middle class family and had been compelled to join the ranks of the 'retail peasants' in order to survive.

I was to find out later that it was only by the most freakish chance that he came to be working for Dunn & Co. At the time he had been living in 'digs' in Maida Vale and had decided to get a job with *Meakers*, a rival Gents' Outfitters. I mentioned earlier *Meakers* had two shops next door but one to each other in Kilburn, the middle unit being occupied by Dunn & Co. Mr Buckingham, like others before him, assumed the central doorway to be the main entrance of *Meakers*, entered and applied for a job. He was interviewed by 'Jumping Jack' and taken on as a West End assistant. And from what I was told I would have loved to be a fly on the wall during that interview.

'D'you play the violin?' Jack had squawked. 'Your hair's long enough to be a violinst.'

'Only if it is a Stradivarius,' Mr Buckingham had purred back.

Despite being of diminutive stature Victor Buckingham more than compensated for this by his very self-assured manner. He was so laid back

as to be almost horizontal and referred to himself as 'perfection in miniature'. It was easy to imagine this languid person with the drawling manner
of speech more suited to the Regency Period of the Nineteenth Century
rather than the present day. Not that he was stand-offish or difficult to get
on with but I had never worked with such a singularly vain creature before.

Gwyn got on with him quite well enough, but he could get on with
anyone except 'Jumping Jack'. Gwyn and I worked as equals and shared
the manager's holiday reliefs between us. Saturday after work we would
pop over to the *Greenhill Bar* situated over the Granada Cinema for a
convivial pint or two … or three. Vic, or 'Mr B' as we compromised on
calling him, was never in a hurry to go home. He had recently married and
lived in a bijou cottage in Elstree, and Joyce, his poor wife, must have had
the patience of a saint trying to work out what time he would be home for
dinner.

Then came the nationwide crisis which was known as the Three Day
Week. Electricity strikes, you name it. Everything was thrown into chaos.
Due to power cuts we often had to shut the shop early or rely on cheap
paraffin lamps to work by. These lamps would be condemned out of hand
as unsafe and I nearly had a terminal experience of this situation.

The shop had just been plunged into darkness. I had gathered the
paraffin lamps together on the shop table so that Vic could fill them. This
done, I struck a match to light the first one when Vic, who had neglected
to replace the cap on the paraffin can, dropped it on the floor and I found
myself standing in a rapidly spreading pool of paraffin with a lighted match
in my hand! The fact that I am here to tell the tale is proof enough that the
worst didn't happen, but it was a very near thing.

Another incident during the Three Day Week involved an unsought day
at our Piccadilly shop. 'Mr Flashman's on the phone,' Vic told me. 'He
wants you to help out at Piccadilly this Thursday. I explained that it is your
day off and he wants a word with you about it.'

I decided to play it with kid gloves after the previous episode and told
Jack quite truthfully that I had a Blood Doning session to go to in the
afternoon no later than 4.30.

I must have said the right thing. 'That's all right, Mr Howard,' he
squawked. 'I've got Mr Miles standing beside me and he'll let you go at
3.30.'

Well that seemed to be settled. I arrived at Piccadilly as arranged and all
went well as far as the morning was concerned. About noon there was a
power cut and the hit-or-miss emergency lighting came into operation.
Then about three in the afternoon Mac, the Assistant Manager, who was
as tolerable as the manger was intolerable, glanced at his watch. 'You'd

better get your skates on, Mr Howard,' he reminded me. 'It's just about three o'clock.'

Thanking him, I nipped downstairs and collected my hat, coat and briefcase. Then as I prepared to leave Derek Miles intercepted me. 'Where d'you think you're going, mister?'

'Blood Doning,' I retorted, sensing another whizz-banger of a row gather strength. 'Mr Flashman told you the arrangement.'

Miles scornfully waved this aside. 'We'll be closing at 4.30 because of this power cut.'

'And so will the Blood Doning session,' I pointed out, firmly donning my hat. 'Goodbye.'

'You can't go yet!' he persisted. 'Mr Hale and Mr Brooks have just arrived!'

Sure enough, two of our directors had just come through the door. 'Can't I?' I replied. 'Just watch my feet.'

And that was the last time I ever worked in Piccadilly or any of the West End shops.

Only a few weeks later there was a most unusual sequel to this incident. I had decided to take Mum out for the evening to see a film at the Grenada Cinema. It was *The Poseidon Adventure* and in retrospect it seems a very odd film to drag one's mother along to see. During the film she nudged me and whispered, 'That man in front of us hasn't stopped eating since he got in here. He's had an ice-cream, popcorn, and now he's got a bag of sweets.'

I grunted non-committedly. I was too busy watching Roddy McDowell plunge to his death down the waterlogged funnel of *The Poseidon*. During the interval when the lights went up Mum had another mutter. 'That man's dressed exactly like you. Look — he's just coming back with another ice-cream.'

I was wearing a light fawn elephant-cord belted safari jacket (well it was the Seventies!), brown polo-necked sweater and a pair of slim-cut dark brown trousers. The object of my mother's scrutiny was wearing exactly the same. He obviously shopped at Dunn's. Then my heart and stomach lurched as I glanced at his face. It was Derek Miles, the manager of Piccadilly!

Covered in outraged confusion and embarrassment, I tore off my light-coloured jacket and bundled it under the seat, hoping that my dark sweater would enable me to blend with the shadows, much to my mother's amusement. But the inevitable happened all too soon. Derek Miles happened to glance round and recognised me. 'Mr Howard!' he exclaimed. 'Hang on; I'll join you!' whereupon he quitted his seat and came and sat in our row, next to my mother.

Mum wasn't having that and changed seats with me – thanks very much! I was gutted; the wind blown completely out of my sails. It turned out his wife was having a 'hen party' and he had decided to get out of the way and visit the cinema.

But the worst ordeal was yet to follow. At the end of the programme Mr Miles and I emerged into the brightly-lit foyer looking like a couple of clones. I was totally mortified. Odd things are said about gentlemen who affect exactly the same mode of dress and I most certainly didn't want them said about me. My mother was completely unsympathetic and had utterly given herself up to the Muse of Mirth. Well, I reflected later, even if she didn't enjoy the film she had a damn good laugh afterwards.

COMPUTERS, CRANKS & COMEDIANS

Autumn 1974 ~ Autumn 1978

Several years earlier Dunn & Co had to acknowledge the hard facts of real life and join the rest of the High Street, or 'Marketplace' as they now say, and have Sales. These started with the January Sales but after a few years along came the Summer Sales and, in later years, mid-season sales and various promotions. One thing we still held dear to were our Clear Lines. These were items which were no longer in production and earned double the commission rate which was a pretty good incentive. A Clear Line ticket was marked with three crosses. Some firms called these line items 'Spiffs' but good old Dunn's were a law unto themselves and most reluctant to follow the herd.

Much the same could be said of their cash sheets. Plus amounts were always in red ink and deficits in black. And yet how often do we hear about businesses losing money and 'being in the red'? I have never been able to fathom out Dunn & Co's reasoning on that one. Perhaps they thought that red ink was a more cheerful colour.

Another stage in our evolution was the computer. There was some apparatus at Head Office which they had used for years called a comptom-eter. I never found out what this was but to me it had the onomatopoeic sound of something steam-driven.

Our computer was nothing like the slick software of the present day and it was mainly used for stock allocation. We all gave thanks that the Wages Department never got hold of it as it was a complete disaster. Our computer used punchcards; squarish and about 3" by 4" with the usual details printed on. This was for the benefit of we humans as they would mean nothing to the computer which read the varying formations of small perforations on each card. The punchcards varied in colour depending on the garment. Blue for hats, orange for caps, white for coats, pink for suits, green for jackets and yellow for trousers and waistcoats. Special factory orders were white with a pink stripe. At the end of trade each day the punchcards of sold items were posted to Head Office with a branch card attached by an elastic band, bearing the branch name and date. These were fed into the computer so that they could be deleted from our stock holding. Well that was the theory anyway.

But as we know, when the human factor is involved, theory becomes fantasy – especially where long-serving Dunn & Co staff were concerned. Men who still used fountain pens and looked askance at ballpoints as a cheap and shoddy gimmick. To ensure that the card would be fed quickly into the computer the right way up, each top left-hand corner was cut at an angle, so it was necessary to band the cards together with all corners correctly aligned. But certain shops did not understand this and got over the problem by cutting the left hand corner off with a pair of scissors whether they had been banded correctly or not. Still others could not get out of the habit of using the sales spike to impale the punchcards on which made a jolly mess of the perforations and it was anybody's guess as to what the computer made of that. This got 'Jumping Jack' Flashman foaming at the mouth and he would pounce on any sales spike he found, violently bend it double and hurl it into the wastepaper bin.

It was obvious that our first venture into computerisation was a bit shaky. The signs did not auger well as the saying goes and the final catastrophe came about one night at Head Office when the computer regurgitated every single punchcard of every single item in every single shop. It has to be also mentioned that we did not employ regular trained computer programmers at the time. Rumour had it that the programming was done by a van driver and two ladies from the cap factory.

For some months the firm licked its wounds and we returned to the old method of stock control. Then in the Summer of 1974 the firm got their act together and had another crack at it. This involved going in on a Sunday which was unheard of at Dunn & Co. The only other time I can recall this happening was back in 1962 when some purchase tax readjustment made it necessary to re-price every garment.

Vic, Gwyn and I, along with a 'happy camper' from Wembley, soon got the job done. All it involved was listing the price of each garment, reference name or number and size. We were out by noon in time for a pub lunch.

There's nothing like smooth running to make your job fun. We still nipped over to the *Greenhill Bar* for a drink on Saturday but these sessions tended to drag out a bit more than they needed to. Vic was the culprit; he never hurried anything, Gwyn was engaged to be married so he had a social life to consider. But our regular appearance at the *Greenhill Bar* every Saturday obviously attracted other regulars which meant that our little group of three would be five or six instead.

Gwyn's Stag Night was something to remember – if only I could remember it clearly. I know I went back with Vic to his home in Elstree beforehand for dinner and then on to a pub in Arkley. No drivers should have been drinking that night, especially as it was very foggy. I would have been happy to have curled up and gone to sleep as Vic is very strong on dinner wines – and only an hour later I was quaffing ale with Gwyn and several others.

A darts match was suggested which I tried to duck out of. But after one turn it was unanimously decided that it would be safer for everyone in the bar if I kept away from the darts. I don't blame them; I felt very odd indeed. Then it was into the cars and back to Gwyn's home at Edgware. Someone suggested a fish and chip supper; a suggestion I didn't relish, but somehow I got through it without any mishap and was given a lift home.

About this time Mr Flashman, on one of his visits, took me to one side. I didn't fancy what I was going to hear one little bit. Probably another marathon tour of the West End or even some posting to a provincial branch which would have entailed living in 'digs'. But it was neither of these things.

'Mr Howard,' began 'Jumping Jack' in his usual breezy, no-nonsense way, 'what are your views on management?'

That was one thing I hadn't thought of. I decided, knowing what a canny beggar he was, not to give him any of what is politely termed 'bullshine' but tell him the truth. 'Well, Sir,' I began, 'I really feel that I would be doing both the firm and myself more of a service as a senior assistant.'

'I'm very pleased to hear you say that, Mr Howard,' I was surprised to hear him say. 'Too many young men assume the mantle of responsibility which is not suited to them. I fully approve of and respect your attitude.'

So you see there was more to 'Jumping Jack' than being a hectoring tyrant. Good managers were born and not made. They need to have a little bit of the 'killer instinct' and I, whether it be good or bad, was always more ready to see the good side of a person. And I couldn't give an order to save my life. Once in a while you got an exception like good old Bertie Benson, but when they made him they broke the mould.

Not long after Gwyn's marriage he was frequently moved to other branches, usually Wembley, which left Vic and I running Harrow. We did have the odd transient junior helping us now and again but really we managed to get on better without them. One dreamy character whom I'm sure was narcoleptic, had only to sit down and he would fall asleep.

Some Saturdays when there were only the two of us Vic dealt with the situation quite positively. At noon he would lock the shop door, hang up a notice saying 'Re-open at 1 o'clock' and we would both have our lunch hour in peace and quiet. In any case I had got into the habit of taking my lunch with me on Saturdays as I could record the morning's sales in the staff room which helped to save time in the evening.

It soon became evident that Gwyn was finding things difficult. His wife was one of those people who wanted the best of everything at once if not yesterday, never mind the expense and poor old Gwyn was flogging himself to death trying to make ends meet. He applied for management but was offered nothing. To be fair this was obviously because there were no openings available at the time and no reflection on his capabilities. He was a good book-keeper and a first class salesman. He didn't care for display work much but neither did many of our managers. In desperation he applied for a transfer to our Kettering branch. He had the chance of a new home there which would be cheaper than where he was living in Edgware. All to no avail. There were no vacancies at Kettering. Sadly it came to the crunch and Gwyn left, moving to Kettering where he got a job as a milkman. He still kept in touch though, and came to Harrow for a festive drink just before Christmas.

The Christmas of 1976 was a hoot as far as convivialities were concerned. It was decided that the staff from Harrow, Wembley and the two Watford shops would meet at a pub called *The Fisheries* near Aldenham reservoir and go on for a meal at a restaurant called *The Old Barn*. Just imagine the scene. All the regulars are having a quiet drink when half a dozen cars pull up outside and about fourteen men in dark hats and coats suddenly appear. They must have thought that 'The St Valentine's Day Massacre' was about to be re-enacted, especially after one glance at John Greer the manager of Watford Parade. He was a dead ringer for Reggie Kray!

The dinner at *The Old Barn* really lived up to the name of the place. It was just like having dinner in an old barn! The place was gloomy and cold and the food much the same. To add insult to injury, as we finished our meal they closed the bar!

Emotions ranged from anger to panic. Never in the history of a Dunn & Co gathering had anyone been faced with a 'dry' evening. Then Mickey Preen had a bright idea. 'I know where we can go,' he announced. 'Just follow my car.'

We all piled into our respective vehicles and drove off into the night along the motorway – and found ourselves at a ghastly little transport café at Scratchwood. Mickey's idea of a drink was a cup of coffee which tasted suspiciously of petrol and judging by the rainbow tints among the bubbles where the fluorescent light caught it, I had a strong feeling that the kitchens were located very near to the petrol pumps.

The New Year was quite a milestone – or landmark depending on your perspective. Not only was 1977 the Jubilee Year, it was the year that Dunn & Co ventured into other items of clothing. We now stocked shirts, ties and shoes. Alas, we also 'stocked' a new junior assistant, Mark Abbott, who nearly drove me mad. Thin, fair and lanky, he was his own fan club. The term 'all mouth and trousers' springs to mind. He just couldn't keep his mouth shut for more than five seconds and his inane and often insulting prattle would have made a saint swear.

One day I'm ashamed to say it really reached the limit and I just snapped. 'Just shut up that bloody stupid row!' I screamed at him. The shop fell silent; more so than it had done for weeks. But it did the trick.

'Well I must concede that your outburst got results,' Vic grudgingly admitted, from which I gather he didn't approve of my shock tactics.

But the real showdown was yet to come. The 'Saturday drinkies' as Vic termed it still took place after work every Saturday. I had become disenchanted with the routine. For one thing there were about half a dozen of us. And that odd custom of each taking a turn to buy a round of drinks was too much. One pint I was happy with; two I could comfortably manage but three I didn't enjoy. Also some of the hangers-on would want scotches which meant an expensive round.

The other reason I ceased to enjoy these sessions was they went on too long. Getting home at 8.30 for a meal I didn't really want wasn't my idea of relaxing. It was too early to call it a day and too late to start anything else.

One evening I had just downed my third unwanted pint when 'Mouth Almighty' Mark Abbott plonked a brimming pint pot down in front of me. 'Drink that,' he said.

'I've had my quota, Mark,' I replied. 'Thanks very much.'

He towered over me, 'I said drink it!' he snapped.

'And I said I don't want it!' I roared back, getting up and staring nose to nose at him.

I don't know what the outcome would have been if Ken the barman hadn't intervened to pour oil on troubled beer. But as far I was concerned that was the end of 'Saturday drinkies'.

Other changes came about that year. Raymond North had retired as had Mr Pedrick our Managing Director. The Chairman, Mr Butterworth, had ascended to that throne. We also had a new Area Supervisor, 'Jock' Finch, a sharp-tongued Scottish gentleman. We didn't have the dubious pleasure of him for long as he was spirited away to Head Office, promoted to Sales Director and replaced by Mr Mayne. I always found Jimmy Mayne an easy man to get along with. He never did me a bad turn and I never gave him cause for complaint.

With the arrival of the Winter stock we found that we were hard pressed to find room for the fur hats in the drawers and shelves so we arranged them in a corner of the counter by the cash office. Bearing in mind a science fiction film that was currently around plus an idea I had been dying to try out I just had to wait until a customer asked if we had any Winter hats. 'Yes, Sir,' I replied. 'On the closed end counter – of the furred kind.'

I should have saved my breath – probably too subtle.

In 1978 our staff strength was doubled by another senior assistant and part-time junior, Bobby Stevens, whose father had managed our Liverpool Street shop. Bobby was a nice little chap and a good worker with a quiet but cheerful manner. He was of slight build with a mop of curly black hair and a welcome replacement for the previous junior, Mark Abbott. He also did me a very good turn by re-recording a great number of my audio tapes onto more reliable cassettes, a task that took several months.

Bobby wasn't with us for very long afterwards and really surprised us all by becoming a Police Cadet. Some year later I met him. No more the slim little lad with the cherubic smile. Now he was a brick wall of a man, taller than me and a damn sight fitter looking, with a fierce black moustache and a voice so deep it must have come from his boots. Goodness knows what they feed them at the Hendon training school. Also he was sporting Sergeant's stripes on his sleeve and told me that he was in line for promotion to becoming a Police Inspector. Thinking back to those earlier days, who would have thought it.

I could have done with Bobby on hand one day in the Spring of 1978 when Vic was on holiday. There was just one other assistant at the time; Phil Ansell from Ealing, when in came this belligerent character, complaining about a hat Vic had sold him the previous week which had shrunk in the rain.

Without doubt the man had a legitimate grievance as it was a cloth hat and, to make matters worse, a small shape which was unsuitable for a man of his stature. Vic had obviously 'flogged' it to him. The customer demanded a felt hat in exchange and I tried to explain that I couldn't hand out a new hat without it being authorised by Head Office. He demanded a new hat straight away so I said that in the circumstances I would short-cut the system, ring Head Office and see if I could get anything done about it.

I had just got through to Complaints Department when a pair of strong hands seized me by the throat and dragged me out of the office. 'Ye bloody sneak!' be bellowed. 'Phone the police, would ye?'

'Let me go, you stupid prat!' I choked. 'I'm phoning Head Office!'

I had dropped the telephone receiver and Phil, not wishing to be involved, had taken refuge in the staff room. Still the mad strangler did his level best to choke the life out of me.

At last I managed to get free. The telephone was squawking in panic, 'Mr Howard! Are you all right?' I seized it and panted down the receiver, 'The bloody idiot's tried to wring my neck!'

'Give him a new hat, Mr Howard!' the reply almost shouted back. 'Get him out of the shop!'

I gave him a new hat and he had the temerity to offer his hand to me – one of the pair that had nearly choked the life out of me. 'Here's your hat,' I told him. 'Now clear off.'

Many years later I saw him in Harrow with his wife. Some impish impulse urged me to say hello as we passed in the street. He just stared at me owlishly, not remembering me but his wife, out of natural curiosity, asked, 'Do I know you?'

'Probably not,' I smiled back, 'but your husband tried to strangle me in 1978. Good day.'

The other member of staff who joined our ranks that year was David Hopton from the Strand. This was something of a surprise as it was the very same David Hopton whom I had met on my first day at work all those years ago when he was based at Wembley. Mr Mayne explained that Dave had asked to be transferred somewhere nearer home. He had a progressive eye problem and found travelling difficult. To his credit Mr Mayne asked if I had any objection to him working at Harrow which I thought very considerate, myself being only 'rank and file'. When I asked him why he thought I might object, he said that he wondered if I might not be happy about the commission being split for a third member of staff. Well it always had been when Gwyn was with us and Dave was Dunn & Co through and through. The only objection I could think of was that, with another staff member at Harrow the firm might take it into their heads to send me to all points of the compass at a moment's notice.

'That won't happen, Mr Howard,' Mr Mayne assured me. 'As far as I am concerned this is still a two-man shop; yourself and Mr Buckingham. Mr Hunter has been moved here for health reasons as he is unable to travel.'

And he was as good as his word. Not once during the time that Jimmy Mayne was our Area Supervisor did he move me – not even for the odd day at Wembley.

Working with Dave Hopton was quite an experience and it is strange to reflect that although I had known him since 'Day One' we had never worked together. Despite his serious eye problem his book work was faultless and meticulous. Being aware of his disability he took more care. Also he was a good Salesman and had a knack of 'slowing down' a sale to a pace he could cope with.

As for the question of commission, we were allowed to work out our own system. In many shops – certainly the West End – it was every man for himself which could make it a very cut throat business. We opted for the pooled system which was quite simple. In all our branches the managers got 'house commission' whether they sold anything or not. This was fifty percent plus anything he sold himself. The other fifty percent was divided equally between the staff. The only way this system could be abused was if a member of staff was not pulling his weight, and in a shop like Harrow it was much fairer. For instance I might have to go to the bank, post office or the alteration tailor's when they might have a real belter of a day's trade at the shop and which I otherwise would have missed out on. But there never was any problem about commission as we all pitched in.

The thing that struck me most about David Hopton was his sense of humour. He was slightly built and walked with a stoop. His speech was as slow as his movements and he would peer through those thick bottle-bottomed glasses, twitch his unkempt and straggly moustache then utter some unique – and often quite profane – observation. He could find his way around the shop without too much trouble because he knew where everything was.

But one Saturday while I was having my lunch break in the staff room I heard Dave greet a customer. 'A jacket, Sir? Yes, our Harris Tweed jackets are in the Sale. The normal price is £79.99 but they've come cerrashing down to £59.99. If you'll just follow me.'

Then came a mighty crash – and it wasn't a Harris Tweed jacket. A chair had been moved from its accustomed place and poor old Dave hadn't seen it. Undaunted, I heard him say, 'I'll be with you in a moment, Sir, when I've finished falling over the furniture.'

Another time one of those bright and somewhat arrogant young men who were known as yuppies strutted into the shop. Ignoring Dave's polite greeting, he brushed past him, executed a swift tour of the shop, then announced, 'see-uits! I'm thinking about see-uits!'

Dave fixed him with a myopic glint and stroked his ratty moustache. 'Yes,' he murmured, 'and they've been thinking about you, too, Sir.'

Dave's sense of humour was unique. It wasn't simply just dry; it was bizarre. One day a new consignment of hats arrived. They were very distinctive, Tyrolean style with ornate feathers in the bands and the soft, green velvety felt had a silky sheen, enhanced with fine red, gold and purple threads woven through the felt. Not risking climbing up the front of the fixture to place the hats on the top shelf, Dave got the ladder out and, at his usual snail's pace, ascended the ladder and proceeded to put the hats away. There he stood at the top with one of these hats in his hand, utterly unaware that a customer had entered the shop and stood at the foot of the ladder.

'This hat's beautiful,' Dave crooned. 'It's beautiful. I think I'm in love with it.'

The customer looked at me with a mixture of amazed amusement, then put a finger to his lips, signalling me not to speak. He also had a sense of humour.

'I want to marry this hat,' Dave droned on. 'I want it to bear my children.'

Neither the customer nor I could hold back our laughter. Dave, completely unflustered, gazed down at us. 'Did I say something funny?' was his only comment.

About that time not only had 'Jumping Jack' Flashman retired but also the Staff Director 'Long John' Neville. I always felt a bit sorry for him. He was an aloof man who wanted to be accepted but didn't know how to relate to other people. The suspicion that he was just a figurehead of authority without any practical function was verified by the fact that he was not replaced. Poor old 'Long John' was just a sinecure.

Apart from staff changes we had seen quite a succession of alteration tailors. Joe Weiss was with us through the early Seventies and I always chuckle about one of the last times I saw him. Arriving at his flat in Kenton to collect something for a customer, I was shown upstairs to his workroom by his wife who was as placid as he was excitable; a slightly plump middle-aged lady with silver hair and a kind and friendly disposition. She was helping out with some sewing when the telephone rang.

'Who is it?' Joe asked when she returned.

'Oh, just Miriam,' replied his wife. 'She rang to ask about the baby.'

I was stunned. 'Mrs Weiss,' I blurted out. 'I didn't know! Congratulations! Is it a boy or girl? Have you decided on a name yet?'

Mrs Weiss blushed. 'No,' she laughed. 'It's my granddaughter.'

Joe glared at me from his ironing board. 'You cheeky young sod!' he declared.

'Oh, I don't know, Joe,' murmured Mrs Weiss, returning to her sewing with a strangely enigmatic little smile. 'I think it's rather nice.'

'You can take that look off your face,' Joe retorted. He thrust the newly-pressed trousers at me. 'And you can clear off before she starts getting broody.'

After Joe Weiss there were several local tailors until one actually opened up a shop beneath my flat and on the face of it the arrangement seemed good. Every Saturday evening I would take the alterations home in a case the firm supplied specifically for alterations. This was a cumbersome affair but made of some lightweight metal alloy. I would drop the alterations in on the way to work Monday morning and collect them as they were due during the week. That was the theory but that tailor wasn't the quickest of workers. Also he and Vic Buckingham didn't get on and after a few months the arrangement was terminated.

Our next tailor was one who had done Vic's work when he was managing Edgware. Morrie Cohen was probably the most scruffy tailor I had ever set eyes on but that seemed to be the normal thing with that particular calling. The more untidy they were, the better their work.

Morrie was well past retirement age but that detail was academic. He collected and delivered the work every Monday, Wednesday and Saturday. He would prowl into the shop with all the bearing of an alley cat in a disreputable light-coloured shortie raincoat. His grey hair was almost Biblical in length and a pair of severe, very executive-looking glasses rested on a jutting nose which looked more like a miniature battering ram. And somehow a wild-looking grey moustache managed to flourish beneath this formidable edifice.

But what he lacked in appearance Morrie more than made up for in character. He was in every sense a gentle man and had a quietly wry sense of humour. 'Would you like a cup of tea, Mr Cohen?' I would ask. To which he would reply, 'Yes please, but only half a cup. The top half.'

He was also a devotee of Beethoven and his wife always made sure he took an extra handkerchief if he went to a Beethoven concert as he would inevitably be moved to tears.

One Wednesday he slunk in to the shop with his bundle of alterations, dumped them on the table and shook them out of the bag. Something fell on the floor with a soggy plop. This was one of the few times I had ever seen Victor Buckingham lost for words. 'What the hell's that?' he spluttered.

Morrie glanced down at the offending object. 'Oh, that?' he replied off-handedly. 'The wife's plum cake.'

That was Morrie all over. Another time he phoned Vic up in a panic. 'I've made a terrible mistake with those two pair of trousers you wanted shortening, Mr Buckingham. I've shortened them to fourteen inches instead of twenty-eight. What are you going to do about it?'

'More to the point, Mr Cohen,' Vic suavely replied, 'what are *you* going to do about it?'

Poor old Morrie had to cough up for two pairs of trousers but I did console him by reminding him that he had two pairs of very good quality Bermuda shorts, even if the material was a bit on the thick side. But how did he come to make such an error? He had been listening to a Beethoven concert on the radio. Enough said.

Vic thought it might be a good idea if I took the work home with me on Saturday and Morrie, who was always to and fro through Harrow, could pick up the alterations from my home on Sunday. Happily this arrangement didn't last long. Morrie was one of those people who go to bed with the chickens and rise with the dawn chorus. At 7.45 on Sunday morning the doorbell was violently assaulted, rousing me from my slumber so suddenly that I suffered a nervous trauma. Donning my dressing gown, I made my way very unsteadily downstairs and opened the front door. There was nobody there. A bit early for practical jokes, I thought as I struggled back upstairs. Then just as I reached the top the doorbell pealed forth again. Back down I went and opened the front door. Still no one there. This time I ventured out on the step and took a squint along the road. There was Morrie Cohen, fighting a one-handed battle with a newspaper rack outside the newsagent's because he was too lazy to take his other hand out of the pocket of that terrible shortie raincoat.

'I rang before,' he told me, looking slightly outraged that I should still have been abed.

'Yes, I heard you,' I retorted, thrusting the bag of alterations into his arms. 'See you Wednesday – at the shop.'

I think he took the hint and the Sunday service ceased to be.

Yes, Dunn & Co had its fair share of characters both sides of the counter and I wouldn't have missed it for the world. I recall reading an interview in one of the daily papers concerning Mr Pedrick when he retired from his exalted position of Managing Director. One thing which stuck in my mind was the comment which the lady journalist had made about our shops which I found as amusing as it was true. 'On entering a Dunn & Co shop,' she had written, 'one is immediately aware of an atmosphere of dozy serenity.'

Well that summed them up and was most likely the reason I stayed with the firm.

THE NEW BROOM

Autumn 1978 ~ Winter 1983

The 1970s saw a number of changes in Dunn & Co. Probably the one which stands out most of all was the abolition of half-day closing. This was instigated by the departmental stores and supermarkets and most businesses had no choice but to follow suit. The only shops which retained the early closing day were jewellers, who had to clear their window display each night and re-dress them the next day; they opted to close for one weekday. Also small private businesses where they had limited staff cover.

At Dunn's we simply staggered our days off. Vic, the manager, had Tuesday, I had Thursday and Dave had Friday. Arthur Hall covered for Vic's day off until 1980 when yet another rule was relaxed and I was allowed to assume the mantle of day relief manager for Harrow. Poor old Arthur. He told me that before he moved to his digs in Bushey he had lodgings in Oxhey for a couple of weeks. The landlady apologised for not having the time to prepare his room and told him that if there were any unwanted bits and pieces lying around he could feel free to dispose of them. Arthur, being extremely tidy, did so.

Some months later when he had moved to Bushey he ran into one of his fellow lodgers from Oxhey who asked him if he had seen a little man in a straw hat and alpaca jacket wandering about the place when he was at Oxhey. Arthur hadn't and asked about it, only to learn that a doctor who had been the previous tenant of his room, but had since died, fitted the description.

'He was cremated and wanted his ashes buried in the back garden,' came the explanation. 'What with one thing and another we never got around to it. But now we can't find his ashes and it seems that he is haunting the place.'

Poor Arthur. He didn't admit it but he remembered a small cardboard box with grey dust in it which he consigned to the dustbin. And even more, I think he regretted telling us about it because it was all round the North London Branches within a week; the Haunted Dustbin of Arthur

Hall. Normally a placid man, the one thing which was guaranteed to get his back up was to ask him if there was anything interesting in his dustbin.

Another innovation was the introduction of the Request Order Book. Previously customers' orders were noted in a book and on Monday morning it was quite a marathon getting them sorted out after a busy Saturday. That was usually my job and it often took almost the entire morning to complete.

I had my own system. I would go through the order book and sort out the orders in their various categories; suits, hats, jackets, etc and then telephone each department at Head Office. If they had the item to hand it would be in our next delivery. If they hadn't, which frequently was the case, they would give me a list of branches which were showing the required item on their stock. The next step would be to cross-reference the items where possible. For example, they might say that our Birmingham shop had a suit we wanted and they might also have been put forward for another of our request items. Two birds with one stone. Eventually I would work my way through the lists and noted the sending branches down in the order book but it was a long and arduous business.

The new system was simpler; a book with four carbonised copies. The top white copy would be posted to Head Office with the second and third blue and yellow copies while the fourth white copy stayed in the book for the branch records. The blue copy was then returned, advising us of the sending branch and the yellow copy was sent to that branch instructing them to transfer the required item to us. At least it must have cut down the telephone bills.

Yet another change was the relaxing of rules regarding dress. We were still required to wear a suit but no stiff white collar. Pastel toned shirts were acceptable but the biggie was the hats – or lack of them. Nothing was ever put into print but we were no longer compelled to wear the Sacred Hat. A far cry from the early days when we had to put our hats on just to go out and look at the shop window.

The reason for this was obvious. Hats were in gradual decline. Current hairstyles among the younger generation were taking their toll ever since the days of the Beatles when the teenagers started to grow their own hats! Also cars were having a detrimental effect too. More people than ever owned a car and that vehicle dramatically effected men's clothing more than we thought it would. Not only was it unnecessary to wear a hat in a car but the same applied to overcoats. True, we still sold hats and over-coats but not to the same extent. Even so, I personally regretted this and felt that a hat made a nice finish to the appearance.

But there was a bigger shock in the late Seventies and it was a very sad one. Since Gwyn Roberts had left the firm in 1976 and moved to Kettering he kept in touch with us and we would all meet up for a drink just before Christmas when he came down to visit his parents. Then in December 1978 he phoned to say that he wouldn't be able to make it as he was working as a bus driver on a seven day week shift until the New Year. A week later his family telephoned to say that he had died. Whether it was a heart attack or cerebral haemorrhage I do not know, but he was found unconscious in a telephone box.

It hit me hard as Gwyn and I had been great mates but it didn't seem to affect Vic Buckingham. He was a cold fish in many respects and only believed in himself. And as far as religion was concerned he didn't believe in anything.

But there was one occasion which shook his air of superiority and really brought the house down. We had a contract with the Kodak Recreation Centre, supplying the stewards who worked in the bar with lightweight cream jackets. One day an order arrived and Vic telephoned Kodak to advise them that their order was ready to be collected. 'Good afternoon, madam,' I heard him say. 'I now have your bar stewards' jackets to hand.'

Then he went pink and started stuttering. Evidently the young lady on the other end had misheard 'bar stewards' and put the worst interpretation on it. Well Dave and I thought it was funny even if it did ruffle Vic's fine feathers.

Towards the end of the Seventies Dunn's brought out the safari suit; a far cry from Dunn's traditional merchandise. These were very elegant garments and the jackets and trousers could be sold separately or together like a suit on a 'mix and match' basis which made everything so much easier from the size point of view. There were three colours; stone, lovat green and blue. The stone was a sell-out as we knew it would be and the lovat green sold quite steadily. But the blue was an utter no-no. We weren't at all surprised. For one thing the blue was neither light nor dark; it was an odd mauvish, mid-powder blue. Also the pointed pocket flaps were too military in design. It looked like a cinema attendant's uniform.

Then one day a young lady came into the shop enquiring about the sartorial Cinderella. She worked for an engineering firm and was looking for a uniform for their representatives to wear when they went abroad. And her firm's logo was of the same peculiar blue as these suits.

It was a gift from the gods. One jacket and two pairs of trousers would be needed for each rep. How many could we supply? It worked beautifully. We didn't even have to sell them. At the end of each month Vic would send in a bill and we would get a four-figure cheque back by return of post. And a sum like that was quite a fortune in those days.

For several months all went smoothly. There were any amount of the jackets at Head Office and gathering dust in the other branches, but the crunch came when we put an order in for more trousers. 'Be reasonable, Mr Buckingham,' grumbled Mr Cranshaw the Director in charge of the Trouser Department. 'You've had your allocation of those trousers for the year. I've got the other branches to think if.'

'But they're not selling them,' Vic pointed out.

'That's not the issue,' the other voice huffed and puffed down the phone. 'We have to plan ahead for the Sale.'

And that was that. No more trousers and the contract fizzled out. And to add insult to injury all those unsold trousers had to be reduced to a knock-down price to clear them. All due to the empty rattling of tin gods.

But there was one more explosive incident during the Winter Sale of January 1981. A directive from Head Office stated that we were not to send in request orders for the first three weeks of the Sale. For Harrow this was bad news. We were a small shop and couldn't carry anything like the volume of stock held in other branches. Then Vic hit on a compromise. 'We can still take the orders,' he decided. 'We simply explain to the customer that there will be a delay of a couple of weeks or so but they will still get their orders at sale discount.'

The customers were quite happy with this and, for the most part, appreciated the situation. Also we found it paid to check through the stock deliveries each week as a requested item would frequently turn up quite by chance.

At the end of the three weeks Vic sent in the 'frozen' orders but even he was knocked sideways when we counted them out. There were one hundred and twenty of them! Mentally crossing ourselves, we sent the weighty package off to Head Office and waited for the explosion. It came the next day – Jock Finch the Sales Director – in full spate. No wonder Hadrian built that wall.

He was almost screaming down the phone but Vic, to his credit, kept his cool. 'You never said anything about not taking any orders,' he calmly pointed out. 'We explained the situation to our customers and they are quite willing to wait.'

More Caledonian splutterings down the phone. 'As you have taken these request orders we are duty bound to honour them,' came the vindictive response. 'However, I have noted each and every one of these items you have requested and I want a written and truthful account of the actual items sold in three weeks' time. Also your branch is banned from using the request order system for a month!'

This last bit sounded rather childish, virtually cutting off the nose to spite the face, but we had no choice but to abide by it. Indeed, I wondered if we were all working for the same firm.

At the end of the three weeks we were gratified to find that ninety percent of the request orders had been purchased, so I typed out a very official-looking and detailed letter to that effect, noting each individual sale which they could check with their computer records. Also, just to cock a snook at them, I listed the introduction sales which had been made by those orders which amounted to something like seven hundred pounds. That we had proved our point was without question as we never heard another word from Head Office on the matter.

But the chuckles were still happening at Harrow. Just opposite our shop was a splendid church with a picturesque array of trees. On a windy day many of the leaves would be blown into our doorway. The problem was that these leaves often carried little many-legged visitors with them who found the warmth of our shop – and clothing – quite suited to their taste.

One Saturday I was showing a suit to a customer when a 'daddy-long-legs' or harvest spider scampered out from inside the jacket. The customer's wife screamed. 'It's all right,' I reassured her, thinking on my feet. 'He's only after the flies on the trousers.' Even so, they didn't buy the suit.

Then there was the time when Vic had to have all his teeth out. I think he had gingivitis which effects the gums. The next day he turned up, very self-conscious of his new dentures. Knowing that, being a vain person, he would be extremely sensitive about this, I was reluctant to enquire about his well-being. But I knew I had to say something so as not to appear unsympathetic, so I couched my enquiry in 'Vic-speak' but probably overdid it. 'Mr B,' I ventured, 'did you experience any degree of post-extraction discomfort?'

He glared at me. 'If you mean did it hurt – yes, it bloody well did!' he snapped.

Another instance involved a good example of knowing or remembering a customer. One Saturday a youngish couple came into the shop and asked me to order some item of clothing which we didn't have in stock. 'Certainly,' I complied. 'Mr Royston, isn't it?'

I have never liked the expression but the man looked utterly gobsmacked. 'How do you know my name?' he squeaked. 'I've never been in this shop before!'

'But you used to shop at our Wembley branch, Mr Royston,' I calmly replied.

Another squeak. 'But that must be twenty years ago!'

'Twenty-one to be precise,' I smiled back. 'We like our customers to feel that they are individuals.'

Mr Royston couldn't get over it. Never have I been treated with such awe and respect by a customer. But if he had known the reason I remembered him he wouldn't have been so happy.

On that occasion at Wembley he was a teenager, and a very spoilt one at that. Mummy had brought him in to be measured for a suit and because it needed a slight adjustment to the sleeve length he stamped and screamed like some spoilt brat throwing a nursery tantrum. No, Mr Royston most certainly would not have been happy if I had elaborated further.

But that Summer brought about another change; a reshuffle of Area Supervisors. Out went Jimmy Mayne and in his place a Mr Ferris. I never did know his first name and wouldn't have been at all surprised to discover that he didn't have one. Mind you, we had our own names for him and pretty unrepeatable they were too. And he merited every one of them.

He was definitely 'a new broom', and he even looked like one; a thin, pale stick of a man. Youngish, bespectacled and with about as much personality as a plank of wood. In fact Dave nicknamed him 'The Plank'. On his first visit to Harrow and disregarding the fact that Harrow was officially classed as a two-man shop on account of Dave's disability, he had the temerity to send me to manage our Holloway shop for one day. As Vic pointed out to him, 'If you want to get on the right side of Mr Howard, you're going the wrong way about it.'

That day was a scorcher. It was an awkward journey, involving Willesden Junction High Level to Camden Road and a bus past Holloway Prison. The shop was dismal and the young assistant a rather effeminate youth and I was only too glad to sweat and puff my way home at 5.30.

'The Plank' even managed to upset Dave Hopton. He made a visit one day when a stock delivery had just arrived and started tearing the parcels open to see what stock we had received. Dave blew his top. 'What the hell d'you think you are doing?' he declared. 'All this stock has to be checked in before you start throwing it all over the place!'

After Jimmy Mayne's consideration of not moving me from pillar to post 'The Plank's' tactics were a complete reversal.

One Summer's day – it happened to be Vic's day off – 'The Plank' phoned and told me that I was to manage Wembley from the following Monday for an indefinite period as the manager there was covering for the West End shops for the Summer holidays.

'I can't do that,' I replied. 'I'm managing Harrow then while Mr Buckingham is on holiday.'

'Are you sure about that?' came the reply.

'Yes, you gave Mr Buckingham those holiday dates yourself.'

A short but venomous silence followed. 'I'll ring you back,' he snapped, and hung up.

As good as his word he phoned back half an hour later. 'I've got someone else to relieve Harrow,' he told me, 'so you will be going to Wembley as planned.'

It was sad to see how Wembley had gone down over the years. Trade or lack of it plus staff shortages had caused all stock from the various departments to be crowded in a mass of running rails on the ground floor. It was more like working in a giant wardrobe than a shop. It transpired that the firm was thinking of closing Wembley and the absence of trade was good enough reason. Also I had to run the shop single-handed which was certainly one of the worst periods of my working life. The hours dragged by painfully slow and to add insult to injury I was out of pocket. Had I been doing the Harrow relief I would have done well on the commission side but at Wembley ...

It got to the stage when the highlight of the week was when one of the Head Office departments sent a memo with stock adjustments to be sorted out. At least it was something to do. One can only have so many tea breaks but I was seriously thinking about taking something stronger.

I had hoped that my fortnight's Summer holiday would bring my sojourn to an end – but no. They found someone to cover for the two weeks and on my return from the bracing, wide-open spaces of the Suffolk Coast I was once more incarcerated in the deserted and claustrophobic cloisters of Wembley.

I really despaired of ever getting out of the place and was becoming quite antisocial in my solitary working environment, rather like Ben Gunn, the eccentric castaway in *Treasure Island* and this 'castaway' was not particularly cheered by a visit from Jock Finch our Sales Director.

'What's happened to the trade here?' he asked me, almost accusingly as if it were my fault. After all, they were trying to get shot of the property before they had me hijacked there.

I suggested that he take a look at the other shops. Cheap jewellery shops, short term, cheapjack places; they answered his question.

So the Summer rolled into Autumn and it wasn't until the first week in November that my personal Mafeking was relieved and I returned to the comparative civilisation of Harrow. But 'The Plank', that new broom, hadn't finished with me yet.

STRAWS IN THE WIND

Spring ~ Winter 1984

From a personal point of view I considered 1984 every bit as bad as foretold in George Orwell's book of the same name. I had just finished a week's Spring relief at Harrow when 'The Plank' unexpectedly arrived and said that I was to manage Wembley for an indefinite period – a phrase which I was getting heartily sick of – as 'caretaker' until they finally decided to close the shop. And on my forty-fifth birthday too! I supposed I was lucky in having managed to do the Harrow relief which was well worth it from the financial angle.

This latest session was no great improvement on the one in 1982 but it wasn't quite so bad. Tuesday I had to cover for Vic's day off at Harrow and an assistant from the Watford Parade shop took my place at Wembley for that day. Thursday was my day off – I was covered by poor Arthur Hall – so it broke up my Wembley sentence to Monday, Wednesday, Friday and Saturday.

I did have help on Saturday, or rather a scatter-brained young lady called Carla who was engaged to Reggie Fowler the likeable 'silly ass' type, straight out of a *Bertie Wooster* story, who was now managing our Hounslow shop. It was good to have company but she would keep referring to me as 'Uncle Keighipeggs'. A year or so later they both left the firm and married. Sadly it didn't last. She was 'playing around' as they say and Reggie found out. Poor, harmless Reggie just couldn't cope and he echoed the tragic actions of Nicholas Willoughby some years earlier and shut himself in his garage with the engine running.

My Wembley session limped through Spring and into Summer. It was then that the bombshell fell. There were only Vic and Dave at Harrow; 'The Plank hadn't bothered to cover them with extra staff; even on Saturdays. Well Dave's eyesight was failing and Vic wasn't as vigilant as he should have been and one Saturday a whole bay of blazers, numbering eighteen in all, were stolen.

Jock Finch and 'The Plank' were soon down to Harrow, holding a court of enquiry. In such cases stock losses were deducted from the manager's annual trade bonus. But this loss was a real 'biggie' and more than wiped out any bonuses.

The upshot of this situation was, knowing they had the whip hand, Jock said that they would wipe the stock loss out completely if Vic agreed to take over as manager at Watford Parade when Norman Hurst retired in July. They had wanted him there for some time but he had always dug his heels in. Now he had nowhere to dig them and was forced to accept.

The new Harrow manager was Phil Ansell from Ealing and the stock transfer was on my day off. Rather belatedly they had engaged a new junior assistant which struck me as ironic. If he had been there before those blazers might never have been stolen.

Yet another change occurred which bordered on farce. Not only had Norman Hurst retired but also Arthur Hall, who was based at Watford, been transferred to the City. It was a horrendous journey for him from Bushey and not long after he moved to Epsom and took early retirement. But this meant that Harrow was no longer covered by a day relief manager. When Phil Ansell went on holiday the whole business became crazy. Thereafter a typical week was scheduled thus: Monday I would do the day relief at Harrow and Vic's day off at Watford on Tuesday. In the meantime someone from Watford covered me for those two days at Wembley. Wednesday I was back at Wembley, Thursday day off and back to Wembley for Friday and Saturday. One week they were so stretched for staff because I was the only relief man in the area who was available and it was a toss-up between Harrow and Wembley on the Monday. Harrow won and Wembley was closed for that day.

Very soon I became aware of 'straws in the wind'. While on the phone to some of the other shops I would be asked if I had heard anything about Watford.

'Such as?' I would probe.

'Oh, nothing,' would come the evasive reply. 'Just thought you might have heard something.'

I soon found out what these 'straws' meant. 'The Plank' called at Wembley one day and told me that he had found someone else to take over Wembley as the shop was due to close – and I was being transferred to Watford. It was Vic's doing. Without even asking me when he was coerced into accepting Watford, he said that he wanted me there too.

I don't think I ever resented a transfer so much. Usually after an initial protest I settled in but it took me a long time to lose that feeling of resentment. I think it was because it was all done behind my back. Everyone but everyone knew about it except me.

True, it was a lovely roomy shop to work in but the journey was a nightmare. Trains were frequently cancelled and in the evenings it seemed as if the wretched town had trapped me like a magnet. And it wasn't the Watford I remembered from 1958. The High Street shop had long since closed and many of the other familiar shops were no more. There were three of us; Vic, a young assistant called Simon Harling and myself. Vic was, as ever, amiable enough, but didn't overwork himself and I soon realised that I was doing most of his work for him.

I still did the Harrow day relief on Monday which rankled Vic but pleased me no end. Dave Hopton was still at Harrow and also the new junior, Ben Keeble. Ben was really something else. Very lanky and gangling with tousled fair hair and an almost girlish face and painfully intense manner. There was something almost medieval about his face, like one of those saintly visages seen on stained glass windows in churches. Ben lived in his own fantasy world and was quite harmless and probably one of the most honest youngsters I have ever met. He painted and also wrote poetry – any amount of it. For the most part it was blank verse but it must have meant something to him.

It went with his character that he was something of a loner but he was of an enterprising nature. On holiday in Italy he had run short of funds for his accommodation in the little inn where he was spending the week. No problem. Ben just dashed off some landscape paintings of the locality and the innkeeper accepted them in lieu of payment.

My first Christmas at Watford wasn't a jolly one. Apart from being understaffed – three in that vast shop were not enough for the festive trade and we had lost a junior in very unusual circumstances – I had a heavy cold which turned into laryngitis. Vic wasn't at all happy about that. We had to get the January Sale notices in the window on Christmas Eve and what annoyed him was that when I was trying to paste them on the inside of the window they wouldn't stick. I was running such a temperature that the glass was damp with my body heat.

Regarding the junior we lost under 'unusual circumstances'. This young man, only nineteen years old, had got married but was having mother-in-law trouble. It terminated in a fearful row outside the shop one evening and he pushed his mother-in-law and wife into the ornamental pond, handed his notice in and was never seen again. It happened just before I was moved to Watford Parade. Trust me to miss 'the big picture'.

As I mentioned earlier, it was bad enough getting to and fro from Watford, especially using the local line which meant a long walk up Watford High Street to our shop at the far end. The same gloomy faces every morning and evening and mistakenly boarding a Croxley Green train after work and having to retrace my journey back to Watford and start again. Eventually I found the benefits of the fast Intercity train which only took twelve minutes and in my opinion it was well worth the extra 10p.

Mind you, even then there were glitches, usually on a Saturday evening. On several occasions the indicator at Watford Junction wrongly showed that the train was stopping at Harrow and Wealdstone when it was a non-stop to Euston. This meant that I had to catch – invariably – a slow train back which took ages.

The customers were markedly different to those at Harrow. Watford was semi-rural with quite a bit of money about and some of them were inclined to look down their noses at humble shop staff. One occasion which stands out was when the firm were having a purge on request orders. Quite rightly they had decided that a £5 deposit should be taken with each request order as many had not been collected.

One customer wanted to order three suits. He knew his size, long-fitting 43". Although we did sizes in inches we didn't cut out too many long 43". 'You order them for me,' he said, selecting three different patterns, 'and I might choose one.'

I mentioned the deposit and he looked at me as if I was something the cat had dragged in. 'And why should I leave a deposit?' he coldly demanded to know.

I explained that we had been compelled to introduce this as many orders had never been collected and a large stockpile had steadily accumulated in our shops when they might well be needed for other customers. If the suits weren't to his liking the deposit would be refunded without any bother.

He sniffed disdainfully. 'Other people aren't my concern,' he retorted.

That was the final straw. 'No, Sir,' I replied, tearing up his orders in front of him, 'but they are mine.'

He went as white as the fragmented request orders, glared at me and strode out of the shop. Vic asked me what on earth I had said to the man and to his credit he agreed with me. I suppose we all have our breaking point but this worm had at last turned and if there had been any angry rumblings from Camden Town I would still have stuck to my guns.

Another customer who could be something of a pest was 'Mister Click', so called on account of his ill-fitting dentures which clicked whenever he spoke, or rather brayed. He was quite elderly but fit enough and extremely self-opinionated and always expected to be served first. And when he did laugh – yes, he did laugh but it was usually at his own jokes – it was one of those deafening, braying laughs that turned to a snarl and seemed to go clean through your eardrums.

One day he ordered a pair of made-to-measure trousers, high-waisted with button fly and brace buttons. We were all dreading the day he came to collect them and I fervently hoped it would be when I was at Harrow or on my day off. If not then let it be on my lunch break, I silently prayed, and I will never do or think anything wicked again.

But of course things don't work out like that. He came in, demanding his trousers on a Monday morning – which was damn bad luck for me as Phil Ansell's day off at Harrow had been changed from Monday to Wednesday. Crossing my fingers, I ushered him into the fitting-room and waited for the explosion. Something was sure to be wrong.

It seemed as if my worst fears were confirmed. Puffing and grunting could be heard, interspersed by oaths and blasphemies of which 'bloody hell!' was the mildest, and I wondered if the makers had left one of the legs off.

Finally he emerged from the fitting-room and handed me the trousers. 'Yes, they're okay,' he grunted. 'Wrap 'em up.'

While Watford seemed a respectable enough place during the day it was a real hell-hole during the night. Frequently my telephone would wake me up at 3am and it would be the police, asking if I was the keyholder for Dunn & Co Watford as our window had been broken. Without much hope I would inform them that I was the second keyholder and that the manager was Mr Buckingham. I always got the same reply. They had tried Mr Buckingham's number but nobody was answering.

Vic never did. It was left to me to turn out and get an early train or minicab to Watford where the police were waiting for me outside the shop. Then there were statements to be taken and a glazier to be notified. Then the long wait until the glazier appeared and boarded up the broken window.

One very early Saturday morning I was called out and had to wait until 5.30 for the glazier. I staggered down to the station and got home about 6.30, cat-napped until 7.30 then washed, breakfasted and went to work at the usual time. I had hoped that Vic might let me off early but as Derek Miles, the manager of Piccadilly would have said, 'You're living in a dream world, Mister!'

The fact that I virtually 'crashed out' around 2.30 was of no consequence either. Although Vic never admitted it he must have heard his phone when the police tried to contact him but he wasn't going to be bothered. That was yet another reason why he had me shanghaied to Watford.

Much of the trouble in Watford was due to the clubs. Even as early as the evenings things could get a bit ugly and I was never inclined to hang around the town once the shop had closed.

Vic Buckingham had fancied himself a ladies' man. What he lacked in stature he more than compensated for in ego. Even at Harrow I can remember him cutting in on a sale if it happened to be an attractive lady customer. He used to say that he had yet to find himself a worthy mistress while working in Harrow; a typical self-opinionated joke that wore thinner than the hair on an egg. Then one day while I was on day relief at Harrow I had cause to phone Watford about something. Simon Harling answered the phone. 'Guess what,' he chuckled. 'I think Mister B has got himself a girlfriend.'

In due course Vic came to the phone. 'What's this I hear about your new girlfriend?' I asked, expecting his usual nonchalant reply that no woman could resist 'perfection in miniature.'

Instead he snapped, 'What are you talking about? Of course I haven't got a girlfriend! Utter rubbish!'

I had never heard Vic 'get out of his pram' as Dave Hopton would have said. It seemed as if I had touched upon a tender spot. Maybe he had been brought down a peg or two. Not before time, I reflected. It wasn't so much that his flirtatious technique was offensive; it was so damned corny. He really should change his script.

All in all my Watford period was not among my favourite memories. But there was a little ray of sunshine in the latter part of 1984. Jimmy Mayne returned to us as Area Supervisor and 'The Plank' was demoted to manager and sent up North to one of our shops in Scotland.

From what I later heard he was not long with Dunn & Co. He was sacked for pilfering stock and fighting in the shop with a junior assistant. At least the customers must have enjoyed the floor show and I hoped that the junior wasn't sacked as well. As far as I was concerned he deserved a medal.

But 1985 loomed ahead and looking back I can only say that it is a good thing we do not know what the future holds for us. Such knowledge can seriously damage your health.

DANGEROUS DAYS AND DECEIT

February 1985 ~ September 1987

On February 13th 1985 there were two heavy falls; one of snow and one of Mother. The latter slipped on the former and broke her wrist. I got her to hospital and managed to find a phone and gave Vic Buckingham a ring to tell him that I wouldn't be in work until Monday.

A few weeks later I had to take Mum back to the hospital for a progress report. It was a Wednesday when I was due to cover Harrow for the manager's day off. Well that couldn't be helped and I told him that I would be there as soon as I could, although it would probably be the late afternoon. Dave Hopton and Ben Keeble would be there which would be quite sufficient for Wednesday which was usually a quiet day.

I saw Mum settled back at home and after a quick lunch, went to the Harrow shop. I was in a very disgruntled mood as we had waited ages in the hospital and my humour was not improved when Ben told me that he had to go to Watford as there were only Vic and Simon, the new junior assistant being off sick.

So I was left with David. Not that we had much to do and there was only about fifty pounds in the till in cash. At about quarter to five we had just finished our second tea break of the afternoon and Dave was tidying up in the staff room when two heavily-dreadlocked youths came in the shop. They seemed a bit tense and I had a gut feeling that they might be looking for an opportunity for a little bit of pilfering.

The tallest one – and gosh he was tall, and big with it, too – asked to see some caps. I was watching his friend – or more precisely his friend's hands – so was completely taken by surprise by what happened next. The tall one, who was standing behind me, suddenly seized me in a bear hug and lifted me clean off my feet. Even then for a moment I thought that they were just skylarking about. But when he started to haul me down the shop I realised that it was something more serious. What he intended to do was throw me in a fitting-room and hold the door closed while his accomplice emptied the till.

It all happened so suddenly that I didn't have time to be scared. That, plus the rotten morning I had endured at the hospital and losing Ben to Watford for the afternoon was the limit. I was in a bad mood to start with and this was the final straw.

Fortunately in my younger days I had read the right comics and seen the right films so as I was propelled towards the fitting-room's open door I swung my legs up, braced them against each side of the door frame and kicked back as hard as I could. The result was spectacular. We both crashed backwards with me on top, completing demolishing a trouser rack.

Meanwhile the other villain had prised the till open, grabbed a handful of notes and beat a hasty retreat. Alerted by the crash, Dave appeared in the staff room doorway, waving the teapot and shouting, 'What the bloody hell's going on?'

My assailant panicked. They often do when their plans go awry, and tried to follow after his friend. But the sight of someone who was twice my size actually fleeing from me filled me with intoxicating bloodlust; a phenomenon which can best be likened to a couple of tomcats fighting. I hared out of the shop after him and jumped on his back, bringing him down for the second time. However, this proved the wrong thing to do as we both rolled down the pavement and finished up in the gutter with me on top. We frantically exchanged blows and mutual muttered observations on each other's parentage when he suddenly shouted, 'Max – help!'

Max was obviously my other visitor and to my horror I heard footsteps rushing towards me and a hand grab my jacket collar. As a drowning man's life is said to flash before him so something akin to 'give my love to Peggy and the boys!' as quoted in those splendid old war films came to mind. I honestly thought that my number was well and truly up.

Then the miracle happened. My adversary suddenly yelled in agony, leapt off me and disappeared up the road with his companion. A little Asian gentleman, no more than five feet tall, had seized him by the ears and twisted them violently.

I staggered to my feet surrounded by the inevitable ring of what the Americans call 'rubber-neckers'. I was bloody and dishevelled with my waistcoat burst asunder and the buttons cascading into the gutter. Quite oblivious to my audience I expressed loud and sincere opinions of my attacker and called upon Heaven to witness my outrage and punish my enemies.

Meanwhile Dave had been quick off the mark and phoned 999 because within a minute a police car appeared and I was ushered into the shop to make a statement. Realising that this could be a lengthy business I made a quick call home to let my mother know I would be late and told her that I had some booking-up to finish.

'What's that voice I can hear?' she asked. 'Someone talking about Bravo Oscar Tango.'

It was the policeman's radio so I told her that we had a customer in the shop with a transistor radio. I didn't want to give her a truthful account of events over the phone. She would find out as soon as she clapped eyes on me.

After giving all the necessary details the police said that if I felt up to it they would drive me around the area in the hope that we might spot the thieves. It was a waste of time so they drove me home and suggested that I check in at the hospital in case I had delayed concussion. Thankfully my mother was more angry than shocked by what had been done to her one and only son who assured her that no real harm had been done. But when she pointed out the knife slash across the back of my jacket her one and only son immediately grabbed the brandy bottle left over from Christmas and phoned for a taxi to take him to the A&E Department.

Happily I had no delayed shock and was let out with an anti-tetanus jab. The only thing that did cause me some discomfort was when I was told to strop off and wait for the doctor, having been given the most inadequate white thing to wear with only one useless tape on it. As it was a chilly evening and I had imbibed several cups of tea during the course of the day I needed to know where the toilets were. 'Down the corridor and turn left,' a nurse told me. Not worth getting dressed, I thought and draped my Dunn & Co Harris Tweed overcoat around my shoulders and ran barefoot (and bare-everything) down the corridor. But what the nurse had omitted to tell me was that I had to pass through the out-patients' reception area! Far from being a victim of grievous bodily harm I felt more like a victim of grievous bodily embarrassment!

The upside of this little adventure was amusing for I gained a legendary reputation among the London shops as a retailer's version of John Wayne. Most undeserved but I relished and wallowed in the exaggerations. By all accounts 'Tiger' Howard had single-handedly fought off a gang of thugs, putting them to terrified flight and wrecking the shop's furniture in the process.

On one occasion at the Watford shop two young lads came in and were being a bit noisy. At the time I was in the stock room helping unload the weekly delivery. I innocently glanced into the shop to see what was going on when one of the two delivery men placed a restraining hand on my arm. 'Don't start anything, Keith,' he whispered. 'They don't mean any harm.'

Well nothing could have been further from my mind but I didn't disillusion them. After all, none of us like our little myths and legends exploded.

But if there was any hero in the situation I think it was Dave Hopton. Poor Dave, frail and with his poor eyesight, didn't hang back. He was on the phone to the police within seconds. Unlike Phil Ansell when, several years earlier, that crazy customer tried to throttle me in the shop. Phil ran out and hid in the staff room.

As expected my mother's broken wrist healed but the Fates had not finished with her and she went down with sciatica. But even then there was an amusing side to it. She had just taken down all her 'Get Well' cards – so she put them all up again. But the trouble with sciatica is that you can never tell how long it will last. I had to leave her lunch and a thermos of tea before I went to work, do any necessary shopping during my lunch hour at Watford, then get the dinner sorted out when I got home.

This went on for weeks and not once did Vic let me off early. It wasn't as if we hadn't enough staff cover. As well as Vic there was Simon Harling and Daniel Carver, the new junior. To the contrary, Vic seemed to regard the whole thing as a joke. 'Here comes Mrs Howard with her shopping,' he would chortle as I struggled into the shop, laden with plastic carrier bags.

But one little perk which we enjoyed, staff levels permitting, was an early night. Vic usually had his on Friday, Simon on Monday and Daniel on Wednesday. We closed at 5.30 and just that extra hour of freedom, leaving work at 4.30 seemed like a mini-holiday. When it came to me Vic said, 'instead of an early night, Keith, how would you feel about having a late morning instead? Saturday for instance. You come in at ten instead of nine.'

Well an hour is an hour whichever end of the day it is and it was better than nothing even though I would have much preferred an early night. It did strike me as strange that he should suggest Saturday which was our busy day, especially as I was the only other keyholder. But he argued that we never had supervisory visits on Saturdays so it would be the best day.

This arrangement did have an advantage while my mother was laid up. If I went to Watford at the usual time I could do all the weekend shopping comfortably as *Sainsbury's* was situated just behind our shop. One Saturday I was just about to go into *Sainsbury's* when I chanced to look down the mews to where the rear of our shop was. I saw the back gate open and a frowsey-looking woman – to put it bluntly, a real dog – slip out and furtively scuttle away around the corner. And then I realised why Vic wanted me to have the late morning and also why he bit my head off the time I remarked that he had found a lady-friend.

Although nothing was mentioned I must admit that I had lost a lot of respect for him. This was brought home even more one night when I had gone out to visit some friends. Arriving home about 11.30, my mother said she had received a telephone call from Joyce, Vic's wife, at around 9.15. She was close to tears and wanted to know if I had got home from work all right. Mum said that I had been home and gone out for the evening.

'Well Vic's not home yet,' Joyce sobbed, 'and his dinner is ruined. I've had to throw it out. I don't know where he's got or what's happened to him.'

I could make a very good guess and I was only too glad that I wasn't in when she phoned.

Poor old Mum's sciatica dragged right on through May. One morning after she had had a particularly bad night I phoned the shop to say that I would be in late. That was the last thing I remembered. When I came to I was sprawled on the floor with the telephone on my chest. Nervous exhaustion, the doctor said, and I was strongly advised to take a week off. Happily this proved to be the turning point for both of us. Once Mum had started to recover she did so quickly and things were back to normal.

It was an unwritten tradition at Dunn's around Christmas that we should go out for a meal one evening. Although Watford was a busy town, its eating places were restricted to the usual burger bars and one or two Chinese restaurants. We had tried the latter the previous year and found it an ordeal. Eating seaweed was an art that must take a lifetime to learn. When it was served up it looked like fragments of green foil. Also it was so dark that I mistook the finger bowl for a wineglass and drank it. I also ate something which seemed remarkably tough until I was told that it was still in its shell.

Vic fancied himself as a gourmet but he was hard put to find a suitable venue and finally settled for a place called *The Ponderosa*. He seemed quite happy with his choice but I had misgivings. These were proved when, on entering, we were each told to grab a tray and help ourselves. Not at all what Vic was used to. Our meal was chicken and chips but the biggest laugh came when Vic called a waitress over and asked for liqueurs.

'Wot?' she asked.

'Liqueurs,' Vic replied with a beaming if glassy smile. 'Drinkies.'

'We 'aven't got no lickers,' the girl replied. Then she brightened. 'I can do you a fizzy orange.'

Vic's face was to be seen to be believed.

But not all of us had a laugh that Christmas. Ben Keeble, the young man at Harrow, was of a shy nature and would blush if he had to serve a young lady customer. So it came as quite a surprise when he confided that he had met a young Italian student and fallen for her, hook, line and sinker. They had arranged to spend Christmas together and he would talk of nothing else. One can imagine the cruel shock when she telephoned the day before Christmas Eve and said – without giving any reason – that she didn't want to see him again. It is impossible to imagine how much this must have hurt his sensitive nature and he spent a miserable Christmas at home.

In the New Year, Ben Keeble, Ben the Benevolent, the angelic-faced poet, handed his notice in. This may well have been a reaction to being jilted at Christmas by his girlfriend but he never admitted it. He said he was going to commune with nature and tour the British Isles on foot. He had drawn all the money out of his bank account and intended to hoof it all the way up through the Eastern Counties, right up to the tip of Scotland and return South through Wales and on to Cornwall. He would sleep under the stars and all that rubbish. Yes, it certainly was a case of delayed reaction.

We couldn't let Ben go without giving him a send-off so on his last Saturday, Vic, Simon and I went to Harrow after work and met up with Phil, Dave and Ben in the *Greenhill Bar* for drinkies. Ben waxed lyrical about his pilgrimage through Nature, interrupted occasionally by Dave Hopton who leered myopically at him over his glass of scotch and sneered, 'prat.' Ben was quite impervious to this and we all made our solemn farewells and wished him good fortune.

So therefore it was quite disillusioning when, three weeks later, Ben reappeared on the scene and announced that he had travelled First Class to Edinburgh, stayed overnight at the best hotel he could find, dined on roast duck with orange sauce and spent what was left of his money on a First Class ticket back the following day. He had also secured a job in the Harrow branch of *Sainsbury's*. Well that was Ben. Whatever it was, he had got it out of his system.

The weeks and months of 1986 passed uneventfully but now and again there would be some little incident to brighten things up. Chalk-striped suits had made a come-back. For decades they had been ostracised on account of their public image regarding the 'demob suit' issued to demobilised servicemen after World War II. Now the new generation had discovered them and we were fully stocked up with these sartorial items. Even Simon bought one, but he could be excused as he was much too young to know of the stigma attached to that particular style.

I was serving a customer with one of these suits and had just shown him to the fitting-room when Simon, who had just finished his lunch, appeared in the doorway leading to the staff room. There he paused, deep in thought and gazing down the shop. Now the staff room doorway was at right angles to the fitting-room with a black wooden frame which had often misled customers into thinking it was a full-length mirror. Also it happened that the chalk-stripe suit which Simon was wearing was identical to the one my customer was trying on.

I had a feeling what was going to happen but some devil in me told me to keep quiet and let events run their course. A minute later my customer emerged from the fitting-room and stood before what he thought to be a mirror, gazing at what he also believed to be his reflection. It was too good to be true. The customer stared at what he thought to be his reflected suit while Simon, a cigarette dropping from his lips and completely oblivious of the customer, gazed past him, his mind on other things such as beer and women.

Thus they stood for several seconds. Then Simon, bored with staring into space, turned away and vanished from sight. The customer nearly fainted when his 'reflection' disappeared, but it was well worth watching – and he did buy the suit after all.

Meanwhile there were big changes at our Harrow branch. The shop was due for a refit. The smaller window was to be left intact but the larger one increased in size so that the entrance once again reverted to the original narrow lobby.

They really should have closed the shop so that the work could have continued through the night and be finished that much quicker. But no. The firm opted to stay open for trade and it was chaotic. I still did the Wednesdays at Harrow and it was like working in an air-raid shelter on a bomb site. There were a few duckboards to walk on and the clothing racks were shrouded in dust sheets which really lived up to their name. If they had been anti-dust sheets they would have kept the dust out but these dust sheets seemed to absorb every mote of dust in the air. The shop looked like a Salvador Dali painting with the cash desk tilted at a most un-Dunn & Co angle and the fitting-room was merely another dust sheet held up by poles. For once I was grateful that I was only at Harrow once a week. The Saturdays there must have been horrendous.

Things jogged along much the same as usual but there was a difference. The character seemed to have gone out of the firm. With Ben's departure the last of the eccentrics had disappeared from the scene. Also the firm had brought in an advisory team with very modern ideas to help us weather our way through a particularly sticky patch of recession. It was only a matter of time before they had taken control.

By then we had a new Area Supervisor, Nigel Grant who paid us a visit with surprising news. Nigel was original Dunn & Co stock and I had occasionally worked with him at Harrow in the late 1960s when he used to help out on Saturdays in the good old days of Bertie Benson. He had done well for himself, even managing our Piccadilly branch before being promoted as Area Supervisor; a job to which he was well suited. He had what is known as 'the common touch' and I would stress that this is in no way meant to be derogatory or patronising. He could relate to and communicate to his staff excellently and he was a real workaholic. At heart he was a very genuine, fair-minded man, almost soft-hearted over some things but woe betide anyone who tried to pull the wool over his eyes. He was much too canny.

'Dave Hopton at Harrow is taking early retirement,' he announced. 'His eyesight is getting worse and the firm are quite happy to release him on full pension.'

I was saddened by this. Another link with the old firm had gone, for I had met Dave on my very first day at Harrow. But Nigel's next words caused me to prick up my ears.

'This means Harrow will be without a senior assistant, so I will be sending Simon there.'

To my mind this was completely crackers. Simon Harling lived in Watford and I lived in Harrow. Anyway, I still resented the trick which Vic had pulled on me three years earlier to get me to Watford.

'I don't mind going to Harrow,' I told Nigel, secretly savouring the frown on Vic's face. 'After all, I do live there and Simon only lives around the corner here.'

'I don't mind which of you goes,' Nigel retorted. 'You can start there next Monday.'

And it was as easy as that.

'EL SUPREMO' IN CHARGE

Autumn 1987 ~ Summer 1989

It is said that you should never return to a place where you were happy because you are sure to be disappointed. I have never fully subscribed to this theory but I know it can be true in certain cases. Often this is due to the changes in oneself. Nevertheless I found Harrow a disappointment. I really should have taken heed of what could have been taken as an omen as, during my first few days back at Harrow we experienced that notorious hurricane of 1987. At least I was grateful that I didn't have any travelling to contend with.

Phil Ansell, that gnomish young man, was still managing and the other assistant was an even younger Portuguese, Leon Vargas. Leon was pleasant enough but his sense of humour was as 'subtle as a flying mallet' as Nigel Grant would say, and could wear a bit thin after, say, several seconds.

But the spirit – the Dunn & Co atmosphere – was missing. Phil was easy enough to get on with but he was the sort of person who said what you wanted to hear but never acted on it. Both Phil and Leon were of that type who delighted in spreading depressing rumours no matter how unsubstantiated they were. The general tone of the place was too serious.

Of course, the new team of 'company advisors' was something to do with it. They all had company cars and seemed bent on eradicating the original Dunn & Co image completely. The Camden Town Head Office was no more. 'El Supremo', as we called the leading light of the new team, considered the place 'little better than a rat-hole' and had let the place go on the market for a tenth of its proper value. I never knew the actual figure involved but that block in Camden was a prime site and should have fetched a fortune.

A new state-of-the-art Head Office-cum-warehouse was opened up at Neasden, semi-automated too, whatever that meant. 'El Supremo' was going through the Company funds like a hot knife through butter.

But my return to Harrow was not without certain instances of humour. Leon had a very high pitched, squeaky voice and this led to a very comical incident one Saturday – about the only one I can recall. He had phoned a customer to advise him that the garment he had ordered was ready for collection. An hour later the customer arrived, beaming all over his face. 'Where's the young lady with the sexy voice?' he demanded. 'She sounded a nice bit of skirt.'

Leon took fright and hid in a fitting-room while we concocted a story, saying that the 'young lady' had been called away to another branch.

One bizarre incident made me realise that Watford wasn't such a bad place after all. It concerned one of our regular customers, Mr Deacon. There was nothing particularly unusual about him; middle-aged, tall and with a fondness for Norfolk-style jackets. One day he commented on how nice it was to come into a shop which didn't have pop music blaring out all the time. Trying to be funny I said that if we had to have music it would have to be classical; preferably ballet music by Tchaikovsky.

Goodness knows what he thought I meant but he raised his eyebrows and smiled. 'Really?' he replied. 'You must come and visit me one evening. I have some very nice friends whom I am sure you would like. We play ballet music and dance to it.'

I went hot and cold with terror at the grisly image this conjured up. I mumbled something about having two left feet, decided it was time for lunch and did the disappearing act.

The next day was my day off but when I returned on the Friday Phil showed me a stack of old LP classical records which Mr Deacon had left at the shop for me. He had also brought in a bottle of champagne and suggested to Phil that they should share it in the staff room. Somehow Phil politely but firmly put him off but sheer terror reigned. Well it did from my viewpoint anyway. Those records swiftly found their way to the nearest Oxfam shop and after a year at Harrow Fate kindly intervened on my behalf.

Nigel Grant said that I had to be transferred back to Watford as Simon Harling had handed in his notice and Daniel Carver would be sent to Harrow in my place. After a somewhat disappointing year at Harrow I was highly relieved.

Vic was as urbane as ever and we had a new junior, Mark Hemmings, a little, shifty-eyed, pale-faced character. But soon after my return to Watford I began to experience stomach pains and hair loss. It wasn't just thinning out; it was coming out in tufts. The hair loss was alopecia but the doctor assured me that it would grow back again but not the same colour. He was right to hedge his bets. It grew back profusely but not dark brown as it used to be. It was as white as the driven snow which was quite embarrassing as I am sure people thought I had bleached it. Eventually it toned down to what it is now – a sort of 'hermit grey'.

As for the stomach pains, I had suspected a hernia but the doc had a surprise for me. I had two of the beggars; one on each side. A double whammy. I was checked in for an operation but as they hadn't strangulated I was put on the list. In the meantime take it easy. Don't strain or lift anything heavy.

Vic's attitude hadn't improved during my year's absence. One busy Saturday he slammed a cap drawer shut as I was about to remove a cap for a customer to try on. The heavy oak drawer caught the top joint of my left index finger with a most unpleasant and painful scrunch. 'Did that hurt?' grinned Vic. No apology. He considered any form of apology as a sign of human weakness. To this day that finger has never properly straightened out and still causes me typing errors.

His laid back attitude was as bad as ever. Casual just wasn't the word. One Saturday lunchtime I was left alone in the shop serving an elderly couple. Vic was in the stock room enjoying a cup of tea and a cigarette, chatting with Mark and Simon, who had popped in for a visit.

Just then three husky and fit-looking young men in T-shirts walked into the shop. They stood in a row facing the trouser rack. 'One-two-three!' shouted one of them. Then they each grabbed an armful of trousers and rushed off to the door!

My initial reaction was to wave a hand in a futile gesture to give hint that I had noticed them and shout, 'Oi!' in a stage version of PC Plod. Obviously more was required so I dashed down the shop, hoping at least to hold back one of the thieves. Somehow I tripped over my own feet, collided with a tall and very heavy wooden display unit which fell and caught one of the thieves on the shoulder. He stumbled off balance and dropped his trousers – the stolen ones – and fell against his two accomplices. Panic reigned as they all tried to squeeze through the doorway at the same time. They were hefty lads and for a second or two they were wedged. So much for all the 'one-two-three' military precision! They stumbled out into Watford Parade, shedding stolen trousers all over the place and took off at high speed with about half of their 'snatch'.

To their credit Mark and Simon – and Simon didn't even work for us anymore – raced off after them, leaving me the embarrassing task of picking up about twenty pairs of trousers from the pavement, under the astonished scrutiny of the Saturday shoppers. In the meantime Vic remained in the shop, tut-tutting and doubtless expounding verbose observations on the state of society to my deserted and bewildered customers. It goes without saying that the thieves got away but at least not with as much as they thought they would.

One regular customer could cause more than a slight degree of embarrassment. The poor man was mute but able to utter wordless bellows. How we ever discovered exactly what he wanted was nothing short of a miracle but we always managed to find him something and he was a very open-handed shopper. He would walk into the shop – a stocky little fellow with a porkpie hat and horn-rimmed glasses – trailing behind him a small and hairy dog on a lead which looked like a Brillo pad on legs. No one was particularly keen to serve him and would hide in the stock room when he appeared. This may sound cruel but it wasn't on account of his unfortunate speech impediment. Whereas a satisfied customer may shake hands when bidding us goodbye this one wanted to kiss us! Not that he was of that particular persuasion. I think it was just honest to goodness friendliness. But even so we did tend to make ourselves scarce. One day he caught Vic and planted a real smacker on his check. I wouldn't have missed the spectacle for anything. That frozen grin on Vic's face. But I must give him full marks for recovering his poise. 'If you must do that,' he remarked, 'I would be grateful if you would shave first.'

One Tuesday – and it happened to be Vic's day off – I arrived at the shop a couple of minutes late to find Harry Saunders the Assistant Sales Director on the doorstep, and he had taken lessons in irascibility from his senior, Jock Finch. He grumbled about me being late and grumbled about my staff – numbering one, Mark Hemmings – being even later. When Mark did arrive Saunders took a bite out of him, too.

'Have you shaved this morning? You haven't. Then you can go back home and make yourself presentable for work. And you'll lose the time it takes out of your wages.'

After he had sent Mark packing he had the temerity to start on me again. 'You will have to make do without any staff until he returns, Mr Howard. You are the relief manager and you should have noticed that he hadn't shaved.'

This was too much and I simply blew up. The kid had hardly walked in the shop! How am I supposed to know whether or not he's shaved before he gets here? I've just about had a gutful of this! For two pins I'd follow him out and let you look after the shop!'

Saunders looked absolutely shocked and I began to feel rather embarrassed. I dislike losing my temper but enough was enough. Just then a customer came in – one of our regulars; a nice chap called Mr Barnes – and bought two – not one but two car coats. He was in a spending mood thank goodness and it was like balm to the soul.

Meanwhile I could see that squat little grey-haired creature muttering on the telephone. He was probably calling for reinforcements because old

Howard had flipped his lid and might turn violent. When he had finished his call he muttered something about having paperwork to do and went upstairs. But I had a fair idea what was cooking and I was right. About half an hour later Nigel Grant appeared and went straight upstairs. A few minutes later he came down and asked me my version of what happened. I told him fairly and squarely and he went back upstairs again. When they both came down nothing was mentioned. In fact they both seemed very affable. Furthermore, on his future visits to Watford, it wasn't 'Mr Howard' and 'Mr Saunders', it was 'Keith' and 'Harry'. Ain't love grand.

But we did have an addition to our staff who proved to be a real nightmare. He was a young Asian called Khalid Desai. He preferred to just be called Desi and he had a technique for getting everyone's back up. He really must have taken lessons at it. Tall and slim with a nose and chin not unlike that of Mr Punch and a grin which was more of a toothsome leer which seemed to stretch around his ears.

The following year, 1989, Vic took his Spring holiday in February and I was left in charge with Mark and Desi. From the very first morning it was sheer hell. They didn't get on and Desi was argumentative and arrogant. Mark threatened to walk out and I had had just about all that I could stand. It got to a point when I threatened to sack Desi if he didn't shut up. Whether I was empowered to do so I am not sure but I had reached breaking point. Desi broke out in a flood of hysterical tears and begged me not to sack him. I found the whole thing sickening but somehow I muddled through the week and I was mighty glad when Vic returned the following Monday.

Desi went from bad to worse. He was too familiar with the customers, grovelling and rubbing his hands and calling the young ladies 'princess'. He was also full of his own self-importance. 'I don't know why I waste my time working for this firm,' he would say. 'I'm a qualified field salesman. To which I would reply, 'then go and sell a bloody field.'

Vic had quite the wrong approach with him. He would try to argue on an academic level with his preposterous statements which only made him worse. The only way to deal with Desi was to tell him to shut up.

One day – and fortunately for Desi it was his day off – a young and very smartly-dressed young Asian came in the shop. 'Does someone called Desi work here?' he asked me.

I said that it was his day off.

'Then he can count himself lucky,' the young man sharply retorted, 'otherwise I was going to smash his face in.'

It transpired that Desi had been annoying a young Asian lady cashier in our bank with his unwelcome attentions and the young man was her boyfriend. Whatever unsavoury comments and suggestions our young friend had made had reduced the poor girl to tears. What a pity her boyfriend chose the wrong day. It would have been a most enjoyable encounter to witness.

But Desi's days were numbered. He went too far with his insolence which resulted in a customer complaining to Head Office. It turned out that this was but one of many complaints and Nigel Grant came down to sort him out. There were the usual hysterics – alternate pleading and cursing – which moved Nigel not one whit. At one stage a gust of wind blew through the shop, slamming the stock room door shut. 'See, Mr Grant!' proclaimed Desi. 'The gods are angry with you! Be fearful!'

But when Nigel Grant was set on something it was more likely that it would be the gods who would be fearful and Desi was given his marching orders.

Not long after that Mark Hemmings inevitably left the firm. I say 'inevitably' because this was something which I had noticed over recent years and it was rather sad. When I joined the firm it was the usual thing to stay and make a career of it but now the young people were more inclined to 'job-hopping'.

Daniel Carver returned to Watford from Harrow and we also had our first young lady join the firm. Now this was something of an innovation for Dunn & Co shops but times were a-changing. Valerie Stevens was a very bright young lady. Very 'English-looking' with curly black hair and a determined chin. She was the sister of young Bobby Stevens who worked with me at Harrow some ten years ago. Their father Derek Stevens, who managed our Liverpool Street shop, had recommended her for the job as Cashier/Sales Assistant.

Without doubt Valerie was a great asset to the shop. Bright, breezy and good with the customers. But she wouldn't stand for any nonsense. This was brought home to me one Saturday. Despite his dismissal Desi still haunted the place and frequently called in the shop about 4.30 when he had finished his shopping. As nosey and arrogant as ever; it seemed impossible to dent his thick skin. It was the usual thing; him telling us how good he was and how all these different computer firms wanted to snap him up (snap his neck more likely!) and how we should run the shop. This particular Saturday he had inflicted his presence on us but both Vic and Daniel had customers and I had found some bookwork to attend to which kept me out of the way. I was dimly aware of raised voices and an unusually high degree of foot traffic in the shop but paid no heed to it. When I finished whatever I had been doing there was no sign of Desi. Vic had finished with his customer so I asked him where the 'boy wonder' had gone.

'Desi?' he replied in his usual languid manner. 'Valerie threw him out.'

She what? This I had to hear. I found Valerie calmly drinking a cup of tea in the stock room. Her hackles had almost settled down but she confirmed what I suspected. Desi had tracked her down to the stock room and bluntly made some improper suggestion, observation or invitation – take your pick; probably all three. She didn't elaborate and I didn't ask. Her reaction was to pick up his two shopping bags, march to the shop door with them and pitch them into the street.

'You have a choice,' she had told Desi, who stood in the doorway, staring in dismay at his chapattis rolling down Watford Parade. 'You can either walk out of here or go out like your shopping.'

Desi slunk off, never to be seen again. By George, I was proud of that girl! Sadly her time with us went all too quickly for she decided to follow in the footsteps of her twin sister and brother Bobby and joined the Police Force. I could find it in myself to feel very sorry for any villains who crossed her path.

Meanwhile in the larger scheme of things Dunn & Co were enduring – suffering even – some drastic changes. 'El Supremo' was now our Managing Director and had ousted certain members from their places on the Board. Jock Finch the Sales Director was one of his victims. He arrived one morning to find the contents of his office thrown out into the passage. Our new master was one of those 'concept' characters. A shop couldn't just be a shop; it had to express something else. In the case of Watford a smoking room in a gentlemen's club. In came the decorators and a lot of fake antique furnishings and pictures; even a load of tatty old books to put on the shelves. Also a gigantic green leather Chesterfield sofa. Everyone raved about it but I found it too low to sit in with any comfort. Not that I had much time for sitting in it anyway.

Ties were to be displayed in neat rows on a massive oak table instead of the more practical revolving racks. Not a good idea as they looked a terrible mess within a few minutes of trading. Mind you, the revolving tie rack had to be treated carefully. I recall one Saturday at Harrow when a very toffee-nosed couple condescended to inspect our ties. Full of airs and graces they were until 'modom' revolved the tie rack rather faster than it was used to and sent the whole lot crashing to the floor where they all tangled up in a multi-coloured Gordian Knot. But that wasn't the only thing which crashed. The aloof composure of 'Sir' slipped more than a few notches when he rounded on his wife and bellowed, 'You stupid, clumsy cow!'

Even so, I preferred the tie stands to the table display, especially as the current trend was for floral designs. You either liked them or loathed them. I'm a 'spots and stripes' man myself and it was like working in a garden centre.

'El Supremo' liked the idea of open evenings when the shop would stay open until 7pm. This was not for sales as the idea was for the public to view the merchandise. Happily the idea never caught on despite the wine and crisps laid out. Most people didn't want to linger in Watford in the evening as it could become dangerous once the clubs and pubs livened up.

I had occasion to be in Watford after hours and a hair-raising experience it was, too. But this wasn't due to the threat of physical violence. It was something much more sinister.

I have described the first floor of the shop where the display school was at the front with a bewildering complexity of passages and rooms at the back. It was spooky up there and there was one passage in particular which ran parallel with another passage each side of the central storeroom which Mark Hemmings called the 'Ghost Passage'. There always had been some talk about that place and we all teased him about this, but I for one, mentally crossed my fingers when I did so.

Then one day someone said that they had sensed a strange presence up there – and this was someone who had never been in the shop before. It was evidently the spirit of a mentally retarded young woman; quite harmless but very unhappy. As far as we knew the building had originally been one of those up-market strawberry and cream tea establishments who employed young girls as waitresses. That all seemed to fit in too well for my liking.

One Winter evening I stayed on in Watford for a meal and a drink with a friend. On my way home to Watford Junction Station I remembered some display items which I had promised to drop into the Harrow shop the next morning on my day off. There was nothing for it but to return to the shop. The back streets were dark and silent and inevitably I recalled the stories about the store rooms upstairs. Once you get a bad idea in your mind it's stuck there mid-way between your ears and nothing will shift it. At one stage of my reluctant return I even started to hallucinate. I had really got myself psyched up. There's no such thing as ghosts, I told myself. Maybe there isn't when there's more than one of you but on your lonesome you tend to leave a pretty wide margin for doubt. I even had a split-second image of this face – a young girl's face but somehow shining as if it was moulded out of crumpled silver paper – and I hadn't even reached the shop!

As of thirty years ago in the foggy cobblestoned alleys of Kentish Town, I felt like the first victim of a horror film. I let myself into the shop and locked the door behind me. I didn't give myself time to think and dashed down the shop and into the stock room where I could at least put the light on. Then it was through another door, up the twisting stairway and along a short passage to the packing room where the 'Ghost Passage' was located on the left. No doubt squeaking the 23rd Psalm, I darted up the other parallel passage and into the large schoolroom, seized the Harrow package and retraced my steps like a bat out of Hell, which is faster than a rat up a drainpipe. We are funny creatures. Once it gets dark all the old primeval myths come flooding back. And we call ourselves civilised!

Another of 'El Supremo's' bright ideas was for each shop to telephone their Area Supervisor at the close of business on Saturday with the week's trading figures. This simply amounted to speaking to an answerphone which was grandly referred to as a 'voicebank'. Now Nigel Grant was a tough nut but easily embarrassed and the first Saturday we used the voicebank was hilarious. Vic asked me to phone the figures over, I dialled the number and heard Nigel's recorded but self-conscious voice announce, 'Hello. Welcome to my Voicebank.'

I just couldn't speak. I put down the receiver, convulsed with laughter. It took me three attempts before I could speak coherently. It reminded me so much of that old 1950's creep-show *Inner Sanctum* when his doom-laden tones announce 'Welcome to my Voicebank.'

I only met 'El Supremo' three times. The first occasion was when he attended a directorial meeting in the training school above the shop. I had expected a tall, suave, maybe slightly foreign-looking character in a designer suit. What I did see was an undersized and arrogant little runt with steel-rimmed glasses and spots. He had all the warmth of a deep-frozen fish finger and I immediately decided not to add him to my Christmas card list.

The second time I met him was by default. By that I mean it was Vic's fault. All the managers in the London area were to attend a meeting at our Guildford shop to discuss the firm's future policies. Vic made some excuse and said that I would go in his place. Well it was a day out and Guildford is a nice little town.

When I arrived at the shop most of the others were already there. There was a woman – I believe her name was Marlene – enthroned on one of the shop's pseudo antique chairs. I say 'enthroned' because she was doing a pretty fair imitation of Queen Victoria and not looking one bit amused. She was one of 'El Supremo's' special team and about as friendly as a viper.

Then the Great Man himself arrived and talked ... and talked ... and talked. We didn't get a chance to say anything. Staff wouldn't wear suits anymore, he decided. We would all wear double-breasted navy blazers and dark grey trousers. He had even selected a tie for our uniform; a hideous blue and yellow thing which looked like the rag Picasso cleaned his brushes on. It really was a great waste of time, money and material.

The third – and thankfully – final time I was to encounter 'El Supremo' was late on a wet Saturday afternoon at Watford. We had been doing a very brisk trade in a batch of reduced raincoats when in marched 'El Supremo'. He looked a complete and utter mess. A crumpled blazer, open-necked denim shirt, jeans and a pair of scruffy trainers. 'What the hell are they doing here?' he demanded to know, pointing at the now-depleted rack of reduced raincoats. 'This is one of the "new concept" shops. You're not supposed to stock reduced goods. It's bad for the image.'

'But it's good for the till,' Vic suavely pointed out. 'We've sold any amount of them today.'

'I don't care how many you've bloody well sold!' raved our sartorially-challenged lord and master. 'Get them off the shop floor at once! Marlene's in charge of stock control. What the hell does she think she's doing?'

And without further ado he was on the phone to the poor woman, screaming at the top of his voice the most disgusting and filthy tirade I have ever heard.

And what was Your Hero doing all the time this was going on? I was serving a very nice gentleman with a sports jacket and feeling more than a little mortified and embarrassed.

The customer gazed at me in shocked astonishment. 'Who is that fellow?' he asked.

'Our Managing Director,' I replied in a ghostly whisper.

The customer rolled his eyes heavenwards. 'That creature?' he murmured. 'You and your colleagues have my profound and heartfelt sympathy.'

But that was 'El Supremo's' style – or lack of it; rule by terror. If he wanted to put the frighteners on some unfortunate manager whose shop was going through a bad patch, he would turn up with his team of yes-men and heavies around him like mobsters out of a gangster film.

But he came unstuck with Steve Lyle, the manager of our Strand shop. One evening after hours he called a meeting of all the West End managers to tear them off a strip about the drop in trading figures. Now the West End shops relied heavily on the tourist trade and it was recognised nationally that year that the tourists just weren't touring. Steve was ready for this and had contacted the Tourist Board beforehand and equipped himself with all the facts and figures. But he had made himself a marked man.

One of 'El Supremo's' female team members went into the Strand shop on a very rainy day and complained to Steve about an umbrella display he had put in the window. It was quite the same story as the raincoats at Watford and she got quite nasty about it. 'You can be replaced,' she threatened.

'Don't bother,' Steve retorted, handing her the shop keys. 'I've had enough. You can find yourself another mug.'

They lost a good one when Steve left. For a West End manager he was quite young and with his knowledge of the retail business he could run rings around 'El Supremo' and his gang.

Then one day Nigel Grant vanished from the scene, to be replaced by Joe Biggs. Joe had been my assistant all those years ago when I did managing relief at Fulham in 1969 and had done very well for himself, ultimately being promoted to manager of Kingston and then Area Supervisor.

Vic challenged 'El Supremo' on Nigel's disappearance but the question was side-stepped. Eventually we found out the truth. 'El Supremo' had told Nigel Grant that the Brighton shop was to be closed down.

'But what about the staff?' Nigel had objected. 'Some of them have been there years.'

'Sack 'em' came the brusque retort. 'And if you won't do it you can kiss your own job goodbye!'

Knowing Nigel, he probably told 'El Supremo' to stuff the job and walked out. But it didn't end there. It was rumoured that Nigel took 'El Supremo' to court – not the firm mind you – and sued him for wrongful dismissal. And what is more, he won.

THE END OF AN ERA

Autumn 1989 ~ Summer 1991

There were a number of comings and goings towards the end of the 1980s at Watford. Mark Hemmings had left, as had Desi – he didn't jump, he was pushed. Daniel Carver left as well as our Amazon cashier Valerie Stevens.

So who was left besides Victor Buckingham and little me? We had acquired a new cashier who had recently moved from Enfield to Hemel Hempstead. This was Doreen Sherman, originally from Yorkshire. Doreen was the complete opposite to Valerie. She was brash, blonde, irritatingly good-natured, loud, flirtatious and extremely talkative. She also was no lightweight with – to put it politely – a rather low centre of gravity. She reminded me of an electric light bulb, bayonet end uppermost.

To her credit she was good at her job, didn't have moods and the customers liked her. Well they wouldn't have dared not to. Even our irascible 'Mr Click' took a shine to her and asked if she would consider doing a spot of house cleaning for him – the dirty dog!

Although they were culturally and socially poles apart, Vic and Doreen got on famously. Probably it was because Vic liked to be flattered and she could pour it on by the bucketful. But she was rather vain and had a high opinion of herself. In all fairness she had once won a beauty competition – how many years ago I couldn't say and it would have been ungallant to ask – but she showed me a photograph of this sylph-like blonde in a bikini and I just marvelled at how people can metamorphosis. It must be something in the water.

In retrospect I suppose she meant well. She was one of those overpowering, gushing characters, forever rattling on about her two sons, 'our Jason' and 'our Craig'. She was always short of money – or so she kept telling us – but that didn't stop her staggering into the shop every day with half a ton of *Sainsbury's* shopping bags.

It wasn't the most comfortable time of my life. I was still waiting for a hospital appointment and those hernias could really play up. I suppose cars feel much the same when their suspension goes. One Saturday they hurt so much I had to hand my customer over to Doreen and go upstairs to the display schoolroom. I lay in one of the dummy windows for twenty minutes and gently managed to get my insides back inside and not outside by the method demonstrated to me at the hospital. Having done that I phoned Northwick Park Hospital and asked if there was any likelihood of having my operation before I died of old age. After a long wait and three chamber music concerts while they put me on hold I was brightly informed that I was halfway up the waiting list. I mean to say! How long is a piece of string?

One lunchtime Doreen was holding forth about some man who tried to chat her up on the bus the previous night. This seemed to happen with monotonous regularity. She may have been good natured, heart of gold and all the other clichés but she had no small opinion of herself. You would have thought that she was the only woman in Hertfordshire.

'He followed me off the bus,' she announced. 'I think he must have been drunk and didn't know what he was doing, but he kept on trying to grab me bum.'

Vic, who was standing in the connecting doorway to the shop, shook his head sympathetically. 'Poor man,' he signed in mock regret. 'He'll never know what he missed.'

'Or how much,' I muttered through my Marmite sandwiches.

Vic picked it up instantly. 'A fiver not to tell her!' he hissed.

Joking apart, Doreen was a generous soul. At Christmas she bought us personalised coffee mugs with our names on and we retaliated by buying her one of those most impractical teapots fashioned to look like an old English cottage.

However, 1991, the following year would prove to be the Year of Change. We hadn't any heavy snow for years but one Friday night in January more than made up for it and we had the grandfather of all snowstorms. I knew I would have trouble getting to work on Saturday. Harrow and Wealdstone Stations had no trains running and it would have been hopeless to wait for a bus. The only thing for it was to muffle myself up in my anorak, Ruski hat and heavy duty wellies and scramble and slither my way up to Harrow-on-the-Hill Metropolitan Line.

The station was chock-ablock with 'wanabee' commuters but the trains were running. Eventually a Watford train struggled in and we all struggled on. But that line has a tendency to meander. It meandered through North Harrow, Pinner, the two Northwood stations, Moor Park and Croxley Green before it finally got to Watford. And even then it wasn't the part of Watford I wanted. It was the residential area, well over a mile from the shopping centre.

The time was 10am when I arrived at Watford and I had a long and difficult trudge through the snow to look forward to. At the time I wondered at the stupidity of having the end of the line in such a back of beyond location but I have since been informed that the line was originally intended to go on further and terminate at Market Street which would have placed me only a five minute walk to the shop.

Resolutely gritting my dentures I set off at a slow and steady plod, arriving at the shop at 10.30. The place was in darkness and locked up. As soon as I got in the telephone shrilled. It was Doreen. ''Ullo luv, I can't possibly get in. There's no trains. It's been snowin', y'know.'

I knew full well it had been snowing, I told her. I'd walked through and fallen in tons of the bloody stuff to get to work.

A nervous giggle, and 'I'll see you Monday, chuck,' was the only reply.

The Vic phoned. 'Sorry, old boy,' he drawled. 'Can't possibly get in. The snow. No buses running.'

So I was stuck with a Saturday in Watford on my own with a sale to put on which meant going through endless lists of merchandise and marking all the prices down. I fully expected it to be quiet owing to the snow, but I was wrong. Customer after customer – there were customers everywhere! But I was to see the upside of the general public that day. Fully appreciating that I was running the shop single-handed, they patiently waited their turn and in some cases served themselves so that all I had to do was take the money and wrap up the purchases. It proved to be a bumper day's trading. Over £1,000 – and I had even completed the sales lists!

I knew there wasn't much hope of getting out on time so I took it easy and finalised the bookwork. I felt very pleased with myself and a customer had told me that Watford Junction was open and the trains were running so I would have an easier and much more direct journey home.

At about 6.45 I locked up the shop, banked the money in the night safe and set off down Clarendon Road to the station.

As a rule I preferred to wend my way there via the back roads past the Police Station in Shady Lane (yes, there really is a Shady Lane) as Clarendon Road is one of those long, boring roads flanked on each side by equally boring office blocks.

What is often termed as a rude shock awaited me. Watford Junction was closed. There were no trains running from there so there was nothing for it but to retrace my steps. This entailed another long trek up Clarendon Road and all the way back to the Watford Metropolitan Line. Thankfully those trains were still running and I stumbled indoors at about 8pm.

Fortunately that was the one and only snowfall we had and the weeks passed uneventfully into Spring. But the wind of change was blowing through Dunn & Co and it was an ill wind. Various straws in that wind rumoured that the firm was not doing very well. Initially I disregarded the rumours. We had been through critical periods before and had always managed to weather them. Then we heard that 'El Supremo' was no longer with the Company and had moved on, doubtless to ruin other business enterprises.

Evidently the bank had advised the Board of Directors that 'El Supremo' had financially gutted the firm and they would be better off without him. Ron Hale, our Chairman – a gentleman in every sense of the word and one of the old Dunn's stock – had now assumed control and 'El Supremo' was, presumably voted off the Board. But the damage had been done, although most of us in the shops were yet to realise just how much.

But at that time such things were not known on the shop floor. There had been subtle changes which should have given me a hint as to how the land lay – or rather how it was slipping away. With the gradual refurbishment of all our branches the hat steamers had been removed and, for the most part, our greatly reduced hat stock consisted of cheap, pre-blocked wool felt trilbies. We all knew that headwear was in decline as were many of the heavier topcoats. More people owned cars and both these items of clothing were largely redundant because of this.

Also, about Easter we should have been receiving our Summer headwear. Genuine Panama trilbies made in Ecuador or the less expensive versions known as Braids – all stacked in cellophane hoods with cardboard collars to prevent the hat bands from creasing. In their heyday we did very well with the Panamas. Some were extremely stylish porkpie shapes in various muted colours with pleated hatbands which were known as puggaree bands. We never stressed this last piece of information to a customer in case he was hard of hearing and might have misunderstood!

One Tuesday on Vic's day off Mr Hale paid a visit. He drifted around the shop like a grey ghost. Difficult times ahead, he murmured, or words to that effect. He looked lost and bewildered. There would be changes but we could pull through. Even then I realised that these words were but hollow wishes but I responded with the same empty reassurance in similar vein. We would overcome the crisis. Dunn & Co had been going for over a century, survived two world wars and the Depression. But I think we both know that we spoke like phantoms reliving our mortal existences. The damage had been done. We had been well and truly holed below the waterline and were sinking fast. Then Mr Hale left to haunt another branch and I never saw him again.

It was easy to blame our predicament on 'El Supremo' with brash, grandiose but ruthless ideas; well they certainly didn't help. But there is never just one reason; there are several. A bad year's trading for the retail business in general would surely cause some damage and some said that in our case this was partly due to our merchandise. Not that it was lacking in quality; far from it. Maybe it was too good and lasted too long. I was reluctant to admit to this as it is something to be proud of but it does give a new slant to the many customers who proudly announced that they had bought a Dunn's suit, jacket, etc and it had lasted ten years. Well no business can survive if the customer only makes a major purchase once every decade and if that was the case it was a miracle that we had survived all those years. On the other hand 'El Supremo' tried drastically to change our image with more modern merchandise such as T-shirts and swimming shorts when there were more than enough of our rivals selling such things. It was also a contradiction of our image when all our branches had been made to look like a lounge in an Edwardian gentleman's club.

Many blamed the buyer. Well he was what you would call a soft target and buying stock for a year ahead is something I wouldn't have cared to do unless I was gifted with clairvoyant powers. I think much of it was to do with the fact that we had lost our image.

Up until the 1980s it had been comparatively easy; 'the mixture as before' but times were a-changing. Things had become more casual and maybe Dunn & Co did fail to keep up with the changing scene. But it must have been like walking a tightrope. Too much change and we would lose our well-known image and also our regular customers. But those faithful old customers were dying off. In the past 'Dad' would bring his son along for his first 'grown-up' suit, and so it had been ever since Dunn & Co had been in existence. 'Son' wore the same clothes as 'Dad' but in a smaller size. But not anymore. Fashion hype, peer pressure – call it what you will – the new generation had different and more modern ideas and poor old Dunn's just hadn't been able to come to terms with this.

The crunch finally came in the Summer of 1991. Dunn's had gone into receivership and the creditors were descending like a flock of vultures. It was then that Mr Hale, together with a few other directors and Head Office staff including Mr Armstrong the Chief Cashier and Denis Breese, made amends, to my mind at any rate, for allowing 'El Supremo' to devastate the firm the way he had. They ringfenced the firm's pension fund and formed it into an independent business so that the creditors couldn't get their claws on it. Oh, the howls of rage and despair which went up from those financial grave robbers. But they had done the right thing by the hundreds of employees who had been with the firm for most, if not all, of their working lives.

Phil Ansell was seconded to help our new Area Supervisor, Jeff Green, in the unenviable task of touring the London shops which would be closing first, much like travelling executioners and booking out the stock to the warehouse. I was transferred to Harrow in Phil's absence to manage the shop for three weeks on my own. There was no staff; it was like being back at Wembley seven years earlier. But what surprised me – even shocked me – was what passed for stock. Thanks to 'El Supremo's' plans for 'updating' Dunn & Co there was nothing but T-shirts and swimming shorts. A far cry from the old days of sober suits, stacks of elegant hats and ranks of Harris Tweed jackets!

There was supposed to be an assistant but thankfully he was conspicuous by his absence. I say 'thankfully' because I had met this gentleman during my one year stint at Harrow three years earlier. He was an old schoolchum of Phil's who had done part-time work at Harrow when he felt like it. His name was Doug and he was a thug and I make no apology for the accidental poetical element. He was one of those sweaty-faced, hefty young men, built like a brick wall and possessed of a very uncertain temper. You could imagine him downing ten pints of lager and tearing the head off someone because he didn't like the colour of their shirt.

I recalled the Christmas I was at Harrow with Phil and we went to a local Chinese restaurant for our Christmas meal. Dangerous Doug came along too and nearly had a fight with one of the waiters. Phil wisely settled the bill after the first course and we made ourselves scarce before any serious trouble started. I really couldn't understand why Phil had got him a job at Dunn's. I later found out that Doug had just completed a spell in Brixton Prison for Grievous Bodily Harm and I really cannot admit to any great surprise except that Phil put his own reputation on the line by recommending him for the job with us.

Yet an even bigger surprise was to follow. Doug had been promoted to day relief manager to cover several of the smaller North London shops. This meant that he had the keys to all those shops so that he could open them up for business when the managers had their days off. One Sunday he visited all the shops on his round, cleared the cash out of each till and disappeared. Having learnt that I found I didn't really mind working single-handed at Harrow. When it came to lunch time I simply locked the door and hung up a notice saying 'Re-open at 1.30'.

During my third week at Harrow all the shops were told what our fate was to be. A menswear chain based in Swansea had put in a bid for forty of our shops. Lucky for some but not for most of us as there were about one hundred and eighty branches. That meant some one hundred and forty would close. But there was some sort of back-handed compliment involved. *Hodges*, the firm that had come to our rescue, were to adopt the name of Dunn & Co for all their shops so in a manner of speaking it was a case of 'the King is dead – long live the King'!

Then on the Thursday all managers of the Greater London shops were to attend a meeting after hours at our Oxford Street branch to find out who still had got a job and who hadn't. When I phoned Vic about this at Watford he was quite unconcerned. 'Oh, I'm not going, old boy. I've heard that the new people are definitely keeping Watford open so there really isn't any point in me travelling up there.'

I wasn't so sure about that and even if it was the case I thought it only right to go and represent Watford. It was a strange feeling that evening, seeing all those managers and senior assistants gathered together. A very sombre reunion indeed for I knew quite a few of them and hadn't seen them for years. It felt like a wake after the funeral.

'I bet you wish you were going, Keith,' grinned Lennie Hollis who was the new manager of our Holborn shop.

I stared at him in surprise. He was comfortably settled in one of 'El Supremo's' pseudo-Victorian armchairs, looking very pleased with himself. 'They're closing Holborn?' I gasped.

'They're closing all the West End and City branches,' he replied, 'but there's a nice redundancy packet in it for us.'

Our new Area Supervisor, Jeff Green, was presiding over the gathering and he looked absolutely gutted. I didn't envy him his job that evening. One by one our destinies were revealed and the manager of each shop that was to close was given a large brown envelope with his redundancy details inside. I think the firm must have dealt with them very fairly as there were no complaints. But there was one surprise; Harrow was to be kept open. I think Phil Ansell was quite disappointed about this but I thought that the reason was for its size it did very well and the overheads were low as it was virtually on a 'peppercorn rent'.

At least I still had a job and these new people seemed to be much on a par with Dunn & Co but on a smaller scale, having only about eighty shops throughout Wales and the West Country. But it was a sad occasion, bidding farewell to many people I had known for years and worked with. But at least the firm had looked after them well. I wasn't at all surprised really. On Dunn's a retired member of staff could make a purchase and get a discount of seventy-five percent.

Having finished my stint at Harrow I returned to Watford. I felt a lot happier about things in general and the only cloud on the horizon was that wretched hospital business. I was still having quite a lot of discomfort and wondered just how far up the waiting list I was. So I telephoned from work one morning and surprisingly got through to someone who seemed to be on the ball. 'Who is to do your operation?' she asked me.

'Mr Cox,' I told her. 'I saw him just over a couple of years ago.'

She gasped. 'He's been retired over a year!' Paper rustled and then she came back to me. 'I've just been checking up on this. I'll see if I can get things moving.'

'I'm on holiday for the next two weeks,' I hastily pointed out. I wasn't going to have that messed up and gave her the dates. At least she sounded a lot more positive than some I had spoken to.

The two weeks in Suffolk were blissful. Good air, peace and quiet and a gentle pace of life. When I returned home there was a letter from the hospital awaiting me. I had been booked for my operation at the end of August.

From then on it was countdown time. Although the shop didn't open for business on August Bank Holiday Monday we went into work as the *Hodges'* auditor was coming to check stock. Doreen Sherman the cashier was moving to Southend and had applied for a transfer to our shop there and then there was only Vic's day off on the Tuesday. Wednesday would see me in hospital and when I would eventually be allowed to return to work it would be to a very much changed Dunn & Co.

A WELCOME IN THE HILLSIDE

Summer ~ Autumn 1991

It was a strange coincidence that two of the most important things in my life should occur at the same time; namely the takeover of Dunn & Co after more than a century of trading and my hernia operation after a wait of over two years. I would also be off work for the transitory period of the takeover. On reflection though it wasn't a bad thing. Victor Buckingham would have to do some work for a change and the system should be up and running by the time I returned to work.

I was only in hospital two days but told to take at least six weeks convalescence. Literally just what the doctor ordered! I phoned Vic at Watford and told him that I had been stitched back together again.

'Good show, old boy,' he drawled. 'When are you coming back to work?'

I told him that I would be off for the best part of two months.

'That long?' he protested. 'With the modern surgical techniques patients are up and running in a few days.'

'Well I'm down and sitting,' I retorted, and rang off.

Those six weeks were truly idyllic. The Summer weather stretched into September without being too hot and the whole world seemed to take on a different perspective. But at least three times a week Vic would phone up and ask when I was coming back to work.

Finally in late October I decided to go back. I still felt a bit shaky and probably should have had another week but nothing came unsewn and I stayed in one piece. But the changes at work were incredible. *Hodges*, who were now running Dunn & Co were paper-driven to the extreme. I had never seen so many forms, and Monday mornings were completely taken up with complicated sales account forms for the previous week.

Apart from our own standard retail accounts we had made-to-measure, contract sales, catalogue sales, hire wear and concessions sales. This last section was itself split into several different groups which were franchises with different manufacturers. Rainwear by *Dannimac*, suits by *Centaur* (who also did our made-to-measure), trousers by *Gurteen* and also *Farah*, shoes by *Stirling & Hunt* and also *Rhode*, gloves by *Dents* and accessories such as wallets, cufflinks and – would you believe it – back-scratchers! – by *Sophos*.

All these different makers had to be stock checked at regular intervals which wasn't as bad as it sounds; a simple matter of counting the items. But with our own stock it was very much different. Although we still traded as Dunn & Co our new masters in Swansea impressed their own system on us. Their branch checks were the total monetary value of merchandise. I never rated that system because it was virtually impossible to isolate what particular item was over or short.

We had forms which we had never heard of before. Weekly Sales Analysis forms for comparing the current sales with the previous year. Also we had to order our own stock which was a very time-consuming job. This entailed noting down what sizes we had in lines which were selling well and ordering the missing ones. Whether we got them or not was another matter. In fact the impression was that *Hodges*, which was a comparatively small company compared with the original Dunn's, had bitten off more than they could chew.

Even worse was the Hirewear; the Highland Wedding outfits in particular. I never realised there were so many bits and pieces involved. The black velvet jacket, kilt, white shirt, lace jabot, belt, sporran, sporran belt, socks, sock tabs, buckle-fronted shoes and even a knife – or dirk to use the proper term – stuck down the sock.

Children were a nightmare to measure up for any form of hirewear. The average small boy is a peculiar shape, rather like a sausage as his waist and chest size are about the same. And finding their shoe size would try the patience of a saint. The little monsters were usually in a fractious mood, having been dragged to the shop on Saturday when they could have been vandalising something instead. To make matters worse they had the most irritating habit of growing by the time the order was required.

Staff were transitory on my return to Watford. When either Vic or I had a day off we would borrow an assistant from Hemel Hempstead but usually it was just the two of us.

I had only been back a week or so when it was announced that a staff dinner was to be held at Swansea to welcome the Dunn & Co personnel who had survived the takeover. This meant shuffling staff around the shops as we would have to travel by train to Swansea, stay overnight and catch a train back the next day and return to our respective shops. It was to be a 'black tie' do and it was rumoured that *Hodges* were well into this sort of thing. That being so I used my suit allowance on a dinner suit instead of hiring one, reckoning that it would pay for itself in the long run, rather than keep on paying out to hire one. As it happened the dinner was a one-off and that suit has only been worn once since. I probably couldn't even get into it now.

We all met up early at Paddington Station that Thursday morning, probably about twenty of us from the London area alone, and caught the train for the long journey to Swansea. On arriving we were met by a bored and shifty-looking person holding a card with *DUNNS* scrawled on it. Then we were all shepherded into a large van which looked suspiciously like a 'Black Maria' and driven off to an industrial estate where our Head Office and Warehouse were located.

It was the usual treatment with all the directors acting like jolly uncles – the 'honeymoon period' or the 'sugar on the pill'. We all knew that after a few weeks, or even days, it would be business as usual and decided to make the most of it while we could. Six of us – myself included – were told that we were 'overflow'. The hotel where the dinner was to be held was fully booked and we would be taken by taxi to another hotel at the far side of town and collected when the social gathering was due to commence.

I was to share a room with Pete Mortimer, the manager of our Hounslow shop, and it took us a full two hours to get into our 'glad rags' and wrestle with our bow ties. On arriving at the hotel we were told that a glass of champagne would be served to each of us as a welcoming drink. You can imagine our shock and dismay when we discovered that there was none left for the 'overflow six'. Oh yes, there had been; it had all been carefully worked out. One glass of bubbly per head. But what nobody had taken into account was a certain manager in the main group who had polished off the six glasses reserved for us.

'Sorry, old boy,' smirked Vic in his usual complacent tone. 'I've always been partial to champers and it might have lost its fizz before you arrived. Couldn't see it go to waste.'

Well I might have guessed. Typical Vic Buckingham!

The dinner was excellent but for one thing. Our hosts, being Welsh, burst into full-throated Gaelic song. It sounded terrifying and the thought crossed my mind that it may be a prelude to a blood sacrifice of Dunn & Co staff to some Druidic god. Eventually they got all the emotional stuff out of their systems but worse was to follow; namely the speeches. First of all the Chairman made a speech of welcome. He was a short, bald little man and to hear him you would have thought that he was Dr Barnado and Mother Theresa rolled into one, welcoming the poor Dunn & Co waifs into the fold. It sounded too good to be true – and it proved to be the case in later days. He was followed by *Hodges'* oldest inhabitant who had evidently worked in the shop from an embryo to his present age which looked and sounded about two hundred years. Doubtless he got tanked up beforehand because he became quite maudlin. I wouldn't have been at all surprised if had suddenly burst into *Land of my Fathers* or *We'll keep a welcome in the hillside.* Finally they managed to shut him up – probably electrified his zimmer frame, and then it was the Managing Director's turn.

Mr Fleet was certainly more lively, though that wouldn't have been too difficult, and by all accounts his speech was a bit on the racy side. But I didn't take in much of what he was saying; I was too staggered by his attire. Mr Fleet was probably the youngest of the directors, thin and heavily moustached. Also he was not Welsh; he was a Liverpudlian and reminded me of Ringo Starr. But it was his suit which impressed and horrified me. The dinner suit was early 1970's cut; wide lapels and flare-bottom trousers – and what is more the trousers were too short, skimming about an inch above his ankles. I never cared for the style but to look correct flared trousers should err on the longer side as, being wider bottoms, they have to touch the instep of the shoe. And just to compound the bizarre image his bow tie and cummerbund were emerald green. At that moment I meditated in deep nostalgia on how different the Staff Training Course dinner had been all those long twenty-seven years ago at Watford.

But one thing I was grateful for. I had opted for an ordinary white dress shirt with a turn-down collar. Many others present had gone for wing collars which, I observed with sardonic amusement, had a tendency to lose their crease so that the two little triangles straightened out as room and body temperature increased, resulting in a somewhat Dickensian appearance.

At last the speeches were over and the presentations commenced. One by one the Dunn & Co staff were called forward and presented with a watch by the Beloved Chairman, appropriately engraved on the back, commending us for our many years of service, dogged determination, missed tea breaks and so forth.

This was followed by the photo session where we were all lined up – tallest at the back; shortest at the front – with our Beloved Chairman dead centre. This was delayed by the absence of Vic Buckingham who had disappeared in the direction of the 'Gents'. Well he had consumed six glasses of ill-gotten bubbly.

After the photo ordeal we were permitted to socialise. This was more like it. Vic inevitably gravitated towards the ladies and those silly women were fussing around him as if he was their patron saint, Richard Burton. The others latched onto the executive staff but I had learnt from my experience at the Watford dinner to be a bit leery of such folk. Loose tongues can cause all sorts of trouble when the party is over. I had already met a couple of the van men who did our weekly run at Watford. They were honest to goodness types with no axe to grind and we got along famously.

Then our Beloved Chairman called for our attention. 'Would the six gentlemen who are staying at the other hotel please go to the lobby,' he announced. 'Your taxi driver is waiting to take you back.'

Great! It was only 10.30 and that was that! 'Hard luck, old boy.' Vic called out from the harem of winsome Welsh women. 'See you in the morning.'

It was a disgruntled 'overflow six' who returned to their hotel that night. To console myself I had a look at my watch. That only made matters worse; I couldn't wind it up.

'What's wrong, mate?' Pete called across from his bed.

'It's this watch,' I growled. 'The bloody thing's busted. It won't wind up.'

'Don't suppose it will,' came the sleepy reply. 'It's battery-powered.'

After a good breakfast we all met at Swansea Station and boarded the train back to Paddington. I felt very chirpy. I'd had a good night's sleep and was looking forward to returning to familiar territory. I sat next to Vic in the train, as excited as any child, which was probably relief that the ordeal was over, and chattered non-stop about all manner of trivia.

After a while I noticed that there was a definite lack of response, and glancing at Vic, I saw that his normally healthy fair-complexion held a decidedly greenish-yellow hue.

'Didn't get to bed until 3.30.' he croaked.

It didn't need a genius to read the situation. He had the great-grandfather of all hangovers. So there was a God in Heaven after all! From that moment I was unmerciful.

'Did you have a good breakfast, Vic? We did; fried bread, lovely fat bacon and eggs. I like my eggs with the yolk all runny; they've got more flavour.'

My reminiscences were punctuated by groans but even after I had exhausted the subject of food there were plenty of other things to talk about. 'What about old Fleet's green bow tie and cummerbund? It was enough to turn your stomach. Almost bilious green.'

Yes, I had decided not to give him one moment's rest. 'Vic, look at those cows. Does it mean it's going to rain if they're lying down. But some of them are standing up. Gosh, look at those ducks! What's Welsh for "duck" …?'

Oh, I could keep up the inane chatter for as long as needed. And it's a very long way from Swansea to Paddington …

SHOCK TIME

Autumn 1991 ~ Autumn 1992

With the run-up to Christmas we Dunn & Co survivors were to find out just how frugal the Yuletide season was to be for the rank and file; no bonuses, no Christmas Box. I suppose I was lucky to still have a job and as far as we were able we still ran the shop on the old established Dunn & Co lines.

The week before Christmas, among other festive items for the seasonal window display, was a large wicker hamper. Obviously some display gimmick, I thought, and put it out of my mind. Some days later I noticed that it had disappeared. Andy, our assistant on loan from Hemel Hempstead, enlightened me. 'It really was a hamper. Each branch received one. A Christmas cake, pudding, mince pies and a bottle of sherry. They were for the managers.'

That explained everything. Vic had taken the whole lot home. Fair enough, it was for the managers, but I knew full well if this had happened on the original Dunn's there would have been a share out of goodies for the staff. But not with our Victor. It was just the same as with the champagne at the Swansea dinner. But apart from that it simply showed what our new masters thought of the rank and file – nothing! We were just cyphers and didn't count. And just to rub our faces in it the current newsletter carried a piece penned by our Beloved Chairman of his first class flight to the States and what an enjoyable (and expensive!) holiday he had there. Not the most tactful thing to put before the minions.

But 1992 was a year of trauma; a year I would not forget in a hurry. The trouble started just before Easter. I had been experiencing acute back pains which the doctor eventually diagnosed as shingles. Nevertheless he said I was fit enough to go to work and I did – more fool I!

By Sunday it was worse. I knew I was unfit for work but I also knew that the paperwork at the start of the week would be vast. Much against my better judgement – as well as my mother's wishes – I decided to go into work on Easter Monday. I hadn't any plans for the holiday so I might just as well put the time to good use and at least complete all the concession forms. Mum forced a compromise and insisted on accompanying me which was just as well as I could hardly put one foot in front of the other on the way home from the station. Then, with a clear conscience, I phoned Vic and said I wouldn't be in work on the Tuesday. Hard lines on Vic; Tuesday was his day off, but I had had enough.

My recovery took all of three weeks and, inevitably enough, Vic rang every other day to find out when I would be returning to work. At the end of the third week I made the effort but found that I tired very quickly and a fourth week would have been of great benefit.

On my return, I found that we had a new member of staff, a part-timer called Sam Isaacs. I confess that I didn't take to Sam; in fact I didn't trust him. He was in his mid-fifties; a fat and self-opinionated know-all. He bragged about how he used to 'work late' at the office in his previous job. Well that's what he used to tell his wife. But he did have a young secretary. I felt that if he cheated on his wife he would cheat on anybody. But we needed another pair of hands at the shop to help cover for days off and he was the best we could get.

One Tuesday, Vic's day off, we were particularly busy. We had just had a stock delivery and had taken about a thousand pounds by early afternoon. In the middle of all this profitable chaos our Beloved Chairman paid a surprise visit. Oh dear, he was not at all a happy bunny – or should I say Welsh rabbit? He tut-tutted about the shop being untidy and how disappointed he was. 'Get a pen and notepad, Mr Howard,' he told me. 'I want you to take down some notes about the shop. I really am most disappointed in Watford.'

'Sir,' I pointed out, 'if you would care to check the day's takings you will see that we have taken over a thousand pounds already – and we've had a stock delivery to contend with as well.'

Most of the *Hodges'* shops were in small towns and anything over five hundred pounds on Saturday was reckoned to be very good indeed. His eyebrows shot up in amazement like jet propelled prawns. 'Well that puts a different complexion on the matter,' he admitted after checking the file to make sure that I wasn't telling 'porkies'. One thousand pounds! Very good! I was all ready to give you a rocket – but no. Well done!'

So off he went in an aura of best malt liquid lunch and I thought that would be the end of the matter. But I should have known better. The little wretch reported me to the Area Supervisor. No different from Dunn's Mr Pedrick who always said that shops that were too neat and tidy meant that they weren't doing the trade. True words of wisdom and he had never worked on the shop floor in his life.

But if I thought that was bad there was worse to follow; much worse. *Hodges* employed auditors to carry out stock checks every six months or so whereas in the good old days of Dunn's stocktaking was done every six weeks by the Area Supervisor. That June an auditor came to check the stock with this miraculous little hand-held calculator-cum-computer which had what appeared to be a miniature loo roll attached to it. He spent most of the morning checking every computer ticket on every sales item, then retired to the stock room to check the results.

Some time later he emerged, looking decidedly serious. 'A shortfall,' he announced. 'I'll have to check through the invoices.'

I gathered by 'shortfall' he meant stock shortage of some sort. So that meant the afternoon would be written off while he went through the books. I hadn't much faith in those state-of-the-art computer gadgets. When I checked stock I did it the simple way with a piece of paper ruled out in a grid, filled up the quantities and added them up. But it seemed that nobody was capable of doing the simplest sum without pressing a button first. Of course, Dunn's checked the quantity of items whereas *Hodges* checked the total monetary value which probably justified the computer. But times were changing and I daresay I was reluctant to change with them. For one thing I didn't care for the modern jargon. Stock shortage was good grammar but *Hodges* had invented a new word for stock being over. They called it an 'overage'.

It can be deduced that I didn't have much faith in their stock checks and even less in their findings. At any event the stock would have to be checked again and that would mean another day wasted. They didn't even know what the shortage consisted of and that was because they couldn't check the quantity of garments; only the total cash value.

The auditor tuned up later with Jeff Green the Area Manager and they went through the whole rigmarole again. By lunch time they had finished and there followed tense phone calls to Head Office and subdued mutterings. Then the balloon went up. Looking somewhat white around the gills, Vic calmly told me, 'It seems that we are short of stock to the value of twelve thousand pounds!'

I couldn't believe my ears. That amount of stock missing would leave a hole big enough to drive a bus through. What happened next was a nightmare. Vic had to hand his keys over, was suspended and sent home. Surely they didn't believe that he had stolen twelve thousand-pounds worth of stock? And it couldn't have been pilfered – not a vast amount like that. I didn't put any significance on it at the time but Sam left. Being a part-timer he didn't have to give notice. He just said that he wouldn't be coming in.

'I know how sick you must feel, Keith,' Jeff Green sympathised, 'but Vic never did you any favours. You carried him.'

In retrospect I think he was right but I still felt shattered. I had worked with the man for eighteen years. He hadn't exactly been sacked, I told myself, just suspended. He would probably be back in a few days when they got this mess sorted out. I was due to go on a fortnight's Summer holiday that weekend – and by Harry I needed it! Jeff arranged for Leon from Harrow to manage the shop while I was away which did little to ease my mind. Leon was a bit of a scatterbrain and I wondered what I would be returning to.

It's a complete myth to believe that a holiday away from such a situation is a good thing. In such circumstances it is much better to stay on the spot and see the whole business through. As it was, I had the worst holiday ever, wondering just what sort of a mess I would be going back to.

My fears were fully justified. The shop looked like a tip and there was a Summer Sale to be put on that very day. No preparation had been made and Leon just handed me the shop keys and went back to Harrow.

As it happened, Daniel Carver, who had left the firm some years earlier, had rejoined and this was his first day back. Even so, the workload of a fortnight was too much to catch up on and Jeff Green sent on his 'floating' senior staff to take over. Stewart Halliday was officially based at our Portsmouth shop and he certainly looked like it with his nautical beard, reminiscent of the sailor on the old cigarette packets. But he was a great help and we soon got things organised between us. He also had some good news which came as a welcome bonus. The firm had taken on a new manager for Watford; none other than our ex-Area Supervisor, Nigel Grant, who had the splendid audacity to take on 'El Supremo', the executive hatchet man with his case for wrongful dismissal.

'You'll enjoy working with Nigel,' said Stewart. 'He's a workaholic but you'll enjoy it.'

I didn't doubt it. I remembered Nigel from our first meeting when he was based at Slough and used to help out at Harrow in the late Sixties in the halcyon days of dear old Bertie Benson. A lanky, round-faced fellow whose sales pitch always reminded me of a used car salesman. But he was red-hot at his job and as straight as a die. Stewart was right. He was a workaholic and I did enjoy working with him. He brought a sense of order and control to the job and you really felt the shop was in capable hands at last.

Nigel drew up a work programme for the week. Monday was obviously 'paper shuffling' which, with *Hodges* and their obsession for all things to be listed and tabulated, pretty well wrote off the entire morning. Nigel hated bookwork although he never admitted it. 'Have a sit down in the stock room, Keith,' he would say, handing me a bundle of forms and ledgers. 'Have a go at these and make yourself a cup of coffee.'

He wasn't fooling anyone and I didn't mind. His first love was serving customers, along with display work and it all ran very smoothly. He was something of a chain smoker and I have known him to have two ciggies on the go at the same time; one in his office and another in the stock room. Also, Nigel wasn't one to hang around after 5.30. We were all out of the shop like rats up drainpipes. After all, he did have quite a long drive home, all the way to Maidenhead.

Tuesday was stock delivery day which took the entire day by the time everything was checked and sorted out. Then the customers' orders would be dealt with along with Catalogue orders and any Hirewear outfits which were due to be delivered.

Wednesday we would check the stock which wasn't such a task as it might sound initially. *Hodges* had no real system of stock checking and it was left to the bi-annual visits of the auditor. Nigel didn't think much of this and being a Dunn & Co man through and through, devised a system to check it each week. He simply drew up a book, listing the totals of all the garments in their different categories, plus deliveries and minus sales and stock transfers so we could monitor things more accurately.

'It won't stop anything getting nicked,' he said, 'but at least we will know what's missing instead of some cash shortage which could be anything.'

And he was quite right. Many discrepancies which occurred were simply innocent errors on the delivery notes which were easily corrected. As far I know we were the only shop to adopt this system and it worked very well for us.

Thursday was my day off and Nigel had Friday. His Friday was sacrosanct as he played golf then as if his life depended on it. Nothing would come between Nigel and his Friday golf when he would meet up with Joe Biggs, now an ex-Dunn crony who had risen to Area Supervisor before the takeover had made him redundant.

One Monday morning, right out of the blue, Jeff Green phoned to send me to our Luton shop for the day. Shades of 'Jumping Jack' Flashman! It really was like old times again. I was needed at Luton for three Mondays to help out with the bookwork. Luton's new manager was quite out of his depth with it and they wanted me there to sort it out.

Luton was about the farthest I had been and being the naïve but incorrigible little rascal that I am I simply hopped on a bus with 'Luton' on the front. What I didn't know was that it went via Harpenden and did a grand tour of Bedfordshire before finally arriving at Luton.

I got to the shop somewhere around lunch time. They were so pleased to see me that they didn't quibble about my late arrival. The branch gave the impression of an antique shop. It was crammed with captain's chairs and dinky little leather-topped wine tables cluttering up the place. Oh, yes, there was some stock squeezed into various areas just to remind me that this really was a Gents' Outfitters. Obviously all the furniture was left over from 'El Supremo's' era. No wonder the original Dunn & Co went bust.

The shop was divided into two halves with a structural wall down the middle, necessitating the use of security mirrors at each end. At some time we must have extended the original shop to take over the next door premises. What with that wall and all the repro furniture there was hardly room for customers.

But the biggest surprise of all was the manager. Joe Montana was built like a nightclub bouncer. He was also a North American Indian. His face, like the pitted surface of a mountain, broad nose and slicked back black hair was belied by his almost childlike, friendly nature. I found him a most likeable person with no 'attitude' problem but he was utterly at sea with most of the bookwork.

Together we worked through the routine balance sheets and he quickly grasped the facts. But there were two things he wanted done; stock profiles and the stock ordering system. Stock profiles were not a regular thing. Once a month Head Office would require a stock profile of suits and the next time it would be of some other item of clothing. This time it was shirts. Not a difficult task but extremely tedious. It entailed listing every range number and every size in those ranges, including the ones in the windows. I finished it about three in the afternoon.

'Gee, you worked hard!' Joe thanked me. 'It took me until after closing time to finish it last Monday.'

'What was it last week?' I asked him.

'Shirts,' he replied innocently. And if it wasn't for the thought that he might still have had a scalping knife tucked away in his hip pocket I could have hit him. Joe assumed that a stock profile of shirts was required every Monday!

The next comedy was the stock sheets. As mentioned earlier, with *Hodges* we had to order our own stock each week.

'I've done the suit sheet,' Joe told me, 'but we could do with some extra sizes in the navy blue suits.'

'Then rub out the ones you have in stock and order a full range,' I suggested.

Joe looked at me with those artless, oily black eyes whose ancestor had probably given General Custer his terminal haircut. 'Gee! D'you mean we can fudge the sheets?'

'If you fudge the sheets,' I retorted, 'you can wash them.'

Joe was very decent about my travelling. He let me off at 4.30 and suggested that instead of travelling back by bus I should pick up the Jetlink coach at Luton Station as it would be much quicker. He was right, too. Hardly anyone on it, comfortable seats and arriving at Watford Junction about the same time I would have got there when working at Watford.

The next Monday I caught the Jetlink coach at Watford and arrived at ten in the morning which is what I had intended the previous week. Things went off much more smoothly although I did make a complete clot of myself in the afternoon. I had to phone Nigel at Watford about something and the telephone was one of those repro affairs with a gleaming brass receiver and a numbered dial. I tried to dial Watford's number, but in vain. 'Hey, Joe,' I complained, 'your phone's busted. The dial won't move.'

Joe pointed out that the dial was only for show and I should press the numbers instead. I wonder how many palefaces have had to be told how to use a telephone by a Red Indian?

The third and final Monday was a complete no-no. I got to Watford Junction for the coach at 8.15 and was still waiting at 9.00. Another cobwebbed person-in-waiting told me that it was not unusual for it to turn up around ten. I decided to phone Nigel so that he could let Joe know that I would be late.

'Never mind that, Keith,' Nigel replied. 'You just come back here. I can find you plenty to do. I'll ring Joe at Luton and let him know you won't be coming.'

So that was the end of my Luton trips but it certainly was a worthwhile experience and helped to jog me out of all the tensions of the earlier part of the year.

But another storyline had threaded its way through my life since Nigel took over at Watford. I had been receiving at least four phone calls a week from Vic Buckingham. He had taken his case to the Tribunal with the intention of suing the firm for wrongful dismissal. He felt very sorry for himself and not without good reason. Although he hadn't done me any favours I sympathised with his problem. It was a horrible thing to happen after all the years of service he had put in and although he could be accused of negligence he most certainly was no thief.

Then a breakthrough occurred during late Autumn. I was upstairs in the 'haunted' and now unused rooms of the Watford shop, ferreting through some old ledgers for some invoices when I came across a box of receipt books. Then I recalled all those cash adjustments which Vic had put through whenever the till came over. He could never be bothered to find out what had caused these and, to be fair, it would have been difficult under the *Hodges'* method of stock control to isolate the problem when only the cash value was checked.

I took the books home and went through them that evening. The total of cash adjustments was staggering. Admittedly it was nothing like the twelve thousand pounds he was found short but it was a hefty three-figure amount.

I never mentioned this to Nigel or anyone but I got photocopies of all those till adjustments and posted them to Vic. Evidently this must have sent out ripples and I experienced some nervous moments over the next few weeks. There were mutterings in the firm, wondering how Vic had managed to produce this evidence and Jeff Green, without making a big thing about it, casually asked me if Vic had been in the shop since his dismissal. It was with great relief that I was able to truthfully say that he hadn't. Not that I had done anything wrong; I had only brought to light facts which had been overlooked. But I certainly wouldn't have been 'flavour of the month' with our Beloved Chairman!

Ultimately the action had a positive result and Vic telephoned me with the good news. 'Thanks a bundle, old boy. The Tribunal really gave the *Hodges'* representatives a roasting. What sort of firm were they running where they could dismiss someone without a proper investigatory enquiry? Why hadn't they got a Personnel Department? Surely a man who would bank cash adjustments which amounted to hundreds when he simply could have pocketed them couldn't be considered responsible for their heavy losses?

'In short,' he told me, 'it amounted to a real grilling for the firm and their cash-orientated system of stock control was severely criticised. Anyway, I've been awarded maximum damages and the Tribunal said that if it had been in their power they would have made it more. Many thanks for what you did, Keith. When my cheque comes through I won't forget what you did.'

Well, being Vic, he did forget. Over the years I've had the usual Christmas card from him but no phone calls. But as I said, Vic never did me any favours.

ALMOST LIKE THE OLD DAYS

Spring 1993 ~ Spring 1995

Working with Nigel Grant was never boring. It was hard work but never boring. Nigel was a man of the people. He never put on any airs or graces and was plain spoken and to the point but I never once heard him swear. In fact he picked up our part-timer, Daniel Carver, on that several times.

Nigel's chronic grumble was leaves. We had a number of large trees outside the shop in Watford Parade and in the Autumn the shop doorway was littered with fallen leaves. I didn't mind as they gave the shop a pleasantly rustic look but Nigel growled continuously about them and I wouldn't have been at all surprised to see him arrive one morning with a lumberjack's axe.

His down-to-earth manner was so much easier to live with than Vic Buckingham's sophistry but he hadn't got a very ready sense of humour. It was there but not readily active and I did have a few moments of wicked fun at his expense. He was bewailing the fact one day that we didn't have a proper cashier. He wanted an efficient, sensible, middle-aged woman instead of some blonde scatterbrain, who could take on all the administrative work that he loathed so much. 'I want a woman!' he bellowed after a lengthy discourse on this problem.

I flapped my wrist at him and retorted, 'Well don't look at me, duckie.'

Nigel didn't know what to make of it. He just glared at me and said, 'wot?' And he said it the way it would be spelt phonetically; W-O-T. That was Nigel all over.

But to his credit he was a great believer in the real value of things. He even insisted on having a Christmas tree in the shop; a massive great artificial thing which nearly reached the ceiling. And as far as Christmas was concerned he insisted on having his family together on Christmas Day. I just couldn't imagine anyone daring to challenge him on that.

Ever vigilant against shoplifters he fitted up three video cameras in the shop. Well they looked like video cameras but they were dummies with batteries to make a little red light flash on and off in the hope of deterring the more light-fingered elements of the community. Then he promptly ruined any deterrent effect by hanging a showcard right in front of one of them.

But not all the thieving came from the usual shoplifting. Early one Saturday a customer came in and queried the fact that he had not been given a shop receipt for a pair of trousers he had bought on the Friday afternoon which was Nigel's day off. 'A young, fair-haired chap served me,' said the customer. Obviously Daniel. And being a part-timer he wasn't due in until 10 o'clock.

'Did you pay by cash?' Nigel asked the man.

The customer produced a slip of paper. 'No, I paid by credit card. Here's the card receipt but I didn't get a shop receipt.'

'Aha!' And with that triumphant snort and no further ado Nigel wrote out a shop receipt, backdated it and the man left the shop, quite satisfied.

'I'll have a few words to say to Master Daniel when he arrives,' Nigel grimly announced. 'He's been trying to pull a fast one.'

'But the customer paid by credit card,' I objected. 'I don't see how he could have done.'

'Was your till correct when you cashed up last night?' Nigel asked me.

'To the penny,' I replied, still not understanding. But Nigel's next words took the wind right out of my sails.

'Daniel took the cash equivalent of the sale out of the till, and by not making out a shop receipt you would have no record of the sale when you cashed up. Nine out of ten people who pay by credit card wouldn't have bothered just as long as they got their card receipt. But that man was the tenth.'

Put that way it made sense but I couldn't really believe it. I had worked with Daniel for over a period of several years, but sad to say that is just what had happened.

On Daniel's arrival Nigel called him out to the stock room and they were out there for over an hour before Daniel owned up. Nigel sacked him on the spot and sent him home but I was still somewhat stunned. That he could have done this while I was in charge of the shop on Nigel's day off was hurtful. Daniel did have the good grace to apologise to me but that was the end of his job with us. A very silly boy. He had it in him to be good at the job but a momentary lapse had cost him that self-same job.

At least it proved that Nigel Grant was a manager worth his salt. A strange mixture really. He could be very sentimental about things like having his family around him at Christmas but he was as sharp as a needle when it came to business. I could well believe the speculation I had heard voiced about him the days before 'El Supremo' came on the scene. He would definitely have made it to the Board of Directors, if not the Chairmanship.

Working life at Watford had now settled down into a happy routine, almost like the old days. But there was one factor of the business which I could well have done without and that was Hirewear. Deadlines were so important as most functions were weddings and so many people expected a tailored fit. And even when we got the garments in on time they might show signs of too much 'mileage', having been cleaned after every use. There was so much stress involved on both sides I would have been quite happy if the firm had relinquished that side of the business, even if it meant forfeiting the commission on each order. Many of the Hirewear customers didn't even know how to knot a tie and as for the top hats, well they just clowned around with them, stuck on the back of their heads. Some of their colour selections were pretty grim too. Peach-coloured cravats with light blue waistcoats. I began to realise that a strong stomach was needed when it came to choosing accessories.

One classic case where everything went wrong turned into a waking nightmare. A party had ordered several Highland outfits for a wedding in Scotland. As the day for collection approached we contacted the Hirewear firm to confirm the delivery date. All in hand, we were assured. The outfits would be delivered to us within the next few days. Well they weren't. But now the customers were becoming understandably apprehensive as the wedding was only three days hence. So Nigel telephoned the Hirewear people again – only to discover that they had lost the order!

Panic stations! We now had just two days to the deadline. Nigel really leant on them and the upshot of it was that a special plane was laid on to fly the outfits down from Glasgow for a special courier to pick them up and deliver them to us at the shop. We had no choice but to wait and they didn't arrive until 6.30. During that time we both reflected on the irony of the situation. The wedding was to be in Scotland and the Hirewear firm was in Scotland. A pity some sort of arrangement couldn't have been made for them to pick them up there. But I suppose that would have created its own problems.

As soon as the orders arrived Nigel phoned the customer who lived at Carpenders Park and said that he would deliver them personally that evening. 'Where's Carpenders Park?' Nigel demanded of me after he had committed himself to this errand of mercy. I told him that it was just the other side of Bushey and Oxhey and we set off in his car with me as navigator. We found the address without difficulty and staggered up the front path with the boxes of Highland wear. Those Caledonians must have been tough chappies to charge around the heather in all that heavy plaid with a knife tucked down their socks. No wonder that William Wallace gave us all the run around all those years ago.

The family were overjoyed to see us and the poor bride-to-be was red-eyed with weeping. I will admit to wallowing in an air of smug self-righteousness at being party to the rescue mission, seeing myself as a certain angel who paid a nocturnal visit to some shepherds a couple of thousand years ago. But it was Nigel who came up with the Grand Gesture. He presented the family with a bottle of champagne for all the anxiety they had been put through. It must be said though, that the champagne came out of the firm's petty cash. Nigel may have been soft-hearted but he certainly wasn't soft-headed.

'I'll give you a lift home,' he said as we left the premises. Very kind of him but I knew that he had a long journey home and it was already 7.30. If he dropped me at a railway station that would be good enough. The euphoric mood which still held me in its thrall made me feel no end of a guy. So what if the trains weren't running? I would simply spread my angel wings and fly home along the track.

Next morning, however, this little ministering angel was to hear something that clipped his wings and brought him rudely down to earth. 'You know what we forgot?' Nigel asked me.

Well it couldn't have been the fee because the customers paid up front when they placed the order. 'A corkscrew for the champagne?' I jested, still extending peace and goodwill in all directions.

'No; the invoices. They were still in the packages. And without them we can't claim the commission.'

And that is when this little angel said a word which, I am sure, no angel has ever given voice to.

That Autumn some bright spark in one of our shops really let us in for something. *Children in Need Day* was fast approaching and he had thought up a way in which the firm could contribute. I had no argument with his sentiments; on the contrary I applauded them. Rather it was his suggestion how this could be done. A member of staff standing outside the shop by a trestle table laden with a stack of our catalogues at a pound each, to be collected in a plastic bucket. But the member of staff would have to be togged up in a morning suit – complete with top hat.

That particular day there would only be Nigel and myself at Watford – and he was quick off the mark to wriggle out of it. 'You can do that, Keith.' There was no question of arguing; the decision had been made.

The next thing was to order the outfit. Black tailed jacket and waistcoat, grey trousers, white wing collar shirt, grey cravat – and that damnable hat. I am sure that the Hirewear people must have been very pleased at getting these orders for our shops all over the United Kingdom but they didn't exactly put themselves out. They obviously sent out the kits which had done the most mileage and were due to be scrapped. The top hat especially was a bit on the tatty side and could probably tell a few interesting stories of drunken bacchanals.

The dreaded day dawned. Under Nigel's eagle eye I set up the trestle table in the Parade outside the shop, taking as long as possible. Then I put the plastic bucket and made quite a prolonged job of that. Then the catalogues, taking as long as I could to arrange them in a neat pile. Passersby stared at me in curiosity – and I wasn't even in costume yet. No, I had put that off until the very last minute. If they were boggle-eyed at me simply setting up a table I shuddered to think what their reaction would be when they saw me in all my sartorial glory. But it could be put off no longer. I slunk out, feeling like a giant beetle in that black tailcoat, finding the pavement strangely interesting to stare at. There was a display card of the table advertising *Children in Need* with a picture of a teddy bear with a bandage over one eye. I stood as close to that bloody bear as I could, hoping that it would fully explain and excuse my bizarre appearance to a thunderstruck public. I did not exactly fall in with the charitable mood and will only say that I would have cheerfully arranged for that bear to have a bandage over the other eye.

Then strange as it may seem, after the first ten minutes I didn't even care. There are so many oddly-dressed people about one more wouldn't make any difference. As the morning passed and the contributions clanked into the bucket I even found I was enjoying it. Having worked in Watford for nearly ten years I had got to know quite a few people there and some of them paused to pass the time of day in amicable conversation.

I packed up at midday for lunch but was back on my pitch at 1 o'clock, breaking the afternoon session to make Nigel and me a cup of coffee. In the meantime Nigel had to run the shop single-handed practically all day – the operative word being 'run'. It was quite funny to see him, a lanky, shadowy figure, darting back and forth in the shop like the proverbial blowfly with the indigo posterior. Finally by 4.30 he had had enough. 'Okay, Keith,' he called out. 'You can come in now.'

'Are you sure,' I replied. 'I'm quite all right out here. This morning coat is nice and warm.'

'Never mind the nice warm morning coat,' he growled. 'You come back in here.'

I knew I would have to but a little gentle winding up was always fun where Nigel was concerned. It had been a very interesting experience. In the course of that day I had had three proposals of marriage – one of them from a fellow!

In due course the *Children in Need Day* featured in the firm's magazine, along with several photographs, but not of this faithful servant at Watford. Not that I minded but what did rankle was that in all the published photographs every one of those collectors had chickened out of wearing the top hat!

During the mid-Nineties our Beloved Chairman retired, no doubt jetting around the world from one fun spot to the next on the accumulated proceeds of the blood, sweat and tears of his staff who never got so much as a Christmas Box. He was succeeded by two faceless 'grey suits'. I never did get to meet either of these two gentlemen but it didn't spoil my night's sleep and I don't think that I missed much. At least they didn't try to turn the business inside-out and upside-down as 'El Supremo' had done.

In the Spring of 1995 that old spectre loomed again; rumours in the wind of change. Whether or not it was an ill wind remained to be seen. Then Nigel was 'invited' to a meeting with the Directors at our 'flagship' branch. The firm had scraped enough money together to re-open just one shop in the West End and this was in Regent Street, but a few doors along from where we were originally. I was soon to learn the outcome. It was an interview which Nigel passed with flying colours, to take over as manager at Regent Street. Well he certainly deserved it if anybody did and after all, he had managed Piccadilly in the Dunn & Co days before he was promoted to Area Supervisor.

Selfishly I was not happy. Who would Watford's new manager be? Even worse; what if Nigel insisted in dragging me along with him to Regent Street as Vic Buckingham had done when he was transferred from Harrow to Watford? Much as I enjoyed working with Nigel Grant this enjoyment was far outweighed by having to travel to and fro to London every day and endure the impersonal West End trade.

Then it all came out. Nigel had definitely been promoted to the position of manager of Regent Street. Evidently the existing manager, one Euan Cansdale, had severely blotted his copybooks. His staff found him difficult to get on with as he was paranoid about his subordinates being after his job which was ridiculous. He also had a bad record of absenteeism, evidently on health grounds. So much time off from work was bad enough as far as the rank and file were concerned but in a West End manager it just couldn't be tolerated.

So who was to replace Nigel at Watford? None other than Euan Cansdale – thanks very much! And when would he take over at Watford? A Saturday in March; to be precise the 11th of March – my birthday – thanks again!

Some birthday present, I thought. But then I had never had much luck on my birthdays during my working life.

On the Friday, Nigel's last day at Watford – yes, he had even put aside his weekly golf session – we went out for a quick drink. Needless to say I was sorry to see Nigel go; not only on account of his daunting replacement. I had very much enjoyed working with him. But now I had to get this new character sorted out the next morning. Happy Birthday, Keith!

THE LAST LAUGH

Spring 1995 ~ Winter 1996

So that was my birthday present for 1995; a bespectacled bald head with a moustache, below which was a mouth that whinged. He whinged about how hard he had worked at Regent Street and how ill he had been with any number of allergies; all this within five minutes of coming into the shop. All the time I got the impression that he was sizing me up, wondering if I would present a challenge to his authority. I had a fair idea of how it had been in the West End. A matter of dog eat dog; hostile and competitive. I also knew the real reason he had been ousted from Regent Street was due to his chronic absenteeism. Whether his claims to ill health were genuine or not no firm could afford to have a West End manager who was only conspicuous by his absence.

Anyway, I had sorted out my own way of playing it. For the most part there would only be the two of us and there was no room for friction. He was a bit leery of me at first but I let him understand that he was the manager and we would work as a team, and after that we got on very well.

Not that I could ever say that I counted him as a friend. He was fanatically intolerant of smoking and hated cats. But as we hadn't got a cat on the payroll the latter problem was academic. In all fairness I must say that he was a first class salesman and when it came to made-to-measure you would have thought he had been trained in Savile Row.

All in all we got on very well which must have come as something of a surprise to both of us. The only problem which arose, and one that I couldn't very well object to as he was the manager, was that he chose to have Thursday as his day off and I was compelled to take Friday. Just a little change of one day can really throw things out of kilter. By the time Thursday came I was almost dead on my feet. Okay, I had the Friday off but it was back to a busy Saturday twenty-four hours later.

Fortunately I got lucky and the problem ceased to be when Euan was transferred to Enfield which was nearer to his home, after only two months at Watford. But I must say that in those two months Euan only had one day's sick leave.

The new manager was a complete outsider. He had worked in retail but not for Dunn's so he was an unknown quantity. My first impression of Ivor Simpson was of a somewhat sinister character. Slightly-built, black hair and glasses, he had a rather furtive way of looking at you out of the corner of his eye. I was to learn that this was just his quirky way and his long suit definitely was humour. This made a welcome change from Euan who was almost paranoid about anything that moved. Ivor was a true vulgarian; a Max Miller of the retail trade. With his chirpy manner he could get away with virtually anything, whereas if I had attempted the same patter I would have been sacked for insulting behaviour.

'I'm looking for a hat,' a customer would ask.

Ivor would adjust his glasses and innocently enquire, 'Yes, Sir? Which way did it go?'

On another occasion a lady came in and rashly announced that she wanted to rummage through our underwear. Ivor studied her solemnly from beneath furrowed brows. 'Are you sure you wouldn't care to re-phrase that, madam?' he replied.

Then it was my turn to become involved in this French farce. A lady asked what I had in pyjamas. Before I could blurt out something harmless and innocent which wouldn't incriminate me, Ivor chipped in with, 'Don't answer that, Keith! Whatever you do, don't answer that!'

Ivor was up to all sorts of tricks too. One morning when I arrived after my day off he said, 'Have you seen what is in the front of the window, Keith?'

I went outside and looked. Right in the front were a set of false teeth and next to them was a hand-printed notice which read, 'Should the owner wish to claim these dentures which were left in the shop on Thursday, please come inside and ask to see our Lost Property Officer Mr Howard.'

How they came to be left in the shop has always remained a mystery as they were never claimed.

One thing that Ivor couldn't and wouldn't tolerate were bad manners. He had the patience of a saint – probably the only saintly thing about him – but he wouldn't stand for discourtesy. If someone pointedly ignored the customary greeting of, 'Good morning, Sir,' Ivor had his own way of dealing with such ignorance. 'Hello there, Keith,' he would call out to me in front of the customer. 'How are you?'

'I'm fine thanks, Ivor,' I would respond, falling in with the game. 'How's the wife?'

'She's fine but I had to give her a good kicking last night.'

'And how's the cat?'

'He's fine too. He's just had pups. I'm a bit worried about him. I think he's bi-centennial.'

Yes, Ivor had a quirky sense of humour and we had a lot of laughs. But there was one time when he was really embarrassed. He was due to go on a fortnight's Summer holiday at the end of his first week at Watford. It had been booked months beforehand but he felt a bit guilty about it. To make amends – not that I was complaining – he handed me the shop keys at 4 o'clock and said that I could have an early night as I would be in charge for the next two weeks and wouldn't be able to have a day off as there was no staff cover. I was well pleased with this as I hadn't had an early night since ... ever? The trains actually cooperated and I was home by 4.40.

'There's a telephone call for you,' my mother greeted me as I breezed indoors. 'It was your new manager. He apologises but would you please go back to Watford as he gave you his keys, forgetting that he should have handed them over to you when the shop shut at closing time.'

Poor Ivor. Well I should have realised it, too. There was nothing for it but to return to Watford, and this time the trains really did play up. I finally reached the shop around 5.45 where a totally mortified manager awaited me, full of apology.

What the hell, I told him. We all get our wires crossed now and again. I once did it myself on day relief at Harrow. Trying to lock up the shop at closing time I discovered to my horror that I was using Watford's keys. I must have picked up the wrong set when I left for work that morning! What to do? I couldn't go home for them and leave the shop open for any villain to plunder. There was nothing for it but to ring Phil Ansell the manager and ask him to come over with his own set of keys. As he lived out at Hanwell this was no small request but to his credit he complied without complaint – not that he really had much choice.

But just as he was locking up the shop he paused. 'How did you get in this morning?' he asked.

Good question. Time for meditative pause. I felt through my pockets and you will never guess what I found. The set of keys for Harrow! I had picked them up as well as the Watford ones. I like eggs, but not on my face.

Ivor was very much into nostalgia. He often said that he wished he had been with Dunn's in the old days. A couple of times he invited me back to his home for dinner at North Watford and showed me the den he had made in his attic. Glass display cases ranged around, containing all manner of memorabilia from war souvenirs to Dinky toys. One corner was set aside for his wife, Carol, where she could do her sewing and they would spend many an evening up there with their two black tomcats, Pipsqueak and Wilfred. He was also a rabid Manchester United supporter and the staff-cum-stock room was festooned with all sorts of Manchester United posters, mirrors and so forth. To display such a preference in the heart of Watford was, to my mind, courting certain death.

Ivor was a man of many parts and his nostalgic interests even embraced the popular music of the Sixties. In fact he was a drummer in a pop band which frequently did gigs at various clubs on Saturday nights.

As we were sharing an assistant with the Hemel Hempstead branch to cover for days off we felt we were justified in approaching our new Area Supervisor, Owen Powell, for a third member of staff, preferably a cashier. He agreed and an advert was duly placed in the Job Centre. A few days later Owen paid us a visit to say that he would be interviewing for the post of cashier at Watford; a young Belgian lady.

Right on the dot this apparition appeared in the shop. I never did catch her full name; it was Marie something-or-other. I know the last part was hyphenated. Petite and elegant with an attractive 'chocolate box' face and wearing a well-tailored and expensive-looking jacket and skirt — what we used to call 'costumes'. A cape of the same material covered her shoulders but what was most striking was a chic Robin Hood-style hat worn rakishly on her dark curls.

Feeling like peasants and no doubt tugging our forelocks, we ushered the vision into the back room where Owen Powell was waiting to interview her. Then Ivor looked at me, for once lost for words except one. 'Blimey!' he muttered.

Several minutes later the telephone rang. It was Owen Powell's wife. Would we ask him to ring her back when he had finished the interview.

An idea struck me. I must have been infected by Ivor's sense of mischief but it did seem to be worth a laugh. 'I'll write him a note and pass it through,' I offered.

'Saying what?' Ivor asked, sensing fun.

I told him and wrote out the note. Then I dutifully tapped on the door, opened it and with a face as grave and solemn as a judge, murmured, 'I beg your pardon,' and handed Owen the note where he sat facing the young lady across the table. I took my leave slowly, giving myself time to observe his reaction as he read the note. A twitching at the corners of his mouth and the ghost of a suppressed chuckle which was manfully stifled at birth was my reward. The note had read, 'your wife wishes you to telephone her at home when you have finished enjoying your Belgian bun'.

Good old Owen. He took it all in good part and it was arranged that Marie would start the following Monday. 'You cheeky buggers,' Owen grinned when she was out of earshot. 'I probably haven't done the poor girl any favours with you two up to your tricks.'

As it happened he couldn't have been more wrong. Despite his cheeky behaviour Ivor was more of a natural gentleman that the grammatically perfect Vic Buckingham who wouldn't have been able to utter a sentence to the girl without some innuendo. We both treated her with friendly respect and she was a cheerful little thing and very efficient with the customers, having worked in the West End.

However, that very Monday lunchtime something happened. I had been having trouble with my glasses. The metal frames had been slightly distorted due to me carelessly tucking them in my shirt pocket and carrying a heavy parcel which may have bent them. I had just made a pot of tea when I was taken by one of those unexpected sneezes. Both lenses fell out of the frames and my dentures followed in the same second.

Marie stared at me in amazement, wanting to laugh but not daring to. But Ivor had no such sensibilities. 'Blimey!' he gasped. 'What else has fallen off?'

I suppose the incident could be regarded as an ice-breaker but I am sure such a method has never found its way into a manual on socialising.

Obviously I had to get my glasses fixed so that afternoon I called at the Opticians who did the repair while I waited. Ivor had suggested that I take Marie with me so that she could acquaint herself with the location of our bank and the Post Office as she would have to know these things whenever he or I had our days off.

The repairs effected, we did the rounds. Then on the way back to the shop Marie disappeared into a very up-market confectioners and emerged a short while later with a large gold-coloured paper bag with tasselled handles. It contained a box of very succulent and every expensive-looking Belgian chocolates. 'For you and Ivor,' she announced. 'You have been so kind and made me so welcome.'

Dear girl. She was a little sweetie herself.

But things were to change the following day. Tuesday was Ivor's day off and I had just opened the shop when the telephone rang. It was Marie. She wouldn't be coming in again. Some weeks earlier she had gone for an interview for a job she had dearly wanted in the West End. They hadn't replied so she came to us. But she had just received a letter saying that she had got the job after all. It was a bit of a disappointment for us but she had herself to think of. Owen Powell took a more jaundiced view, but then again, she hadn't bought him any chocolates.

So we were back to only two staff again but Ivor soon solved that. His friend Dave who also shared a passion for all things outdated, mentioned that his wife, Shirley, was looking for a job. She was a very practical, no-nonsense lady and worth triple her weight in gold. And just for good measure Ivor got her friend, Lynn, a job at our Hemel Hempstead branch. Lynn would help us out at Watford if anyone was away and she was a real joy to work with, having a very cheerful nature. So now the shop was firing on all cylinders again.

In the Spring of the following year Shirley mentioned that Ivor's fiftieth birthday was fast approaching and Carol wanted to plan a surprise party for him. This would be on a Sunday and Dave had got Ivor out of the house on the pretext of looking at a motorbike he was thinking of buying. It worked like a charm. All the guests arrived and awaited Ivor's return. Then we heard him come in. 'We never saw the bloody bike after all,' he grumbled. 'Dave lost his way and forgot the address.'

Then he saw us all, numbering twenty-plus including Lynn and her husband, George, ensconced in his front room with glasses of various alcoholic beverages raised in a birthday toast. But the biggest surprise was when the doorbell rang and a voice announced, 'I've come to check your stock.' It was none other than Owen Powell and his wife Pat who had come all the way from Swindon.

We had another get-together at Ivor's which was his own idea with a very original theme. Although he had never worked for the real Dunn & Co Ivor had a great respect for their ideals and hit upon having a Dunn & Co theme for the day.

His home was decorated with obsolete Dunn & Co display items, a sepia portrait of the founder in his Camden Town Head Office – even old invoice books dotted about and forms used as coasters. As well as Dave, Shirley, Lynn and George, Owen Powell and Pat were there along with Mary from Head Office and a chap I had never met from North Finchley. Phil Ansell from Harrow had been invited and promised faithfully to come but it was no great surprise when he didn't show up. He would always say what you wanted to hear but never follow it through.

One Saturday, near closing time, we had a mini-drama in the shop. Ivor was busy with a customer who wanted his son to have a made-to-measure suit and I was on the phone to a customer when a man dashed into the shop, went straight up to Ivor, demanding to see a pair of shoes. Ivor explained that he was dealing with another customer and would be with him as soon as he could. Still the man persisted, demanding attention and Ivor, to his credit politely but firmly told him that he would attend to him as soon as he could. The man still rudely continued to interrupt and Ivor was compelled politely to put him in his place. At that point the man lost his temper and stormed off, threatening to report Ivor for insolence.

By this time I had finished my phone call and chose to put my two-pence worth in. 'You are out of order, Sir,' I called out to him from the office desk. 'If you report the manager I'll bear witness to your behaviour.'

The response was something on the lines of 'go to Hell,' but we never heard anymore from the fellow.

Things were running very smoothly at Watford. We made a good team and Ivor had happily adopted Nigel Grant's system for checking stock. Occasionally we would hear rumblings and grumblings from the Swansea Head Office but that was nothing new. As far as we were concerned trade was healthy and everything in the garden was lovely – except for one thing.

For me, the Hirewear side of the business had always been the bogeyman of the job. There was too much pressure for comfort. Would the deliveries arrive on time? And even if they did, had we got the sizes right? If there was a problem with this there was only a very narrow deadline in which we could get things corrected. Would the garments be up to standard? There were so many pitfalls the problems could be never-ending and the customers all expected fittings of a bespoke standard. That was a bit of a joke as some of them didn't even know how to knot a tie.

One week when Ivor was on holiday it really did get to me. On the train going to work that morning, knowing that I had a really knotty Hirewear problem to sort out, I felt wretched. I had buzzing in my ears and felt freezing cold, yet the sweat was pouring off my face like raindrops. The next thing I knew was that the train had terminated at Watford Junction. As I was wedged into the angle of a corner seat the other passengers probably thought I had simply dozed off. I still felt shaky but not so cold, so I sat in the train for a couple of minutes until I felt steadier. Then I ventured out onto the platform where the fresh air revived me. Somehow I managed to get the Hirewear orders sorted out but it surely wasn't one of my favourite memories.

The weeks slipped by without any great crisis, through the Summer and into the Autumn. But the bombshell actually fell on Christmas Eve 1996. I had just popped into my newsagent's on the way to work when he drew my attention to an item on the business page of the newspaper. It read, 'Dunn & Co go into receivership.'

THE ELEPHANTS' GRAVEYARD

Spring 1997 ~ Winter 2003

I have known happier Christmases than 1996. Being told that your job may have come adrift isn't exactly conducive to Yuletide cheer. However, after the shock had worn off I was able to view things more philosophically. When the same thing happened in 1991 it was far more worrying. As I saw it this time it was just a matter of sitting tight and waiting to be rescued by a passing ship in the form of another company.

Ivor Simpson the manager viewed it differently and urged me to look for another job but I pointed out that our situations were very different. He had only been with the firm for eighteen months, as had Shirley our cashier. In my case I had years of service behind me and I wasn't going to throw all that away. We would probably be taken under the wing of one of the big established concerns such as Dannimac or Baird and would wag along in our own sweet way. Dannimac were said to be one of the contenders so at least there were interested parties. There was another firm, too, which I had never heard of with an Italian-sounding name which was very dangerous to pronounce if you wore dentures. But Dannimac were the odds-on favourites.

We soon learned our fate in the early weeks of 1997. The Italian-sounding rank outsider had bought us out, lock, stock and barrel. It was said that it was the Swansea warehouse they were after but they were compelled to take the shops as well. They were a comparatively new company and had absorbed a number of other firms in recent years.

Ivor ceased to badger me about seeking another job and we mentally held our breath to see what our new masters would be like. They already had a store in the Harlequin Centre at the far end of Watford High Street and they were geared for the younger, more modern market and we wondered just how Dunn's-orientated bods would fit in with their contemporary scheme of things.

The first thing that scared the life out of me was the arrival of a fax machine. I had heard of them but knew nothing about them. All their stores were equipped with them. The second shock was a massive stock delivery. I had never seen anything like it. The suits looked like something out of the Nineteenth Century with their broad stripes, small lapels and four-button fronts. Evidently this had been the current trend among modern young men. It made me realise what a sheltered life we 'Dunnites' had led. There were also shirts. Crates and crates of them sent in from different branches. I was later to discover that each of their branches had been instructed to send a specified quantity of their surplus stock to all Dunn & Co shops. And it was obvious to see that they had unloaded the dross. They looked more like something from a ladies' boutique store.

There was no denying that we were desperate for stock. The bulk of our merchandise had been concession stock which had automatically been reclaimed by the various firms who supplied it. These events could be quite ugly, for it was said that in some of our larger shops such as the West End, strong-arm boys were employed to collect the concession stock and there were no arguments.

This pointed the way to where the Dunn/*Hodges* business had failed. Initially I had thought that we had been doing well but we were selling the concession items, not the firm's merchandise. And it has to be said that their merchandise was nowhere near the standard of the original Dunn & Co stock.

Also a large percentage of concession sales had to be repaid to the suppliers which left very little in the kitty.

We were soon to meet our new masters. Paddy Pasco, a pleasant enough young man, was to be our new Area Supervisor. He was impressed with the way we dealt with our customers and I thought that if the rest of the executive were like him we would be all right. Unfortunately this this did not prove to be the case. Their Sales Director paid us a visit the following Saturday. He was the 'Jumping Jack' Flashman of the new firm. Everyone was terrified of him. He looked like Dracula with a blow wave.

As Ivor and Shirley were busy with customers it fell to me to give him a conducted tour of the premises. I showed him the labyrinthine first floor area without once getting lost, or mentioning our suspected resident ghost for obvious reasons. In his taciturn way he seemed impressed. 'Yes, great possibilities here,' he murmured when we had returned to the shop floor. 'We can use the upstairs as another sales department and build a central staircase down here.'

It sounded like a good enough idea to me but we would obviously need more staff. But staff was the one commodity which the new people had in abundance.

Over the next couple of weeks we had visits from the staff of the Harlequin Centre store. They certainly weren't Dunn & Co types but they were very friendly. They were all young, certainly no older than the early twenties, and very cosmopolitan and colourful. Royal blue shirts and gold ties seemed to be in vogue as well as very Mediterranean-style beards and moustaches, although this last feature only applied to the male staff. There was a fair number of young ladies on their staff and they were definitely not of the Dunn & Co image. One I recall wore a mini-skirt and black leather thigh boots.

Probably the biggest surprise one afternoon was when two middle-aged Eastern gentlemen called in. They weren't what you would call natty dressers – I thought they might have been gardening – but they were friendly enough, cheerful and unassuming. Ivor introduced Shirley and me to them. 'Keith had been with Dunn's since he left school,' he told them.

'That's right,' I endorsed. 'You'll have to look after me. I'm an endangered species.'

They laughed and smiled politely but I don't think they fully understood me. Which probably was just as well as I discovered later that they were the owners of the firm.

One big difference that we found was that we were not, under any circumstances, allowed to touch our window display. Never mind if a specific display item was needed for a sale, we were not allowed to remove it. In the old days it was an easy job to whip the required garment out of display, sell it and replace it with something else – but not anymore. Mind you, the way the clothes were mangled into arty contortions in the window rendered them completely unsaleable. Also the amount of pins the display team used made me wonder if they were practising acupuncture.

They also had rigid ideas on merchandising the stock on the shop floor. I had spent a couple of hours one afternoon, tidying up the trousers until they were symmetrically perfect. Then at about 4 o'clock in came Paddy Pasco. 'Sorry, Keith, you'll have to do them all again. They've got to be facing the other way round and colour-coordinated.'

I don't know whether or not he expected a fight but he didn't get one. I just shrugged and got on with it. Since we had been taken over our closing time had gone back to 6 o'clock so I might just as well be fiddling around with that for the next two hours as anything else.

In the early Summer the next 'bombshell' fell. Paddy called and said he needed to speak to each of us in turn as they were closing our shop. So much for the high-flown plans for an interior staircase! No, they had a shop in the Harlequin Centre and didn't need another one in Watford.

Ivor and Shirley opted to leave when the shop closed in a week's time. When it came to my turn Paddy said he would reallocate me to their Brent Cross branch. I was ready for that one. 'They're short-staffed at Harrow,'

I replied. 'I'd rather go back there.'

Well that was where I had started all those years ago and it seemed fitting that I should finish there; something like the elephants' graveyard.

And so it was agreed. In the days that followed Shirley got a job in a local departmental store and Ivor with a Gents' Outfitters in Hemel Hempstead. It was a very unreal period for me.

The last days at Watford were something of an eye-opener. We were told to sell all the furnishings! I couldn't believe it. All of 'El Supremo's' retro-antique stuff was up for grabs. The green leather Chesterfield sofa went for one hundred pounds – everything went. Ornaments, writing desks, chest of drawers – the lot!

But one thing I am secretly proud to own up to not selling. I gave it away. Mr Cranshaw, one of the original Dunn & Co directors, occasionally popped in the shop and on several of his visits his wife had admired a particular pseudo-antique vase. It was a massive blue and yellow thing and I personally thought it was hideous. 'It would look so nice in our fireplace,' she said.

To keep the coal in? I thought. But she liked it and that was all that mattered. Unknown to Ivor or anyone else I boxed it up and gave it to them on their final visit. Call it a gesture to one of the Dunn & Co old guard, one of the few survivors of the firm who had treated me so well.

That final Saturday was a poignant day for me. About 5.45 Paddy and several of the Harlequin staff trooped in to transfer our stock out to other branches. Shirley left at six o'clock as did Ivor who had one of his nightclub gigs booked for that evening so it was left for me to complete the bookwork and close the sheets, a job which normally would have been done on Monday. That was no problem but all the while stock was being packed in bags and boxes and the shop was looking emptier with every passing minute.

By about 6.45 I had finished everything. I took a brief tour around upstairs to make sure there was nothing I might have forgotten but really more to say goodbye to the place and also the poor little ghost – if she ever existed. Then I returned to the shop floor, handed over the keys to Paddy and bade Watford farewell.

There isn't much more to tell. True to form, Phil Ansell at Harrow, let me in for sorting out the Dunn's shop at Bedford, which meant being picked up by the relief manager at Watford Junction at 7.30 in the morning. The shop was filthy and verminous. The books were impossible to balance as the previous relief manager had absconded with several hundred pounds and there had been no carry-over figures for weeks. I phoned Paddy and told him his best bet would be to write it off and do a stock check with what was in the shop to get a new opening figure. Anyway I was off on holiday for a fortnight that weekend. And I needed it.

When I returned to Harrow Phil had handed his notice in. We had a succession of relief staff; most of them young enough for me to have been their father – or even grandfather. I felt out of place, like some ancient mascot. The Regimental Goat. So what was a goat doing in an elephants' graveyard?

The whole job had changed beyond recognition. Because I wasn't managerial staff I wasn't allowed to wear a suit. A matching grey shirt, tie and trousers was the rank and file assistant's uniform. It looked like something out of Alcatraz. Customers, generally speaking, no longer wished to be served. We were there just to wrap things up and deal with the transactions. Some of them even objected to being approached. A far cry from Dunn's 'Nine Steps of Salesmanship'.

Try as I may I just couldn't imagine the shades of Ronald Harvey or Bertie Benson haunting the place. Not even a cold shiver of their presence. Old Ronald would have had plenty to cluck his tongue about – and quite rightly so. 'You blokes – sluck. If you had been paying more attention to that customer you could have sold him a suit – sluck.'

And how nice it would have been to hear 'Shall we have a cup of tea, laddie? Ah, thank you.' No Bertie, 'please' and 'thank you' are no longer fashionable.

Hard to imagine 'Jumping Jack' Flashman having one of his famous rants, yapping terrier-like after a slothful junior or rebellious assistant. And poor old 'Long John' Neville on his bi-annual visits, terrifying the junior staff with his steely eye of assassin blue, impeccable in his dark *Crombie* overcoat and bowler hat. A hat which protected a head which, when all was said and done, was full of vagueness.

Norman Hurst, Rupert Higgs, Bill Humbert, Lionel Parr, Ivor Simpson, David Hopton – all gone but not forgotten. Their personalities had been completely erased from the premises.

Six and a half years later the new firm went into administration just three months before I was due to retire. A good number of the larger stores survived for a while but this time Harrow didn't. But in my heart of hearts, I had retired long before then.

Before the last takeover in 1997, before *Hodges* in 1991 and even before then to about the time 'El Supremo' had started the rot which was to prove the final countdown in the late Eighties. Before then I had served the best, worked with the best … and for the best. And there are not many who are fortunate enough to say that.

#0111 - 090718 - C0 - 210/148/13 - PB - DID2243901